Cecil B. Hartley

Heroes and Patriots of the South

omprising lives of General Francis Marion, General William Moultrie, General Andrew Pickens, and Governor John Rutledge

Cecil B. Hartley

Heroes and Patriots of the South

omprising lives of General Francis Marion, General William Moultrie, General Andrew Pickens, and Governor John Rutledge

ISBN/EAN: 9783337195915

Printed in Europe, USA, Canada, Australia, Japan

Cover: Foto ©Andreas Hilbeck / pixelio.de

More available books at **www.hansebooks.com**

SERGEANT JASPER AT FORT MOULTRIE.—PAGE 89.

HEROES AND PATRIOTS

OF THE SOUTH;

COMPRISING

LIVES OF

GENERAL FRANCIS MARION, GENERAL WILLIAM MOULTRIE, GENERAL ANDREW PICKENS, AND GOVERNOR JOHN RUTLEDGE.

WITH SKETCHES

OF OTHER DISTINGUISHED HEROES AND PATRIOTS
WHO SERVED IN THE REVOLUTIONARY WAR
IN THE SOUTHERN STATES.

By CECIL B. HARTLEY.

WITH ENGRAVINGS FROM ORIGINAL DESIGNS,
By G. G. WHITE.

PHILADELPHIA:
G. G. EVANS, PUBLISHER,
No. 439 CHESTNUT STREET.
1860.

Entered according to the Act of Congress, in the year 1860, by

G. G. EVANS,

in the Clerk's Office of the District Court for the Eastern District of Pennsylvania.

PREFACE.

The purpose of the following work is to record the actions of some of the most celebrated of the many heroes and patriots who distinguished themselves by eminent services in the Revolutionary War, in the Southern States of the Union. Among these General Marion, whose life occupies a considerable portion of the volume, was one of the most remarkable characters who figured on the grand theatre of war in those times that "tried men's souls." He was one of those men who are born to command. His active and brilliant career as leader of the famous "Marion's Brigade," has scarcely a parallel in history; and his success in defending the Carolinas against the enemy, at a time when he was almost alone in the field, is due in a great measure to his power of attracting the personal regard of his men, and keeping them in active service, while surrounded by every species of discouragement, and the incessant danger of their utter destruction by the overwhelming force of the enemy. Marion's achievements were of the most heroic and romantic character; and are always read with interest and admiration.

General Moultrie, the illustrious defender of the fortress which bears his name, is not less interesting in his way. He was remarkable for cool courage, invincible resolution, sound judgment, and excellent common sense. The city of Charleston was twice saved from capture by his exertions. His military career was unfortunately terminated when on a third attack the enemy succeeded in taking the place, and the whole of its defenders became prisoners of war. In the life of Moultrie, contained in this volume, we have frequently quoted his own "Memoirs of the Revolution," a most interesting and valuable work.

General Pickens was the companion of Marion in some of his daring enterprises, an able and efficient coadjutor of General Greene, and one of the most useful of all the general officers who assisted in recovering the Southern States from the enemy.

Governor Rutledge was the most distinguished of all the Southern patriots, in the civil line. To his exertions the whole military force were greatly indebted for the success of their operations. As governor and dictator of South Carolina, he rendered services to the cause, of the most important nature, and displayed a character and ability equal to every emergency of those critical and perilous times.

Of several other military commanders and statesmen, we have given but slight sketches, in consequence of the brief space to which we were limited; but we trust that we have been successful in conveying to the mind of the reader a tolerably clear conception of the peculiar nature of the war in the Southern States, and of the characters of some of its leading spirits as displayed in the field and in the cabinet.

CONTENTS.

CHAPTER I.

Francis Marion—Descendant from French Huguenots—Sketch of the history of the Huguenots of France—Repeal of the Edict of Nantz—Emigration of the Huguenots to foreign countries—A party among whom were the ancestors of Marion settled in South Carolina—Sufferings of the emigrants described by Mrs. Manigault—Happy condition of the Carolina Huguenots as described by Mr. Laurens—Jealousy of the English settlers—The French refugees denied political rights—Political rights subsequently granted to them.................. 13

CHAPTER II.

Marion's descent—His grandfather a French Huguenot—His father and family—His feeble childhood—He desires to become a sailor—Opposed by his mother—Goes to sea—The vessel founders at sea, and he has a narrow escape from death—Returns to farming—Parallelisms in the lives of Washington and Marion—Both pass much of their lives as planters—Both serve in the Indian and Revolutionary wars—Some characteristics of Marion... 20

CHAPTER III.

Marion's first military service in the war with the Cherokees—Origin of the war—Horse stealing—Revenge of the Virginians—Attack of the Cherokees on the Carolinians—Marion serves in a troop of cavalry—The Indians send chiefs to Charleston to make peace—Lyttleton detains them and marches into the Indian country—Chiefs shut up at Fort Prince George—Conference with Attakullakulla—Treaty—Small-pox in the camp—Cost of Lyttleton's expedition—Great joy of the Carolinians—Marion has no opportunity for distinction in this campaign... 33

CONTENTS.

CHAPTER IV.

PAGE

Second campaign against the Cherokees—Surprise and death of Captain Cotymore—Murder of the Indian hostages—Terrible revenge of the Indians on the frontier inhabitants—General Amherst sends a force of regulars to Carolina under Colonel Montgomery—Governor Bull succeeds Lyttleton—Arrival of Montgomery—The militia rendezvous at Congarees—Marion with the army—Capture of Indian towns—Difficult march—Action near Etchoe—Return of Montgomery—Siege and surrender of Fort Loudon—Noble conduct of Attakullakulla to Captain Stuart............... 42

CHAPTER V.

Renewal of hostilities by the Cherokees—Expedition of Colonel Grant—Marion serves in the regiment of provincial volunteers a lieutenant under Captain William Moultrie—Advance to the Cherokee country—Marion leads the forlorn hope in the battle of Etchoe—Narrow escape with his life—The Cherokees subdued—Marion's remarks on the treatment of the Indians by the whites............... 53

CHAPTER VI.

Marion and Washington follow farming as a pursuit for several years—Washington's political course—South Carolina takes a prominent part in the Revolution—Organizes a Provincial Congress—Marion a member—Acts of that Congress—Arrival of Lord William Campbell—Activity of the members of Congress—Colonel Moultrie—His account of the acts of the patriots—News of the battle of Lexington—Seizure of arms, gunpowder, and of the royal mail............... 59

CHAPTER VII.

Meeting of the Provincial Congress of South Carolina—State of affairs—The Congress raises an army—Obtains powder—Military ardor of leading citizens—Officers of the army chosen by ballot—The Rangers—Distinguished men among the officers—Colonel Moultrie in command of the second regiment—Marion and Peter Horry captains in the same regiment—Their complete success in recruiting men for their Companies............... 66

CHAPTER VIII.

Noble conduct of Carolina at the commencement of the Revolutionary War—State of parties—Activity of the tories—Marion concerned in

CONTENTS. 7

PAGE

the first act of open hostility—The capture of Fort Johnson—Colonel
Moultrie directs this service—His account of the capture, and of the
events immediately succeeding it.. 70

CHAPTER IX.

State of parties—Captain Thornborough threatens to intercept vessels
bound to Charleston—Meeting of Congress—The first actual fighting
—Regiment of artillery raised—Moultrie drives the British men of
war out of the harbor of Charleston—Two regiments of riflemen ordered to be raised—Marion in command at Dorchester—At Fort
Johnson—Marion promoted to the rank of Major—His excellent discipline—Marion engaged in erecting Fort Sullivan—Arrival of General Lee—His opinion in favor of abandoning Fort Sullivan—Colonel
Moultrie's account of the defence of Fort Sullivan....................... 78

CHAPTER X.

Effect of the battle of Fort Moultrie—Rewards to the victors—Presenta-
tion of flags—Marion promoted to the rank of Lieutenant Colonel—
Another Indian war—Marion sent to Georgia with reinforcements—
Placed in command of Fort Moultrie—Invasion and subjugation of
Georgia—General Lincoln placed in command of the southern de-
partment—Bad state of defence in which he found South Carolina—
He advances to Purysburg... 92

CHAPTER XI.

Change in the aspect of affairs—General Pickens defeats Colonel Byrd
—General Lincoln sends General Ashe into Georgia—Defeat of Ashe
—Its disastrous consequences—Lincoln marches into Georgia—Prevost menaces Charleston—Subsequent operations—Marion at Fort
Moultrie—Siege of Savannah—Obstinacy and folly of Count D' Estaing—He grants delay to the garrison till it is reinforced and compels an assault unnecessarily—Marion takes part in the assault—
The colors of the Second Regiment planted in the British lines—Several officers killed in defending them—Death of Sergeant Jasper—
The siege raised and the expedition totally defeated—Depreciation of
the paper currency.. 99

CHAPTER XII

Marion in command at Sheldon—Stationed at Bacon's Bridge—Siege
and fall of Charleston—How Marion escaped captivity—His retire-

ment at St. John's—Infamous treatment of the South Carolinians by the British—Defeat of Buford—Clinton's proclamation—Cornwallis left in command—His proceedings.. 109

CHAPTER XIII.

Marion leaves St. John's and takes shelter in the woods and swamps—Joins the Continental army in North Carolina—Appearance of his men—Invited to Williamsburg—Appointed Brigadier General—Starts for Williamsburg—Gates's character—His defeat—Success and subsequent surprise and defeat of Sumter.. 117

CHAPTER XIV.

The people of Williamsburg—Their character and proceedings—Mission of Major James to Captain Ardesoif—Bravery and patriotism of James—His report—Formation of Marion's brigade—McCottry and Tarleton—Marion takes the command—His character and appearance at this time—State of the brigade—Arms made of mill-saws—Marion defeats Major Gainey and Captain Barfield—Captures an escort of Maryland prisoners—They refuse to join the brigade—Their reasons—Atrocious instructions of Rawdon and Cornwallis to their officers—Marion's opinion... 124

CHAPTER XV.

Marion's activity—Colonel Wemyss sent in pursuit of him—Marion retreats to North Carolina—Cruelties, murders, and burnings by Wemyss—Marion returns to South Carolina—Defeats Captain Ball at Black Mingo—Deliberates on joining General Greene—Surprises Colonel Tynes and captures valuable arms and stores—Cornwallis sends Tarleton to capture Marion—He is foiled, and returns without meeting him—Marion's brother killed by a tory—Marion entertains a British officer at Snow's Island... 134

CHAPTER XVI.

Greene succeeds Gates—Battle of the Cowpens—Lee and Marion attack Georgetown—Escape of Watson—Marion organizes four new companies—Operations of Horry and Postell—Battle of Guilford—Colonels Watson and Doyle sent to drive Marion out of the country—Affair of Peter Horry—Colonel Tynes defeated—Major McIlraith encountered by Marion—Proposal to fight—Backing out—Encounters of Colonel

Watson and Marion—Watson driven into Georgetown—Doyle plunders Marion's camp at Snow's Island and escapes to Camden—Marion's council with his officers.. 142

CHAPTER XVII.

Retreat of Watson—Siege and capture of Fort Watson by Marion and Lee—Battle of Hobkirk's Hill—Watson escapes to Camden—Siege of Fort Motte—Noble conduct of Mrs. Motte—Marion rescues a prisoner from assassination.. 155

CHAPTER XVIII.

General Greene's opinion of General Marion—Misunderstanding between Marion and Greene—Reconciled—Lord Rawdon evacuates Camden—General Sumter takes Orangeburg—Lee captures Fort Granby—Siege of Ninety-Six—Greene pursues Rawdon to Orangeburg and offers battle—The British garrison evacuates Ninety-Six, and joins Rawdon at Orangeburg—Operations of Greene to cause the evacuation of Orangeburg—Sumter and Marion sent to the posts at Monk's Corner and Dorchester—Colonel Wade Hampton's exploits—Attack on Colonel Coates at Shubrick's plantation—Effect of these operations on the country—Lord Rawdon sails for Europe............... 169

CHAPTER XIX.

State of the southern country—Bitter hostility between the contending parties—Cruel excesses—Moderation of General Greene—Rawdon succeeded by Stewart—Greene prepares to attack Stewart—Secret expedition of Marion—He defeats the British force under Major Frazer, and relieves Colonel Harden—Receives the thanks of Congress—Battle of Eutaw Springs.. 179

CHAPTER XX.

Events succeeding the battle of Eutaw—Marion chosen to a seat in the Assembly of South Carolina—Laws passed by the Assembly—Marion's brigade suffers a severe defeat in his absence—He returns to the brigade and restores order and reinspires confidence—Greene takes post at Bacon's Bridge—Mutiny in his army...................... 186

CHAPTER XXI.

Marion takes post at Sinkler's plantation—Suppresses an insurrection in North Carolina—Second treaty with Gainey—Rescues Butler—Affair of Fanning—Marion defeats Frazer—General Leslie seeks an armistice, which Greene refuses—Leslie's incursions into the country to obtain provisions—Resisted by Gist's detachment—Colonel Laurens killed—Evacuation of Charleston by the British army.............. 198

CHAPTER XXII.

Marion's parting with the brigade—His resemblance to Washington—He retires to his plantation—Finds it desolated—Resumes his agricultural pursuits—Is elected Senator—The confiscation act—Anecdote of his magnanimity—Voted thanks and a medal by the Senate—Appointed to command Fort Johnson—Marion's marriage—His death—His character.. 206

MAJOR GENERAL WILLIAM MOULTRIE.

CHAPTER I.

Family and birth of Moultrie—His services in the war with the Cherokees—Returns to his plantation—Condition of South Carolina—Moultrie takes an active part at the opening of the Revolution—Member of Provincial Congress—Chosen Colonel of the famous Second Regiment of South Carolina—Seizes the king's stores of arms and ammunition—Devises the flag—Drives the British ships out of Charleston harbor.. 213

CHAPTER II.

Invasion of South Carolina by the fleet and army under Gen. Clinton—Defence of Sullivan's Island by Colonel Moultrie—Opinions of General Lee and Governor Rutledge—Presentation of colors to the Second Regiment—Officers who were in Fort Sullivan on the 28th of June—Vote of thanks by Congress—Declaration of Independence read to the army—Lee's expedition to Florida—Moultrie predicts its failure—It fails—Lee's thanks to the troops—General Moultrie's brigade placed on the continental establishment—General Lee goes to the north—Moore succeeds him—Moultrie stationed at Haddrill's Point—Nash succeeds Moore................................. 218

CHAPTER III.

Moultrie attached to Lincoln's army—Moultrie's account of the fall of Savannah, and the succeeding events—Moultrie at Purysburg—Ordered to Port Royal Island—Defeats the British there—Lincoln marches into Georgia—General Prevost enters South Carolina and marches for Charleston—His march retarded by Moultrie—Moultrie defends Charleston against Prevost and prevents its capture—Prevost returns to Georgia... 228

CHAPTER IV.

General Moultrie appointed commander in chief of the Southern army to take the place of Lincoln, who has permission to retire on the plea of ill health—Lincoln however remains with the army—His dissatisfaction at the criticisms on his campaign in Georgia—The correspondence between Jay and Moultrie respecting his appointment—General Moultrie attends the legislature as a Senator—His notice of the siege of Savannah... 238

CHAPTER V

Moultrie stationed at Bacou's Bridge—His force there—Leaves his command and goes to Charleston—Siege of Charleston—Surrender—Coolness of Moultrie—His account of the surrender and the explosion of the magazine—Moultrie sent to Haddrill's Point............................ 244

CHAPTER VI.

Moultrie a prisoner at Charleston—Attempt of Colonel Balfour and Lord Montague to gain him over to the British side—Balfour's letter to Moultrie's son—Lord Montague's letter to Moultrie, and his noble answer—Moultrie's important services while a prisoner in Charleston—Exchange of prisoners—Moultrie goes to Philadelphia on parole—Is exchanged—Returns to his plantation in South Carolina—Is present at the evacuation of Charleston by the British—His description of the scene—Moultrie elected Governor of South Carolina —Close of his life... 254

MAJOR GENERAL ANDREW PICKENS.

CHAPTER I.

Birth and ancestry of General Pickens—His father emigrates to Virginia, and afterwards to South Carolina—Pickens serves in the French war, and in the Cherokee war—Engages in farming at the Long Cane settlement—Serves in the Revolutionary war in the South —Defeats the loyalists at Kettle Creek—Services after the fall of Charleston—At the battle of Cowpens—Attached to the main army—Detached with Marion to North Carolina—Pursuit of Tarleton, and defeat of Pyle... 269

CHAPTER II.

Pickens and Lee besiege and take Augusta—They rejoin the main army—Battle of Eutaw—Pickens's expedition against the Cherokee Indians—Services as commissioner under the treaty of Hopewell—Member of the Convention of South Carolina—Of the Legislature—Member of Congress—Consulted by Washington on Indian affairs—Appointed Major General—Retires from public life—Recalled to the Legislature in 1812—His death and character............................ 280

GOVERNOR JOHN RUTLEDGE.

CHAPTER I.

Birth and parentage of Governor Rutledge—Education—Practice at the bar—Resistance to Governor Boone—Member of the Continental Congress—Member of the Convention—Member of Congress—President of South Carolina—His conduct in relation to the defence of Fort Moultrie.. 291

CHAPTER II.

Rutledge chosen Governor of South Carolina—Member of Congress—His important services—Minister to Holland—Judge of the Court of Chancery—Member of Constitutional Convention—Associate Judge of Supreme Court—Chief Justice of the United States—His death..... 298

GOVERNOR EDWARD RUTLEDGE... 305
COLONEL JOHN LAURENS.. 310
COLONEL JOHN EAGER HOWARD.. 317
COLONEL CARRINGTON.. 318
CAPTAIN O'NEAL.. 319

LIFE OF
GENERAL FRANCIS MARION.

CHAPTER I.

Francis Marion—Descendant from French Huguenots—Sketch of the history of the Huguenots in France—Repeal of the Edict of Nantz—Emigration of the Huguenots to foreign countries—A party among whom were the ancestors of Marion settled in South Carolina—Sufferings of the emigrants described by Mrs. Manigault—Happy condition of the Carolina Huguenots as described by Mr. Laurens Jealousy of the English Settlers—The French refugees denied political rights—Political rights subsequently granted to them.

GENERAL FRANCIS MARION was one of the most celebrated heroes of the Revolutionary War. His fame rests upon the extraordinary nature of his services; and these were owing to the peculiar characteristics of his mind. In person, he was slight and diminutive; and no instance of victory in single combat is recorded among his exploits; but in the strategy required by his position and resources, in the moral firmness, so indispensable to a great commander, and in the personal influence which holds captive the hearts of the soldiery, and commands their most unlimited devotion, he was unrivalled. Even Washington and Napoleon were not his superiors, in this respect. In the South, during his life-time, his popularity was unbounded; and since his decease, his fame has become the cherished possession of his country, destined to endure till the sun of American liberty and independence shall set, to rise no more.

General Marion was descended from the old French Huguenot stock. Better blood never flowed in the veins of heroes, patriots, and martyrs. Among them were men, and women too, who perilled all, sacrificed all, which the world holds dear, for conscience sake. The Pilgrim Fathers suffered for the cause of religion. But their sufferings will not bear comparison with those of the Huguenots.

We trust the reader will pardon us for giving a slight sketch of the history of these noble defenders of the Protestant religion.

The principles of Luther and Zwinglius had gained an entrance into France, during the reign of Francis I. (1515—47). The doctrines of Calvin spread still more widely, although Francis endeavored to suppress them, by prohibiting Calvinistic books, and by penal laws, and, in some instances, by capital punishments.

Under Henry II., the successor of Francis, these doctrines made greater progress, in proportion as they were more violently persecuted. The opinions and influence Queen Margaret of Navarre had no small share in this extension, and the parties at court contributed much to the bloody persecution of the Protestants. One party wished to enrich themselves by the estates of the heretics, who were executed or banished, and the other to gain the favor of the people by their punishment. The parties of the Bourbons and of the five princes of Guise, under the government of the weak Francis II., made use of this religious dispute, in order to advance their own political ends.

The Bourbons belonged to the Protestant party; and the Guises, in order to weaken, and, if possible, to destroy their rivals, continued the persecution of the heretics with fanatical fury. In every parliament, there was a chamber established to examine and punish the Protestants, called by the people the *burning chamber* (*chambre ardente*), because all convicted of heresy were burnt. The estates of those who fled were sold, and their children who remained behind were exposed to the greatest sufferings. But notwithstanding this persecution, the Protestants would not have thought of a rebellion, had not a prince of the blood encouraged them to it, by the promise of his assistance.

In 1560, the conspiracy began. The discontented inquired of lawyers and theologians, whether they could, with a good conscience, take arms against the Guises. The Protestant divines in Germany declared it proper to resist the tyranny of the Guises, if it were under the guidance and direction of a prince of the blood, and with the approbation of the majority in the states.

The malcontents having consulted upon the choice of a leader, all voices decided in favor of the brave Prince Louis of Condé, who had conducted the whole affair, and gladly seized the opportunity to make himself formidable by the support of the Huguenots. The name of the leader was, however, kept secret, and a Protestant gentleman of Perigord, John du Barry, *seigneur* of Renaudie, was appointed his deputy.

It was determined, that a number of the Calvinists should appear on an appointed day, before the king at Blois, to present a petition for the free exercise of their religion; and, in case this request was denied, as it was foreseen it would be, a chosen band of armed Protestants were to make themselves masters of the city of Blois, seize the Guises, and compel the king to name the prince of Condé, regent of the realm.

This plot was betrayed. The court left Blois, the military were summoned, and the greatest part of the Protestants, who had armed themselves to carry the conspiracy into effect, were executed or imprisoned. Few of those who fell into the power of the court, found mercy; and about 1200 expiated their offence with their lives.

The Guises now desired to establish the inquisition, but the wise chancellor, Michael de l'Hopital, in order to avoid the greater evil, advised that all inquiries into the crime of heresy should be committed to the bishops, and that parliament should be prohibited from exercising any jurisdiction in matters of faith; and it was so ordered by the edict of Romorantin (1560).

In the reign of the next king, Charles IX., during whose minority the queen mother, Catharine de Medici, was at the head of the government, the contest between the parties became yet more violent, and their contending interests were more and more used for a pretence to accomplish unholy designs; and it was only from motives of policy that the free exercise of their religion was secured to the Protestants, by the queen, in order to preserve the balance between the parties, by the edict of January (1562), so called. The Protestants thereby gained new courage; but their adversaries, dissatisfied with this ordinance, and regardless of decency, disturbed the Huguenots in their religious services. Bloody scenes were the result, and the massacre of Vassy (1592) was the immediate cause of the first civil war.

These religious wars desolated France almost to the 16th century, and were only interrupted by occasional truces. The suffering which these wars brought upon the people, is to be ascribed to the instability and bad policy of Queen Catharine de Medici, who exerted the most decided influence, not only over the feeble Charles IX., but likewise over the contemptible Henry III. She wished, in fact, for the extirpation of the Huguenots, and it was merely her intriguing policy, which induced her, much to the vexation of the opposite party, to favor the Protestants from time to time, and to grant them freedom of conscience. Always wavering between the two parties, she flattered herself with the expectation of holding them in check during peace, or of destroying the one by the other in war. Both parties were, therefore, generally dissatisfied with the court, and followed their own leaders.

A wild fanaticism seized the people. Heated with passion and religious hatred, they endeavored only to injure each other; and, with the exception of some party leaders, who made use of this excitement for the accomplishment of their own ambitious schemes, their only object was to acquire the superiority for their own creed, by fire and sword.

The horrible effect of Catharine's policy was the massacre of St. Bartholomew's (1572), of which she and her son, her pupil in dissimulation, had laid the plan with their confidants. Shortly before the line of kings of the house of Valois had become extinct with Henry III., and the way was opened for the house of Bourbon, the head of which was the Protestant Henry king of Navarre, the relations of the two parties became still more involved.

The feeble king found himself compelled to unite with the king of Navarre against the common enemy, as the intrigues of the ambitious Guises, who openly aimed at the throne, had excited the people against him in such a degree, that he was on the point of losing the crown.

After the assassination of Henry III., the king of Navarre was obliged to maintain a severe struggle for the vacant throne; and not until he had, by the advice of Sully, embraced the Catholic religion (1593), did he enjoy quiet possession of the kingdom.

Five years afterwards, he secured to the Huguenots their civil rights, by the edict of Nantes, which confirmed to them the free exercise of their religion, and gave them equal claims with the Catholics to all offices and dignities. They were also left in possession of the fortresses which had been ceded to them for their security.

This edict afforded them the means of forming a kind of republic within the kingdom, and such a powerful party, which had for a long time been obliged to be distrustful of the government, would always offer to the restless nobility a rallying point and a prospect of assistance.

Louis XIII., the weak and bigoted son of the liberal and magnanimous Henry IV., allowed himself to be influenced by his ambitious favorite, De Luinnes, and his confessor, against the Huguenots, who were able to offer a powerful resistance, as they had become very numerous in many provinces. But in the first religious war, which broke out in 1621, the Protestants lost the greatest part of their strong places, through the faithlessness or cowardice of the governors. Some of these, however, and among the rest Rochelle, remained to them, when, disunited among themselves and weary of war, they concluded a peace.

Rochelle enabled them to keep up a connection with England; and Richelieu, who aimed to make the royal power, which he exercised under the name of Louis, absolute, used every means to deprive the Protestants of this bulwark of their liberty, and thus destroy every remnant of a league which recalled the times when civil factions had so often weakened the royal power.

Rochelle fell into the hands of Louis, after an obstinate defence, in 1629; the Huguenots were obliged to surrender all their strongholds, and were thus left entirely at the mercy of the king. Freedom of conscience was indeed promised them, and Richelieu and his successor Mazarin did not disturb them in the enjoyment of it; but when Louis XIV. abandoned his voluptuous life for an affected devotion, he was led by his confessors and Madame de Maintenon, to persecute the Protestants, for the purpose of bringing them back to the bosom of the true church.

In 1681, he deprived them of most of their civil rights, and, on the death of Colbert, who had generally opposed violent measures, he followed altogether the advice of his counsellors, who were in favor of persecution—his minister of war, Louvois, the chancellor Le Tellier, and the Jesuit La Chaise, his father confessor. Bodies of dragoons were sent into the southern provinces, where the Protestants were most numerous, to compel the unhappy inhabitants to abjure their faith.

To prevent the emigration of the Protestants, the frontiers were guarded with the utmost vigilance; yet more than 500,000 Huguenots fled to Switzerland, Germany, Holland, and England. Many who could not escape, were obliged to renounce their faith. Lists of Protestants, who, it was pretended, had been converted, were sent to the king, and it was very easy for his flattering counsellors to persuade him that he had gained honor, by having almost extirpated the Protestants in France. Under this erroneous supposition, he revoked the Edict of Nantz, Oct. 22, 1685. But he had still more than half a million of Protestant subjects, and this unjust and unwise revocation robbed France of a great number of useful and rich inhabitants, whose industry, wealth, and skill, found a welcome reception in foreign countries.

It was not till five years after the revocation of the Edict of Nantz, (about 1690,) that a certain considerable body of French Huguenots, among whom were the ancestors of Marion, emigrated to South Carolina, and took up their residence in that province, which had then been settled only twenty years before by British colonists. As they were of the same religion, and were generally poor and destitute, having been robbed of their property before leaving France, they were received with open arms, and had afforded them the shelter and asylum which they sought. They were not the only party of French Huguenots who settled in South Carolina, others having come before them; and others who had settled previously in England, and in the more northern states being destined to come after them. The party of which we speak had escaped from France to England, and then had emigrated to South Carolina.* It consisted of eighty or a hundred families, who settled on the banks of the Santee river, at first; and from them that part of the country in the old maps was called French Santee. They subsequently extended their settlements toward the Wynyah and the sources of the Cooper river.

* The revocation of the Edict of Nantz, fifteen years subsequent to the settlement of Carolina, contributed much to its population. In it, soon after that event, were transplanted from France the stocks from which have sprung the respectable families of Bonneau, Bonnetheau, Bordeaux, Benoist, Boiseau, Bocquet, Bacot, Chevalier, Cordes, Couterier, Chastagnier, Dupre, Delysle, Dubose, Dubois, Deveaux, Dutarque, De la Consiliere, De Leiseline, Douxsaint, Du Pont, Du Bourdieu, D'Harriette, Faucheraud, Foissin, Faysoux, Gaillard, Gendron, Gignilliat, Guerard, Godin, Girardeau, Guerrin, Gourdine, HORRY, HUGER, Jeannerette, Legare, LAURENS, La Roche, Lenud, Lansac, MARION, Mazyck, Manigault, Mellichamp, Mouzon, Michau, Neufville, Prioleau, Peronneau, Perdriau, Porcher, Postell, Peyre, Poyas, Ravenel, Royer, Simons, Sarazin, St. Julien, Serre, Trezevant. *Ramsay's History of South Carolina.*

What sort of trials these Carolina Huguenots had to undergo may be learnt by the following quotation from Ramsay's History of South Carolina:

A letter written in French by Judith Manigault, the wife of Peter Manigault, who were the founders of the worthy family of that name, may give some faint idea of the sufferings of these French Protestant refugees. This lady, when about twenty years old, embarked in 1685 for Carolina, by the way of London. After her arrival, she wrote to her brother a letter, giving an account of her adventures. This letter translated into English, is as follows:—" Since you desire it, I will give you an account of our quitting France, and of our arrival in Carolina. During eight months, we had suffered from the contributions and the quartering of the soldiers, with many other inconveniences. We therefore resolved on quitting France by night, leaving the soldiers in their beds, and abandoning the house with its furniture. We contrived to hide ourselves at Romans, in Dauphigny, for ten days, while a search was made after us; but our hostess being faithful, did not betray us when questioned if she had seen us. From thence we passed to Lyons—from thence to Dijon—from which place, as well as from Langres, my eldest brother wrote to you: but I know not if either of the letters reached you. He informed you that we were quitting France. He went to Madame de Choiseul's, which was of no avail as she was dead, and her son-in-law had the command of every thing: moreover, he gave us to understand that he perceived our intention of quitting France, and if we asked any favors from him, he would inform against us. We therefore made the best of our way for Metz, in Lorraine, where we embarked on the river Moselle, in order to go to Treves—from thence we passed to Cochieim, and to Coblentz—from thence to Cologne, where we quitted the Rhine, to go by land to Wesel, where we met with an host, who spoke a little French, and who informed us we were only thirty leagues from Lunenburg. We knew that you were in winter quarters there, by a letter of yours, received fifteen days before our departure from France, which mentioned that you should winter there. Our deceased mother and myself earnestly besought my eldest brother to go that way with us; or, leaving us with her, to pay you a visit alone. It was in the depth of winter: but he would not hear of it, having Carolina so much in his head that he dreaded losing any opportunity of going thither. Oh, what grief the losing so fine an opportunity of seeing you at least once more, has caused me! How have I regretted seeing a brother show so little feeling, and how often have I reproached him with it! but he was our master, and we were constrained to do as he pleased. We passed on to Holland, to go from thence to England. I do not recollect exactly the year, whether '84 or 85, but it was that in which king Charles of England died, (Feb. 1685.) We remained in London three months, waiting for a passage to Carolina. Having embarked, we were sadly off: the spotted fever made its appearance on board our vessel, of which disease many died, and among them our aged mother. Nine months elapsed before our arrival in Carolina. We touched at two ports—one a Portuguese, and the other an island called

Bermuda, belonging to the English, to refit our vessel, which had been much injured in a storm. Our captain having committed some misdemeanor, was put in prison, and the vessel seized. Our money was all spent, and it was with great difficulty we procured a passage in another vessel. After our arrival in Carolina, we suffered every kind of evil. In about eighteen months our elder brother, unaccustomed to the hard labor we were obliged to undergo, died of a fever. Since leaving France we had experienced every kind of affliction—disease—pestilence—famine—poverty—hard labor. I have been for six months together without tasting bread, working the ground like a slave; and I have even passed three or four years without always having it when I wanted it. God has done great things for us, in enabling us to bear up under so many trials. I should never have done, were I to attempt to detail to you all our adventures: Let it suffice that God has had compassion on me, and changed my fate to a more happy one, for which glory be unto him." The writer of the above letter died in 1711, seven years after she had given birth to Gabriel Manigault, who in a long and useful life accumulated a fortune so large, as enabled him to aid the asylum of his persecuted parents with a loan of $220,000, carrying on its revolutionary struggle for liberty and independence. This was done at an early period of the contest, when no man was certain whether it would terminate in a revolution or a rebellion.*

* Three of the nine presidents of the old Congress which conducted the United States through the revolutionary war, were descendants of French protestant refugees, who had emigrated to America in con-

The French settlers in Carolina formed to a certain extent a separate community. They were settled, as we have already stated, on the Santee river. Mr. John Lawson, Surveyor General of North Carolina, in a book of travels published in London in 1709, quoted by Mr. Simms, in his "Life of Marion," thus speaks of the community of Carolina Huguenots:

"There are," says he, "about seventy families seated on this river, who live as decently and happily as any planters in these southward parts of America. The French being a temperate, industrious people, some of them bringing very little of effects, yet, by their endeavours and mutual assistance among themselves (which is highly to be commended), have outstripped our English, who brought with them large fortunes, though (as it seems) less endeavour to manage their talent to the best advantage. 'Tis admirable to see what time and industry will, (with God's blessing) effect," &c.

"We lay all that night at Mons. Eugee's (Huger,) and the next morning set out further, to go the remainder of our voyage by land. At ten o'clock we passed over a narrow deep swamp, having left the three Indian men and one woman, that had piloted the canoe from Ashley river, having hired a Sewee Indian, a tall, lusty fellow, who carried a pack of our clothes, of great weight. Notwithstanding his burden, we had much ado to keep pace with him. At noon we came up with several French plantations. Meeting with several creeks by the way,

sequence of the revocation of the Edict of Nantz. The persons alluded to were Henry Laurens, of South-Carolina; John Jay, of New-York; and Elias Boudinot, of New-Jersey.

the French were very officious in assisting us with their small dories to pass over these waters: whom we met coming from their church, being all of them very clean and decent in their apparel; their houses and plantations suitable in neatness and contrivance. They are all of the same opinion with the church of Geneva, there being no difference among them concerning the free method of their Christian faith; which union hath propagated a happy and delightful concord in all other matters throughout the whole neighborhood; living amongst themselves as one tribe or kindred, every one making it his business to be assistant to the wants of his countrymen, preserving his estate and reputation, with the same exactness and concern as he does his own; all seeming to share in the misfortunes, and rejoice at the advance and rise of their brethren."

This happy, and peaceable, and prosperous community soon became the object of jealousy to the English settlers. This circumstance is thus noticed by Dr. Ramsay:*

Another source of controversy between the proprietors and the people, was the case of the French refugees. Many of these, exiled from their own country towards the close of the 17th century, had settled in the province; particularly in Craven county.† They were an

---

* History of South Carolina.

† South Carolina, soon after its first settlement, was divided into four counties, Berkeley, Craven, Colleton, and Carteret. Berkeley county filled the space round the capital; Craven to the northward, and Colleton contained Port Royal, and the islands in its vicinity, to the distance of thirty miles. Carteret lay to the south west.

orderly, industrious, religious people. Several brought property with them which enabled them to buy land, and settle with greater advantages than many of the poorer English emigrants. While they were busy in clearing and cultivating their lands, the English settlers began to revive national antipathies against them, and to consider the French as aliens and foreigners, legally entitled to none of the privileges and advantages of natural born subjects. The proprietors took part with the refugees and instructed their governor, Philip Ludwell, who in 1692 had been appointed the successor of Seth Sothell, to allow the French settled in Craven county the same privileges and liberties with the English colonists; but the people carried their jealousy so far that at the next election for members to serve in the assembly, Craven county, in which the French refugees lived, was not allowed a single representative. At this period the assembly of South Carolina consisted of twenty members, all chosen in Charleston.

This was in 1692. In 1696, the same historian thus records the final settlement of these difficulties between the French and English settlers:

The national antipathies against the French refugees in process of time began to abate. In common with others, they had defied the dangers of the desert and given ample proofs of their fidelity to the proprietors, and their zeal for the success of the colony. They had cleared little spots of land for raising the necessaries of life, and in some measure surmounted the difficulties of the first state of colonization. At this favorable juncture the refugees, by the advice of the governor and other friends, petitioned the legislature to be incorporated with the freemen of the colony and allowed the same privileges and liberties, with those born of English parents. Accordingly an act passed in 1696 for making all aliens, then inhabitants, free—for enabling them to hold lands, and to claim the same as heirs to their ancestors, provided they either had petitioned, or should within three months petition, Governor Blake for these privileges and take the oath of allegiance to King William. This same law conferred liberty of conscience on all Christians, with the exception of papists. With these conditions the refugees, who were all Protestants, joyfully complied. The French and English settlers being made equal in rights, became united in interest and affection, and have ever since lived in peace and harmony.

CHAPTER II.

Marion's descent—His grandfather a French Huguenot—His father and family—His feeble childhood—He desires to become a sailor—Opposed by his mother—Goes to sea—The vessel founders at sea and he has a narrow escape from death—Returns to farming—Parallelisms in the lives of Washington and Marion—Both pass much of their lives as planters—Both serve in the Indian and the Revolutionary wars—Some characteristics of Marion.

AMONG the Huguenots who emigrated to South Carolina in 1690, as stated in the last chapter, was Benjamin Marion the grandfather of Francis. Weems, in his "Life of Marion,"* states that he brought money, probably received from his wife's parents, and from the sale of his farm in France; and that, on his arrival in Carolina, they went up into the country, and bought a plantation on Grave Creek, near Charleston. His eldest son, Gabriel, married Miss Charlotte Cordes, by whom he had six children, Esther, Gabriel, Isaac, Benjamin, Job, and Francis. "As to his sister Esther," says Weems, "I have never heard what became of her; but for his four brothers, I am happy to state, that though not

* The Life of General Francis Marion, a celebrated Partisan officer in the Revolutionary War, against the British and Tories in South Carolina and Georgia. By General P. Horry of Marion's Brigade and M. L. Weems, formerly Rector of Mount Vernon Parish.

formidable as soldiers, they were very amiable as citizens."

Francis Marion was born at Winyah near Georgetown, South Carolina, in 1732, the same year which gave birth to Washington. The early life of Marion by no means held forth any remarkable promise of distinction. At his birth he was so exceedingly puny and diminutive, that little expectation was entertained of rearing him to manhood, nor did he ever attain the ordinary stature. But when he had arrived at the age of twelve years, his constitution appears to have undergone a change; he became exceedingly fond of active occupations and sports; and he soon acquired that vigor, hardihood, and power of endurance for which he was so noted in after life. His advantages of school instruction are not recorded; but they must have been respectable for the time and the country in which he lived.*

Marion's spirit of enterprise and his fondness for active pursuits led him, as the same disposition has many other boys, George Washington among the rest, to make choice of the seafaring life as a pursuit. His mother, like Washington's, endeavored to dissuade him from his purpose, but in this she was not so successful as the mother of the Great Virginian At the age of sixteen he shipped on board of a small vessel bound to the West Indies. But the voyage was singularly unfortunate. The vessel was struck by a whale, a plank was started, and the leak occasioned by this circumstance, soon compelled the crew to abandon the sinking craft and take

---

* This we know by the style of his correspondence and his recorded speeches in public, always brief, terse, and to the purpose.

to the jolly boat, in such haste that they were not able to bring off any provisions or water. In this destitute condition, with no food but the flesh of a dog which had followed them into the boat, they were tossed about in the open sea for six days. Two of their number died. The survivors were finally picked up by a passing vessel, and restored to their homes.

Among the survivors of this disastrous voyage was Francis Marion. His slight and delicate frame had already become sufficiently hardened to bear a degree of suffering and exposure which had proved fatal to strong men. Fortunately for his country, he was effectually cured of all predilection for the life of a mariner. He returned contentedly to his former rural pursuits. He became an industrious and successful farmer. His father died in 1757, Francis remained with his mother till 1759. when he removed to the Parish of St. John, where he settled on the plantation, which continued to be his home during the remainder of his life.

There are several parallelisms in the lives of Marion and Washington. We have already noticed one in their desire for going to sea. Another presents itself in the fact that in the early and forming period of manhood they were both devoted to agricultural pursuits. Both were successful planters. Washington was a planter before serving against the Indians, and he spent fifteen years in planting between the close of his service in the Old French War and the beginning of the Revolutionary War. Marion spent a shorter period as planter before his service in the Indian War of South Carolina, and, then returned to his farm, and was engaged in agriculture about thirteen years before he engaged in the Revolutionary contest. We shall see in the course of Marion's life, that there were other points of resemblance; although we would by no means insinuate that Marion is to be brought into any near comparison with the illustrious Father of his Country.

How Marion passed his time in these periods of rural life, we can only conjecture. One thing we know, however, that whatever he did was done earnestly and with a will. His Huguenot blood and education, as well as the character which he displayed in after times, give assurance that he considered the business of life a serious affair; that he regarded his talents and opportunities as gifts from the Creator, of the use of which he must give account hereafter; that he acted in every relation from a solemn sense of duty; and that in all circumstances and situations he was ever alive to the claims of honor and christian charity.

The time was now near when he was to enter the field as warrior, and show the metal he was made of, in the great theatre of public action.

CHAPTER III.

Marion's first military service in the war with the Cherokees—Origin of the war—Horse stealing—Revenge of the Virginians—Attack of the Cherokees on the Carolinians—Marion serves in a troop of cavalry—The Indians send chiefs to Charleston to make peace—Lyttleton detains them and marches into the Indian country—Chiefs shut up at Fort Prince George—Conference with Attakullakulla—Treaty—Small pox in the camp—Cost of Lyttleton's expedition—Great joy of the Carolinians—Marion has no opportunity for distinction in this campaign.

MARION'S first military service was in the war with the Cherokees, which broke out in the year 1759. This war lasted through three campaigns, and was attended with all those circumstances of danger, difficulty, and hardship, which were best calculated to fit him for the peculiar duties of a partisan leader, in which character he was destined to take so signal a part in the more important conflict for national independence.

The war between France and England, which commenced in 1754 or 1755, induced both nations to court the friendship of the Indians. The French were assiduous in connecting a chain of influence with the aborigines, from Canada to the mouth of the Mississippi. The British pursued a similar line of policy, but less extensive. Governor Glen held a treaty with the Cherokees in 1755, ostensibly to brighten the chain of friendship, but really to obtain a cession of their lands and a liberty to erect forts on the western frontier, as a barrier against the French on the south-west. Both were granted.

In the progress of the war the French were defeated in Canada, and compelled to abandon Fort Duquesne. After they had retreated from the latter down the Ohio, and the Mississippi, they had the address to involve the Indians in a serious war with Carolina. By the reduction of Fort Duquesne, the scene of action was changed from Pennsylvania and Virginia to Carolina; and the influence of the French soon appeared among the upper tribes of Cherokees.

An unfortunate quarrel with the Virginians helped to forward their designs. In the successful expedition of 1758, against Fort Duquesne, the Cherokees had sent considerable parties of warriors to the assistance of the British army. While the savages were returning home from that expedition, through the back parts of Virginia, many of them having lost their horses took possession of such as came in their way. The Virginians, instead of asserting their rights in a legal manner, resented the injury by force of arms and killed twelve or fourteen of these unsuspicious warriors. The Cherokees, with reason, were highly provoked at such ungrateful usage; and when they came home, gave a highly colored account thereof to their nation. They became outrageous. Those who had lost friends and relations, resolved upon revenge. In vain did the chieftains interpose their authority. Nothing could restrain the ferocity of the young men. The emissaries of France among them added fuel to the flame, by declaring that the English intended to kill all the Indian men and make slaves of their wives and children. They inflamed their resentments, stimulated them to bloodshed, and furnished them with arms and ammunition to revenge themselves. Parties of young warriors took the field, and rushing down among the white inhabitants murdered and scalped all who came in their way.

The commanding officer at Fort Prince George dispatched a messenger to Charleston, to inform Governor Lyttleton that the Cherokees had commenced war. Orders were given to the commanders of the militia immediately to collect their men, and stand in a posture of defence. The militia of the country were directed to rendezvous at Congarees, where the governor resolved to join them and march to the relief of the frontier settlements. Francis Marion was one of the volunteers who joined the governor's army on this occasion. He served in a company of cavalry, commanded by his brother.

No sooner had the Cherokees heard of these warlike preparations, than thirty-two of their chiefs set out for Charleston to settle all differences. Though they could not restrain some of their young men from acts of violence, yet the nation in general was inclined to friendship and peace. As they arrived before the governor had set out on the intended expedition, a council was called; and the chiefs being sent for, Governor Lyttleton, among other things, told them "that he was well acquainted with all the acts of hostility of which their people had been guilty, and likewise those they intended against the English," and enumerated some of them. Then he added "that he would soon be in their country, where he would let them know his demands and the satisfaction he required, which he would certainly take if it was refused. As they had come to Charleston to treat with him as friends, they should go home in safety and not a hair of their heads should be touched; but as he had many warriors in arms, in different parts of the province, he could not be answerable for what might happen to them unless they marched with his army." After this speech was ended, Occonostota, who was distinguished by the name of the great warrior of the Cherokee nation, began to speak by way of reply; but the governor having determined that nothing should prevent his military expedition, declared "he would hear no talk in vindication of his nation nor any proposals with regard to peace." This highly displeased the Indians.

In a few days after this conference the governor set out for Congarees, where he mustered about fourteen hundred men. To this place the Cherokees marched with the army and were in appearance contented, but in reality burned with fury. When the army moved from the Congarees, the chieftains were all made prisoners. To prevent their escaping, as two had already done, a captain's guard was mounted over them. Being not only deprived of their liberty, but compelled to accompany an enemy going against their families and friends, they no longer concealed the resentment raging in their breasts. Sullen looks and gloomy countenances showed that they were stung to the heart by such treatment.

Upon the arrival of the army at Fort Prince George, the Indians were all shut up in a hut scarcely sufficient for the accommodation of six soldiers.

The army being not only poorly armed and disciplined, but also discontented and mutinous; it was judged dangerous to proceed farther into the enemy's country. The governor sent for Attakullakulla, who was esteemed the wisest man of the nation and the most steady friend of the English, to meet him at Fort Prince George. This summons was promptly obeyed. On the 17th December, 1759, they held a Congress at which the governor, in a long speech, stated to Attakullakulla the injuries done by the Cherokees to the white people in violation of existing treaties—the power of the English—the weakness and many defeats of the French, and then concluded as follows:

"These things I have mentioned to show you that the great king will not suffer his people to be destroyed without satisfaction, and to let you know that the people of this province are determined to have it. What I say is with a merciful intention. If I make war with you, you will suffer for your rashness; your men will be destroyed, and your women and children carried into captivity. What few necessaries you now have will soon be exhausted, and you will get no more. But if you give the satisfaction I shall ask, trade will be again opened and all things go right. I have twice given you a list of the murderers. I will now tell you there are twenty-four men of your nation whom I demand to be delivered up to me to be put to death, or otherwise disposed of as I shall think fit. Your people have killed that number of ours and more; therefore it is the least I will accept of. I shall give you till to-morrow to consider of it, and then I shall expect your answer. You know best the Indians concerned. I expect the twenty-four you deliver up, will be those who have committed the murders.

To this long speech Attakullakulla replied in words to the following effect: "That he remembered the treaties mentioned, as he had a share in making them. He owned the kindness of the province of South Carolina, but complained much of the bad treatment his countrymen had received in Virginia; which, he said, was the immediate cause of the present misunderstanding. That he had always been the warm friend of the English— that he would ever continue such, and would use all the influence he had to persuade his countrymen to give the governor the satisfaction he demanded; though he believed it neither would nor could be complied with, as they had no coercive authority one over another." He desired the governor to release some of the head men then confined in the fort to assist him, and added, " that he was pleased to hear of the success of his brothers the English;" but could not help mentioning "that they showed more resentment against the Cherokees than they did to other nations who had disobliged them. That he remembered some years ago several white people belonging to Carolina were killed by the Choctaws, for whom no satisfaction had either been demanded or given."

Agreeably to the request of Attakullakulla, the governor released Occonostota, Fiftoe the chief man of Keowee town, and the head warrior of Estatoe, who next day delivered up two Indians whom Mr. Lyttleton ordered to be put in irons. After which all the Cherokees present, who knew their connections to be weak, instantly fled; so that it was impossible to complete the number demanded. Attakullakulla, being then convinced that peace could not be obtained on the terms demanded by the governor, resolved to go home and patiently wait the event; but no sooner was Mr. Lyttleton made acquainted with his departure, than he dispatched a messenger after him to bring him back to his camp; and immediately on his return began to treat of peace.

Accordingly a treaty was drawn up and signed by the governor, by Attakullakulla, another chief, and four of the confined warriors, who, together with a few others, thereupon obtained their liberty. By one article of this treaty it was agreed, "that twenty-six chieftains of the Cherokees should be confined in the fort as hostages, until the same number of Indians guilty of murder were delivered up to the commander-in-chief of the province." This was said to be done with their own consent; but as they were prisoners they could have no free choice. If they must remain confined, it was a matter of little moment under what denomination they were kept. One more Indian was delivered up, for whom one of the hostages was released. The three Indians, given up by their companions, were carried to Charleston where they died in confinement.

After having concluded this treaty with the Cherokees, the governor returned to Charleston. Perhaps the Indians who put their mark to these articles of agreement did not understand them, or conceived themselves to be so far under restraint as not to be free agents in the transaction, and therefore not bound by it. Whether either of these or deliberate perfidy was the case, cannot be ascertained; but it is certain that few or none of the nation afterwards paid the smallest regard to it. The treacherous act of confining their chiefs, against whom no personal charge could be made, and who had travelled several hundred miles to obtain peace, was strongly impressed on their minds. Instead of permitting them to return home "without hurting a hair of their heads," as the governor promised in Charleston, they were confined in a miserable hut. It was said they were kept only as hostages until the number of criminals demanded was completed by their nation. It was also said to be done by the consent of the nation, as six of its chiefs had signed the articles of peace; but when the relative situation of the parties, and all circumstances are considered, nothing less could have been expected than that these wild and independent warriors would violate the articles they had signed and retaliate for the confinement of their chiefs.

Scarcely had Governor Lyttleton concluded the treaty of Fort Prince George when the small-pox, which was raging in an adjacent Indian town, broke out in his camp. As few of the army had gone through that distemper, the men were struck with terror and in great haste returned to the settlements; cautiously avoiding all intercourse with one another and suffering much from hunger and fatigue by the way. The governor followed them, and arrived in Charleston on January 8th, 1760. This expedition cost the province £25,000 sterling.

Though not a drop of blood had been spilt during the campaign, yet as articles of peace were signed, the governor as commander-in-chief was received like a conqueror with the greatest demonstrations of joy.*

In this, Marion's first campaign, there was no fighting with the Indians, and as he appears to have held no office, he had, of course, no opportunity for any kind of distinction. But the war was not yet over, and before its conclusion we shall hear of him again.

* Ramsay's History of South Carolina.

CHAPTER IV.

Second campaign against the Cherokees—Surprise and death of Captain Cotymore—Murder of the Indian hostages—Terrible revenge of the Indians on the frontier inhabitants—General Amherst sends a force of regulars to Carolina under Colonel Montgomery—Governor Bull succeeds Lyttleton—Arrival of Montgomery—The militia rendezvous at Congarees—Marion with the army—Capture of Indian towns—Difficult march—Action near Etchoe—Return of Montgomery—Siege and surrender of Fort Loudon,—Noble conduct of Attakullakulla to Captain Stuart.

The rejoicings on account of the peace were scarcely over, when news arrived that fresh hostilities had been committed, and that the Cherokees had killed fourteen men within a mile of Fort Prince George. The Indians had contracted an invincible antipathy to Captain Cotymore, the officer whom Governor Lyttleton had left commander of that fort. The treatment they had received at Charleston, but especially the imprisonment of their chiefs, converted their former desire of peace into the bitterest rage for war. Occonostota, a chieftain of great influence, became an implacable enemy to Carolina, and determined to repay treachery with treachery. With a strong party of Cherokees he surrounded Fort Prince George, and compelled the garrison to keep within their works; but finding that no impression could be made on the fort, he contrived the following stratagem for the relief of his countrymen confined in it.

He placed a party of savages in a dark thicket by the river side and then sent an Indian woman, whom he knew to be always welcome at the fort, to inform the commander that he had something of consequence to communicate and would be glad to speak with him at the river side. Captain Cotymore imprudently consented, and without any suspicions of danger walked down towards the river accompanied by Lieutenants Bell and Foster. Occonostota appearing on the opposite side, told him he was going to Charleston to procure a release of the prisoners, and would be glad of a white man to accompany him as a safeguard. To cover his dark design he had a bridle in his hand, and added he would go and hunt for a horse. Cotymore replied that he should have a guard, and wished he might find a horse as the journey was very long. Upon which, the Indian turning about, swung the bridle thrice round his head as a signal to the savages placed in ambush, who instantly fired on the officers, shot the captain dead, and wounded his two companions. In consequence of which, orders were given to put the hostages in irons to prevent any further danger from them. When the soldiers were attempting to execute these orders, the Indians stabbed one and wounded two more of them; upon which the garrison fell on the unfortunate hostages, and butchered all of them in a manner too shocking to relate.

There were few men in the Cherokee nation that did not lose a friend or a relation by this massacre, and therefore with one voice all immediately declared for war. The leaders in every town seized the hatchet, telling their followers " that the spirits of their murdered brothers were hovering around them and calling out for vengeance on their enemies." From the different towns large parties of warriors took the field, painted in the most formidable manner and arrayed with their instruments of death. Burning with impatience to imbrue their hands in the blood of their enemies, they rushed down among innocent and defenceless families on the frontiers of Carolina; where men, women and children, without distinction, fell a sacrifice to their merciless fury. Such as fled to the woods and escaped the scalping knife, perished with hunger; and those whom they made prisoners were carried into the wilderness where they suffered inexpressible hardships. Every day brought fresh accounts of their ravages and murders. But while the back settlers impatiently looked to their governor for relief, the small pox raged to such a degree on the sea coast, that few of the militia could be prevailed on to leave their distressed families. In this extremity an express was sent to General Amherst the commander-in-chief of the British forces in America, acquainting him with the deplorable situation of the province and imploring his assistance. Accordingly a body of fine picked troops, consisting of six companies of the royal Scots regiment, and six companies of the seventy-second, in which were included the grenadiers and light infantry companies of several regiments, was put under the command of Colonel Montgomery and ordered immediately to Carolina.

In the mean time William Henry Lyttleton being appointed governor of Jamaica, the charge of the province devolved on William Bull. Application was made to the neighbouring provinces of North-Carolina and Virginia for relief. Seven troops of rangers were raised to protect the frontiers, and prevent the savages from penetrating further down among the settlements, and to co-operate with the regulars for carrying offensive operations into the Indian country.

Before the end of April, 1760, Colonel Montgomery landed in Carolina and encamped at Monk's corner. Great was the joy of the province upon the arrival of this gallant officer; but as the conquest of Canada was the grand object of that year's campaign in America, he had orders to strike a sudden blow for the relief of Carolina and instantly return to head quarters at Albany. Nothing was omitted that was judged necessary to forward the expedition. Several gentlemen of fortune, excited by a laudable zeal for the safety of their country, formed themselves into a company of volunteers, and joined the army. The whole force of the province was collected and ordered to rendezvous at Congarees.

Tradition informs us that Marion volunteered and served in this campaign, but Mr. Simms, the most intelligent of his biographers, says that the records are silent on the subject. Many of the records of South Carolina, however, were destroyed in the revolutionary war, and it seems but fair to accept the traditionary accounts of his service in this second campaign.

A few weeks after his arrival Colonel Montgomery

marched to the Congarees, where he was joined by the militia of the province, and immediately set out for the Cherokee country. Having little time allowed him, his march was uncommonly expeditious. After reaching a place called Twelve Mile river, he proceeded with a party of his men in the night to surprise Estatoe, an Indian town, about twenty miles from his camp. On his way there was another town called little Keowee. He ordered the light infantry to surround the latter, and to put every adult male Indian in it, to the sword. He then proceeded to Estatoe which he found nearly abandoned. This town, which consisted of at least two hundred houses, and was well provided with corn, hogs, poultry, and ammunition, he reduced to ashes. Sugar-town, and and every other settlement in the lower nation, shared the same fate. The surprise to every one of them was nearly equal, and so sudden and unexpected, that the savages could scarcely save themselves, far less any little property they had. In these lower towns about sixty Indians were killed and forty made prisoners, and the rest driven to seek for shelter among the mountains. Having finished his business among these lower settlements, with the small loss of three or four men, he marched to the relief of Fort Prince George.

Edmund Atkin, agent for Indian affairs, dispatched two Indian chiefs to the middle settlements to inform the Cherokees that by suing for peace they might obtain it as the former friends and allies of Britain. Colonel Montgomery, finding that the savages were not yet disposed to listen to any terms of accommodation, determined to carry the chastisement a little further. Dismal was the wilderness into which he entered, and many were the hardships and dangers he had to encounter from passing through dark thickets, rugged paths, and narrow defiles, in which a small body of men properly posted might harass the bravest army. He also had numberless difficulties to surmount; particularly from rivers fordable only at one place, and overlooked by high banks on each side, where an enemy might attack with advantage, and retreat with safety. When he had advanced within five miles of Etchoe, the nearest town in the middle settlements, he found a low valley covered so thick with bushes that the soldiers could scarcely see three yards before them.

Through this natural ambuscade it was necessary for the army to march, though the nature of the place would not admit any number of men to act together. Captain Morison, who commanded a company of rangers well acquainted with the woods, was therefore ordered to advance and scour this thicket. He had scarcely entered it when a number of savages sprung from their place of concealment, killed the captain and wounded several of his party. Upon which the light infantry and grenadiers advanced and charged the invisible enemy. A heavy fire then began on both sides, and for some time the soldiers could only discover the places where the savages were hid by the report of their guns. The woods resounded with Indian war whoops and horrible yellings.

During the action, which lasted above an hour, Colonel Montgomery had twenty men killed and seventy-six wounded. What number the enemy lost is uncertain, as it is a custom among them to carry their dead off the field. Upon viewing the ground, all were astonished to see with what judgment they had chosen it. Scarcely could the most experienced officer have fixed upon a spot more advantageous for attacking an enemy.

This action terminated much in favor of the British army, but reduced it to such a situation as made it very imprudent to penetrate further into the woods. Orders were therefore given for a retreat which was made with great regularity. A large train of wounded men was brought in safety above sixty miles through a hazardous country. Never did men endure greater hardships, with fewer complaints, than this little army. Colonel Montgomery returned to the settlements, and in August embarked for New York agreeably to his orders; but left four companies for covering the frontiers.

In the meantime the distant garrison of Fort Loudon, consisting of two hundred men, was reduced to the dreadful alternative of perishing by hunger or submitting to the mercy of the enraged Cherokees. The governor having information that the Virginians had undertaken to relieve it, waited to hear the news of their having done so. But so remote was the fort from every settlement, and so difficult was it to march an army through the barren wilderness where the various thickets were lined with enemies; and to carry at the same time sufficient supplies along with them, that the Virginians had relinquished all thoughts of even making the attempt.

Provisions being entirely exhausted at Fort Loudon, the garrison was reduced to the most deplorable situation. For a whole month they had no other subsistence, but the flesh of lean horses and dogs, and a small supply of Indian beans which some friendly Cherokee women procured for them by stealth. In this extremity the commander called a council of war to consider what was proper to be done. The officers were all of opinion that it was impossible to hold out any longer, and therefore agreed to surrender the fort to the Cherokees on the best terms that could be obtained.

For this purpose Captain Stuart procured leave to go to Chotè, one of the principal towns in the neighborhood, where he obtained the following terms of capitulation which were signed by the commanding officer and two of the Cherokee chiefs: "That the garrison of Fort Loudon march out with their arms and drums, each soldier having as much powder and ball as their officer shall think necessary for their march, and all the baggage they may choose to carry. That the garrison be permitted to march to Virginia or Fort Prince George, and that a number of Indians be appointed to escort them and hunt for provisions during the march. That such soldiers as are lame or sick be received into the Indian towns, and kindly used until they recover, and then be allowed to return to Fort Prince George. That the Indians provide for the garrison as many horses as they conveniently can for their march, agreeing with the officers and soldiers for payment. That the fort, great guns, powder, ball, and spare arms, be delivered to the Indians without fraud or further delay on the day appointed for the march of the troops."

Agreeably to these terms the garrison delivered up the fort, and marched out with their arms, accompanied by Occonostota the prince of Choté, and several other Indians; and that day went fifteen miles on their way to Fort Prince George. At night they encamped on a plain about two miles from Taliquo, an Indian town, when all their attendants left them.

During the night they remained unmolested; but next morning, about break of day a soldier, from an outpost, informed them that he saw a number of Indians, armed and painted in the most dreadful manner, creeping among the bushes and advancing to surround them. Scarcely had the officer time to order his men to stand to their arms, when the savages poured in upon them a heavy fire from different quarters accompanied with the most hideous yellings. Captain Paul Demere, with three other officers, and about twenty-six private men, fell at the first onset. Some fled into the woods, and were afterwards taken prisoners and confined. Captain Stuart and those that remained were seized, pinioned, and brought back to Fort Loudon.

As soon as Attakullakulla heard that his friend Stuart had escaped, he hastened to the fort and purchased him from the Indian that took him; giving him his rifle, clothes, and all he could command by way of ransom. He then took possession of Captain Demere's house, where he kept his prisoner as one of his family and freely shared with him the little provisions his table afforded, until a fair opportunity should offer for rescuing him from their hands; but the soldiers were kept in a miserable state of captivity for some time, and then redeemed by the province at a great expense.

While these prisoners were confined at Fort Loudon,

Occonostota formed a design of attacking Fort Prince George; and for this purpose dispatched a messenger to the settlements in the valley, requesting all the warriors there to join him at Stickoey Old Town. By accident, a discovery was made of ten bags of powder, and of ball in proportion, which the officers had secretly buried in the fort to prevent their falling into the enemy's hands. This discovery had nearly proved fatal to Captain Stuart, and would certainly have cost him his life, if the interpreter had not assured the enemy that these warlike stores had been concealed without his knowledge or consent. The Indians having now abundance of ammunition for the siege, a council was called at Choté; to which the captain was brought and put in mind of the obligations he lay under to them for sparing his life. They also stated to him, that as they had resolved to carry six cannon and two cohorns with them against Fort Prince George, to be managed by men under his command, he must go and write such letters to the commandant as they should dictate to him. They informed him at the same time that if that officer should refuse to surrender, they were determined to burn the prisoners one after another before his face, and try if he could hold out while he saw his friends expiring in the flames.

Captain Stuart was much alarmed at his situation, and from that moment resolved to make his escape or perish in the attempt. He privately communicated his design to Attakullakulla, and told him how uneasy he was at the thoughts of being compelled to bear arms against his countrymen. The old warrior taking him by the hand, told him he was his friend. That he had already given one proof of his regard, and intended soon to give another. Strong and uncultivated minds often carry their friendship, as well as their enmity, to an astonishing pitch. Among savages, family friendship is a national virtue; and they not unfrequently surpass civilized men in the practice of its most self-denying, and noblest duties.

Attakullakulla claimed Captain Stuart as his prisoner, and had resolved to deliver him from danger. Accordingly he gave out among his countrymen, that he intended to go a hunting for a few days and carry his prisoner along with him to eat venison. Having settled all matters they set out on their journey, accompanied by the warrior's wife, his brother, and two soldiers. For provisions they depended on what they might kill by the way. The distance to the frontier settlements was great, and the utmost expedition necessary to prevent any surprise from Indians pursuing them. They travelled nine days and nights through a dreary wilderness, shaping their course for Virginia, by the light and guidance of the heavenly bodies. On the tenth they arrived at the banks of Holstein river; where they fortunately fell in with a party of three hundred men, sent out by Colonel Bird for the relief of such soldiers as might make their escape that way from Fort Loudon.

CHAPTER V.

Renewal of hostilities by the Cherokees—Expedition of Colonel Grant—Marion serves in the regiment of provincial volunteers a Lieutenant under Captain William Moultrie—Advance to the Cherokee country—Marion leads the forlorn hope in the battle of Etchoe—Narrow escape with his life—The Cherokees subdued—Marion's remarks on the treatment of the Indians by the whites.

It might now have been expected that the vindictive spirit of the savages would be satisfied, and that they would be disposed to listen to terms of accommodation. But this was not the case. They intended their treacherous conduct at Fort Loudon should serve as a satisfaction for the harsh treatment their relations had met with at Fort Prince George. Dearly had the province paid for the imprisonment and massacre of the Indian chiefs at that place. Sorely had the Cherokees suffered, in retaliation, for the murders they had committed to satisfy their vengeance for that imprisonment and the massacre of their chiefs. Their lower towns had all been destroyed by Colonel Montgomery. The warriors in the middle settlements had lost many friends and relations. Several Frenchmen had crept in among the upper towns, and helped to foment their ill humor against Carolina. Lewis Latinac, a French officer, persuaded the Indians that the English had nothing less in view than to exterminate them from the face of the earth; and furnishing them with arms and ammunition, urged them to war. At a great meeting of the nation he pulled out his hatchet, and striking it into a log of wood called out, "Who is the man that will take this up for the king of France?" Saloné the young warrior of Estatoe instantly laid hold of it, and cried out, "I am for war. The spirits of our brothers who have been slain, still call upon us to avenge their death. He is no better than a woman that refuses to follow me." Many others seized the tomahawk and burned with impatience for the field.

Lieutenant Governor Bull, who well knew how little Indians were to be trusted, kept the royal Scots and militia on the frontiers in a posture of defence; and made application a second time to General Amherst for assistance. Canada being now reduced, the commander-in-chief could the more easily spare a force adequate to the purpose intended. Lieutenant Colonel James Grant, with a regiment from England and two companies of light infantry from New York, received orders to embark for Carolina. Early in the year 1761 he landed at Charleston, where he took up his winter quarters until the proper season should approach for taking the field.

In this campaign, the province exerted itself to the utmost. A provincial regiment was raised, and the command of it given to Colonel Middleton.*

* The other field officers were Henry Laurens Lieutenant Colonel, John Moultrie Major. William Moultrie, Francis Marion, Isaac Huger, Andrew Pickens, Owen Roberts, Adam M'Donald, James M'Donald, and William Mason, served in this expedition and were there trained to further and greater services in the cause of their country.

This regiment numbered twelve hundred men. Francis Marion was attached to it serving as lieutenant in the company of which William Moultrie, afterwards the distinguished General Moultrie, was captain. The service was precisely of that kind which was best suited to fit Marion for his future arduous duties as a partisan commander.

Presents were provided for the Indian allies, and several of the Chickesaws and Catawbas engaged to co-operate with the white people against the Cherokees. All possible preparations were quickly made for supplying the army with every thing necessary for the expedition. Great had been the expense which this quarrel with the Cherokees had already occasioned. The Carolinians now flattered themselves that, by one resolute exertion, they would free the country from the calamities of war.

As soon as the Highlanders were in a condition to take the field, Colonel Grant set out for the Cherokee territories. After being joined by the provincial regiment and Indian allies, he mustered about 2600 men. On the 27th of May, 1761, he arrived at Fort Prince George; and on the 7th of June began his march from it, carrying with him provisions for thirty days. A party of ninety Indians and thirty woodsmen, painted like Indians, under the command of Captain Quintine Ken-

---

They all served in the Revolutionary war, and in the course of it, the first four were promoted to the rank of general officers. Bellamy Crawford, John Huger, Joseph Lloyd, John Lloyd, and Thomas Savage, also served in this expedition; and afterwards in civil departments, in and after the Revolution.—Ramsay's *Hist. S. Carolina.*

nedy, had orders to advance in front and scour the woods. When near to Etchoe, the place where Colonel Montgomery was attacked the year before, the Indian allies in front observed a large body of Cherokees posted upon a hill on the right flank of the army. An alarm was given. Immediately the savages rushing down began to fire on the advanced guard, which being supported repulsed them; but they recovered their heights.

Under these heights lay the line of march which it was necessary for the army to pursue in their advance; and the men would thus be exposed to a murderous fire from the enemy, concealed by the rocks and trees on each side, which rendered this pass of Etchoe, the most difficult and dangerous defile in the whole Indian country. It was their Thermopylæ. It therefore became a matter of imperative necessity to dislodge them from this post before the army could proceed.

For this important, but exceedingly dangerous service, which could only have been entrusted to an officer of known ability and undoubted courage, Marion had the honor to be detailed at the head of a forlorn hope of thirty men. His conduct in the affair is thus described by Weems:

At the head of his command, he advanced up the hill and entered the defile, every part of which was full of danger. Hardly were they within the gorge, before a terrible war-whoop was heard, and a sheet of fire from savage rifles illumined the forest. The discharge was most deadly. Twenty-one men fell to the ground; but Marion was unhurt. The rapid advance of the next detachment saved the survivors, who fell back and united with their companions. The battle now became general; the regulars remained in order and poured continuous volleys of musketry into the wood; the provincials resorted to their rifles, and with unerring aim, brought down the Indians as they appeared on each side of the pass. The contest was close and bloody; the regulars at length resorting to the bayonet and driving the savages before them. From eight o'clock until two, the battle continued; but the whites achieved a signal victory. One hundred and three natives were slain ere they yielded the ground, and left a free passage to Grant and his army.

The Cherokee town of Etchoee was immediately reduced to ashes, and the whites then proceeded to burn their wigwams, and lay waste their country. The fields, in which the corn was already tasselled and ripening for harvest, were overrun and utterly ruined. Severity may have been necessary in order to break the spirit of the savages; but we cannot regard such devastation without profound sorrow. On this point Marion presents himself to us in an interesting light, and his own words shall be used to prove that to the courage and the firmness of the soldier, he united the tender feelings of a true philanthropist:—"I saw," he says, "everywhere around, the footsteps of the little Indian children where they had lately played under the shade of this rustling corn. No doubt they had often looked up with joy to the swelling shocks, and gladdened when they thought of their abundant cakes for the coming winter. When we are gone, thought I, they will return, and peeping through the weeds with tearful eyes, will mark the ghastly ruin poured over their homes and happy fields, where they had so often played. 'Who did this?' they will ask their mothers; 'The white people did it,' the mothers reply; 'the Christians.' "*

After this war of devastation, the army returned and was disbanded. They had encountered severe toil and bloody conflict; but their object was accomplished. The Cherokees were effectually subdued, and even in the subsequent war with England they gave the Americans but little annoyance. Marion left his regiment and returned to the repose of rural life.

* Marion's letter in Weems, 25; Simms's Marion, 52.

CHAPTER VI.

Marion and Washington follow farming as a pursuit for several years—Washington's political course—South Carolina takes a prominent part in the Revolution—Organizes a Provincial Congress—Marion a Member—Acts of that Congress—Arrival of Lord William Campbell—Activity of the members of Congress—Colonel Moultrie—His account of the acts of the patriots—News of the Battle of Lexington—Seizure of arms, gunpowder, and of the royal mail.

At the close of the Cherokee war, Marion returned, as we have seen, to his plantation at St. Johns, and resumed the quiet life of a farmer. In the cultivation of his land, and in the usual country sports of hunting, shooting, and fishing, he passed his time for the next fourteen years, (1761—1775). Precisely in the same pursuits Washington was engaged at the same time; but as Virginia, with Massachusetts, took a leading part in the political dispute which led to the Revolution, Washington, during this period, was more actively engaged in politics than Marion. During the whole of this period, the illustrious Virginian was a member of the House of Delegates of his native State, and by his voice, his vote, and his pen, strenuously advocated the rights of the colonists, which had been invaded by the oppressive acts of the British ministry and parliament.

South Carolina was not backward in resisting the arbitrary acts of the mother country. When the Bostonians threw the East India Company's tea into their harbor, the Charleston men destroyed the obnoxious article in a less summary but not less effectual manner. South Carolina sent delegates to the first Continental Congress in 1774; and in the succeeding year, organized a provincial congress which adopted the Bill of Rights, and at once placed herself in the front rank of the resisting colonists.

Of this memorable provincial congress, Francis Marion was elected a member, from St. John's, Berkley county. His colleagues were his brother, Job Marion, James Ravenell, Daniel Ravenell, John Frierson, Gabriel Gignilliat. This congress assembled on the 11th of January, 1775, at Charleston, then the residence of the royal Lieutenant Governor William Bull. Their acts were all of a bold and decisive character. Besides adopting the Bill of Rights as declared by the Continental Congress, they adopted the Act of Association recommended by the same body, by which the subscribers bound themselves to prevent the importation of British goods, and to hold no intercourse with colonies or provinces not acceding to the terms of the Association. In imitation of the more northern colonies this congress established a complete system of committees of safety and correspondence, passed resolves for relieving the Bostonians in the distress occasioned by the Boston Port Bill, and fully approved their conduct in resisting the British government.

They also sent a bold remonstrance to Lieutenant Governor Bull, citing the oppressive acts of the British government, and requesting him to summon the General Assembly of the Province. In his answer the royal functionary, of course, refused to recognize their authority, and defined his position.

Without paying any further attention to this representative of the royal authority, the congress proceeded to the decisive step of recommending to the people a complete system of military organization throughout the province.

Bull was succeeded by a new governor, Lord William Campbell, who was received with great courtesy, and the usual demonstrations of loyalty to the king's immediate representative. At this period it was the fashion of the patriots to profess perfect loyalty to the *king*, and to charge all the grievances, of which they complained, on the *ministry*. Washington, in his letters to Congress during the siege of Boston, calls the enemy, the *ministerial army*. This style was maintained, and hopes were entertained of a reconciliation until the Declaration of Independence. These hopes were expressed by all parties equally, but the most ardent leaders, such as the Adamses, Franklin, Patrick Henry, and others, undoubtedly foresaw the end from the outset, and many of them were fully determined that there should be no reconciliation.

Lord William Campbell appears to have been a mild and courteous gentleman, thoroughly ignorant of American affairs, and desirous of peace; and he probably considered the professions of the people who welcomed his arrival as an earnest of attachment to the mother country; but he was destined to be speedily undeceived.

Among the members of the provincial congress were some of the most active and determined patriots in the province, and they by no means confined themselves to their legislative duties; but entered with lively zeal into the execution of the acts which they had passed. After transacting their business as legislators, they adjourned to meet again on the 20th of June, 1775.

Among the members of this congress was William Moultrie, who had been captain of the company, in which Marion served as lieutenant, in the third campaign against the Cherokees. Moultrie had now been advanced to the rank of colonel. In his Memoirs of the "American Revolution," he gives the following graphic account of what passed in South Carolina after the adjournment of the Congress:

Agreeably to a recommendation of the provincial congress, the militia were forming themselves into volunteer uniform companies; drums beating, fifes playing; squads of men exercising on the outskirts of the town; a military spirit pervaded the whole country; and Charleston had the appearance of a garrison town. Every thing wore the face of war; though not one of us had the least idea of its approach; and more especially of its being so near to us, for we were anxiously looking forward to a reconciliation; when, on the 19th day of April, war was declared against America, by the British troops firing upon the inhabitants at Lexington; an account of which flew over the whole continent; and now the hopes of a reconciliation were at an end; and recourse to arms was the only and last resort.

In this situation were we when the battle of Lexington was fought, without arms or ammunition: some there were in the King's stores, but we could not get them without committing some violent act. A few gentlemen went to Captain Cochran (the King's store-keeper) and demanded the keys of him: he said "He could not give them up, neither could he hinder them from breaking open the doors;" this hint was enough; there was no time for hesitation; and that night a number of gentlemen went and broke open the doors, and carried away to their own keeping, 1200 good stand of arms. Lieutenant Governor Bull offered a reward of one hundred pounds sterling to any person who would discover the persons concerned in the business; but to no purpose.

We had now got the arms, but no ammunition; the next thing to be done, was the breaking open the magazines; as we were fairly entered into the business we could not step back, and the next day we broke open the magazines, and found in that at Hobea, 1700 lb.; at the Ship-yard, 600 lb.; some little at Fort Charlotte, in the back country, and in private stores, the whole making about 3000 lb. of powder, which was all we had to begin our great Revolution. On the same day the battle of Lexington was fought, a packet arrived at Charleston from England: the public letters were taken out by the secret committee, the particulars I have from Mr. Corbet,* as follows:

"I was a member of the secret committee of the State; and some time in 1775, a packet arrived from England (it was about the time that disputes ran high with Lord William Campbell, the then Governor, and it was re-

* A member of the Provincial Congress.

solved by that committee to get possession of the mail, that was expected in that packet; and for that purpose the member who should first know of the packet's coming in, should give notice to the others, and be ready at the Post-Office, to get possession of the mail; as I lived at the south end of the Bay, I was the first member who knew of her coming, and immediately gave notice thereof to such as I could first find in time to intercept the mail. On its arrival, William Henry Drayton, and John Neufville, they two and myself, immediately went to the Office, kept then by Stevens, and demanded the mail; he peremptorily refused it, and we as peremptorily demanded it, declaring that we would take it by force if not delivered quickly, having authority for that purpose; he said we might do as we pleased, but that he should not deliver it: we then took possession of it, (for which he entered a regular protest against us,) we carried it to the State-house, and summoned the rest of the Committee. When the mail was opened, it contained (besides private letters) dispatches to Governor Dunmore, of Virginia, Governor Martin, of North Carolina, Governor Campbell, of South Carolina, Governor Wright of Georgia, and Governor Tonyne, of Augustine, (the private letters were all returned to the Post-Office unopened,) the others were opened, and read, and found to contain the determination of England to coerce America; and directing the respective Governors to prepare such provincial forces as they could, to co-operate when they should come. These dispatches were thought of so much consequence, as to be sent by express to Congress; and I have understood that it was the first certain accounts of the determination of the councils of England to subjugate the colonies by force; and the effect was that congress resolved to raise an army, and prepare seriously for defence.

Yours, &c.   Thomas Corbet."

About this time a letter from Governor Wright to General Gage, going to the northward, was intercepted by the secret committee, and opened; in it was found a request to General Gage to send a detachment of his Majesty's forces to awe the people of Georgia; the secret committee took out his letter, and put another in the cover, (with his name counterfeited,) in which they mention to General Gage, "that he had wrote for troops to awe the people, but that now there was no occasion for his sending them, that the people were again come to some order:" thus were the Americans obliged to take great strides to defeat the purposes of the British Government.

The above extract from Moultrie's Memoirs, gives a glimpse of the real spirit of the times. The Charleston men of that period were, verily, *men of action*.

CHAPTER VII.

Meeting of the Provincial Congress of South Carolina—State of affairs—The Congress raises an army—Obtains powder—Military ardor of leading citizens—Officers of the army chosen by ballot—The Rangers—Distinguished men among the officers—Colonel Moultrie in command of the second regiment—Marion and Peter Horry captains in the same regiment—Their complete success in recruiting men for their companies.

On receiving news of the battle of Lexington, which took place on the 19th of April 1775, the general committee of safety of South Carolina immediately summoned the provincial congress to meet on the first day of June.

"At this summons," says Moultrie,* "the people were greatly alarmed, and their minds so much agitated, they were anxiously waiting for the day of the meeting that they might consult with their countrymen, on what was best to be done at this critical juncture; they saw that a war was inevitable; and that it was to be with that country which first planted them in America, and raised them to maturity; a country with which they were connected by consanguinity; by custom, and by manners; by religion; by laws, and by language; a country that they had always been taught to respect and to consider

* Memoirs.

as amongst the first in the world. A rich and powerful nation, with numerous fleets, and experienced admirals sailing triumphant over the ocean; with large armies and able generals in many parts of the globe. This great nation we dared to oppose, without money; without arms; without ammunition; no generals; no armies; no admirals; and no fleets; this was our situation when the contest began. On our first meeting they determined upon a defensive war; and the fourth day it was resolved to raise two regiments of five hundred men each; and some confidential gentlemen were immediately sent to the West-India Islands, in small fast sailing vessels, to procure powder. They were so successful as to bring home ten thousand pounds, which was a very seasonable supply. The military ardor was so great, that many more candidates presented themselves, from the first families in the Province, as officers for the two regiments than were wanted; every one was zealous in the cause; those who through infirmities and particular domestic situations could not take the field, went into the cabinet and other civil employment; and in this way did we divide ourselves in different departments.

"The day after the officers of the first and second regiments of foot were balloted for, it was resolved to raise a regiment of cavalry rangers of five hundred men. The pay and rations of the officers in the British service had at that time; the soldiers had one shilling sterling per day; the rangers had much more, as they were to find their own horses. In regard to the regiment of rangers, it was thought not only useful, but politic to raise them, because the most influential gentlemen in the back country were appointed officers, which interested them in the cause."

In organizing the army, referred to in the above extract from Moultrie's Memoirs, the reader will observe that instead of the company officers being elected by the men as in New England, they were balloted for by congress. Their first duty it appears was to recruit the men required for service.

Among the officers elected by the provincial congress to serve in the first and second regiments, we recognize some of the most illustrious names in American history. Christopher Gadsden was Colonel of the first regiment, and William Moultrie of the second. Among the captains were Charles Cotesworth Pinckney, Francis Marion, Peter Horry, Daniel Horry, Thomas Pinckney, and Francis Huger.

Marion, no doubt, was well pleased to serve in the regiment of Colonel Moultrie, who had been his captain at Etchoe. He had already begun to raise recruits, when (June 21) his commission was made out. In his recruiting service he was assisted by Captain Peter Horry, who belonged also to Colonel Moultrie's regiment.

They were very successful in recruiting, and in a short time made up the requisite number of sixty men for each of their companies. The men were enlisted only for a term of six months. This bad system of short enlistments was followed at that time in all the other colonies. Washington's army at the siege of Boston was very near dissolution at one time from this excuse.

Many of the recruits for the second regiment were of Irish descent. Among them were two soldiers, Jasper and Macdonald, who afterwards became celebrated for their exploits during the war.

"About this time," says Moultrie, "the Catawba Indians were alarmed, and could not tell what to make of it, on seeing such military preparations throughout the country; they sent down two runners to Charleston, to be informed of the reasons. They had been told different stories, and they came down to know the truth. The Council of Safety sent up by them a talk to their nation, acquainting them that our brothers on the other side of the water wanted to take our property from us without our consent, and that we would not let them; and that we expected their warriors would join ours. The Council of Safety informed them that the people of Boston had had a great fight * with the red-coats, and had killed a great many of them. The Catawbas were requested to send the talk on to the Cherokees.

* Battle of Lexington.

CHAPTER VIII.

Noble conduct of Carolina at the commencement of the Revolutionary War—State of parties—Activity of the tories—Marion concerned in the first act of open hostility—The capture of Fort Johnson—Colonel Moultrie directs this service—His account of the capture and of the events immediately succeeding it.

SOUTH CAROLINA deserves infinite credit for the bold stand which she took at the very commencement of the Revolutionary War. Had her leading citizens consulted their own ease, and the safety of their fortunes, they would have joined the royal cause. Georgia did not join the other colonies till July 1777. But South Carolina sent delegates to the Continental Congress of 1774, and never faltered in her patriotism even when the enemy was in possession of every military post in the colony. Her Gadsdens, Pinckneys, Moultries, Marions, and Sumters, had counted the cost of independence, and literally risked "their lives, their fortunes, and their sacred honor in its defence."

This conduct of the Carolina patriots is the more creditable to them from the fact, that through the whole contest they had to encounter the formidable opposition of a powerful party of tories, which pervaded the whole province, and rendered the most active service to the royal cause. In 1775, before the actual commencement of hostilities at Charleston, this party was strenuously opposing the proceedings of the patriots, and endeavoring to intimidate the people, by painting in glowing colors the terrible dangers to be encountered in a contest with so powerful a nation as Great Britain; and their emissaries were already stirring up the Indians on the Western border to take part in the impending hostilities, on the side of the crown.

Relying on the support of this party, the royal governor, Lord William Campbell, still continued to reside in Charleston, and to exercise certain acts of authority, even after the provincial congress had ordered a levy of troops. While these troops were being raised, two British men of war, the Tamar and the Cherokee, were anchored in Rebellion Roads opposite Sullivan's Island; and Fort Johnson, on James's Island, was held by a garrison of the king's forces.

This anomalous state of affairs was undoubtedly owing to the still existing doubt in the minds of both parties, whether open war was really about to ensue. But this doubt was not permitted to continue long. In the first act of overt hostility, Marion was destined to take a part. This was the capture of Fort Johnson situated on the most northernly point of James's Island, and within point blank shot of the channel, and held, as already stated, by a British garrison.

Doctor Ramsay says that this measure was decided, because "about the middle of September, 1775, the general committee became possessed of intelligence, obtained by artifice, directly from Lord William Campbell, 'that troops would be sent out to all the colonies.' On the next evening," he continues, "it was resolved that proper measures ought immediately to be taken to prevent Fort Johnson being made use of to the prejudice of the colony."

This service was entrusted to Colonel Moultrie. His account of the expedition is so characteristic and graphic that we copy it in detail, with the orders, &c. He says :*

Fort Johnson was still garrisoned by the British, under Colonel Howarth's command. I was ordered to send and take possession of it. A day or two before the fort was taken, Colonel Howarth, whom the inhabitants respected very much, was invited to go with a party into the country, to be out of the way, that no injury should happen to his person or character; he went, accordingly, not suspecting our intentions.

By the order I received from the Council of Safety, for taking Fort Johnson,† they must have conceived it a hazardous and dangerous attempt, by the number of men they required for that service.

"In Council of Safety.
"CHARLESTON, Sep. 13, 1775.

"Sir,—You are to detach one hundred and fifty men under such command as you shall judge most proper for the service; to embark this night at a proper time of the tide, to proceed with the utmost secrecy and land at a convenient place on James' Island. Mr. Verree and Mr. William Gibbs will be at Captain Stone's, or in the

---

* Moultrie's Memoirs. Vol. 1. p. 86.
† The garrison we were certain had but six men and a gunner.

neighborhood, attending the landing, in order to conduct the commanding officer to Fort Johnson, which he is to enter and take possession of, with as much secrecy and silence as possible; taking especial care that none belonging to the fort escape, and that no intelligence be given but by his orders. When the officer, who shall be sent upon this service is in possession of the fort, he is immediately to give notice to this board and wait for orders; except only in case the man-of-war* now lying in the Rebellion-road, should make an attempt to attack the fort or proceed towards this town, when he is to do every thing in his power to prevent her progress. Captain Stone, of James' Island, will order his company of militia to join the troops which you send, and the whole are to be detained till relieved by our order.

"By order of the Council of Safety.

"HENRY LAURENS, President.

"WILLIAM MOULTRIE, Esq. Colonel of the second Regiment."

In consequence of receiving this order, I immediately issued the subsequent orders to the troops:

"GENERAL ORDERS,

"14th September, 1775, 4 o'clock, P. M.

"Ordered, that Captains Charles Cotesworth Pinckney's, Bernard Elliot's, and Francis Marion's companies be immediately completed to fifty men each, from their respective corps, and hold themselves in readiness to march in three hours. Colonel Motte is appointed for this command, and will receive his orders from the commanding officer."

* Always in dread of this man-of-war.

The orders given to Colonel Motte were similar to those I received from the Council of Safety.

This detachment went on board their boats at twelve o'clock at night, at Gadsden's-wharf, and, dropping down with the ebb tide, landed on James' Island, a little above the fort, and marched in immediately unmolested; the garrison escaped to the man-of-war, then in the road, but not before they had thrown down all the guns and their carriages from off the platform, which plainly shows that they had information of our intentions to take the fort.

So little were we acquainted with naval affairs, and so highly impressed with the mighty power of a British man-of-war, that although we had got possession of a strong fort and one hundred and fifty good regular troops, and the James' Island company of militia of about fifty men, yet the Council of Safety was so fearful of the Tamar sloop-of-war mounting 14 or 16 six pounders, attacking the fort, that they gave me orders to send down two hundred and fifty men, as a reinforcement to Colonel Motte, which I did by the following order.

"GENERAL ORDERS, Sept. 15, 1775.

"Ordered, that Captains Benjamin Cattel, Adam M'Donald, and John Barnwell's companies of the first regiment, and that Captains Peter Horry, and Francis Huger's companies be completed to fifty men each, and to hold themselves in readiness to march. Major Owen Roberts to command this detachment."

"To MAJOR OWEN ROBERTS, of the first regiment.

"Sir—You are to proceed with your detachment to

Gadsden's-wharf, where you will find two schooners ready to take on board your party; with them you will proceed to Fort Johnson on James' Island; on your arrival there you are to send an officer to Colonel Motte to acquaint him. Then march to the fort and put yourself under his command; you are not to suffer any boats* to obstruct your passage."

"To LIEUTENANT COLONEL MOTTE.

"Sir,—I have sent Major Roberts with two hundred and fifty men to reinforce you. You are to defend the fort from all parties that may attempt to land, but if the man-of-war† should attack the fort, and you find you cannot make a stand against her, you are to withdraw your men to some place of safety, out of the reach of her guns; but you are to take care not to suffer any parties to land with an intent to damage the fort."

At the same time Captain Thomas Heyward, with a detachment of Charleston artillery, went down with gin and tackles and had three cannon mounted immediately.

About this time the Cherokee sloop-of-war arrived. A little time after we were in possession of Fort Johnson, it was thought necessary to have a flag for the purpose of signals: (as there was no national or state flag at that time,) I was desired by the Council of Safety to have one made, upon which, as the state troops were clothed in blue, and the fort was garrisoned by the first and

---

* Fear of the man-of-war boats.

† Every order and every movement of ours shows how fearful we were of the man of-war; all these orders were issued agreeably to the Council of Safety's directions.

second regiments, who wore a silver crescent on the front of their caps; I had a large blue flag made with a crescent in the dexter corner, to be in uniform with the troops. This was the first American flag which was displayed in South Carolina. On its being first hoisted, it gave some uneasiness to our timid friends, who were looking forward to a reconciliation. They said it had the appearance of a declaration of war ; and Captain Thornborough, in the Tamar sloop-of-war, lying in Rebellion-road would look upon it as an insult, and a flag of defiance, and he would certainly attack the fort; but he knew his own force, and knew the weight of our metal; he therefore kept his station and contented himself with spying us.

Lord William Campbell,* the Governor of the province, when he discovered from on board the Tamar sloop-of-war, that we were in possession of Fort Johnson, he sent his secretary, Mr. Innis, in the man-of-war's boat to the fort, to demand "by what authority we had taken possession of his Majesty's fort ;" he was answered, "by the anthority of the Council of Safety," he then made his bow and went off. After we had taken the fort we were in apprehensions, lest these two small men-of-war should attack the fort or the town; on the 16th September orders were issued that all officers belonging to the two South-Carolina regiments should hold themselves in readiness, upon any alarm, to be immediately at the barracks.

Moultrie's account of this affair, the capture of Fort

* Lord William Campbell went on board the Tamar, for refuge, on the day of the capture of Fort Johnson.

Johnson, without firing a shot, shows throughout the powerful effect of the prestige of British power entertained at that time; as well as the undaunted courage of the patriots in setting that power at defiance. The little Tamar was formidable because she was a British man-of-war; but if she attacked the fort its defenders were to meet force by force, &c. The Carolinians soon learned to place a juster estimate on the character of the British navy. The subsequent affair of Fort Moultrie was soon to set that matter in a truer light.

CHAPTER IX.

State of parties—Captain Thornborough threatens to intercept vessels bound to Charleston—Meeting of Congress—The first actual fighting—Regiment of artillery raised—Moultrie drives the British men of war out of the harbor of Charleston—Two regiments of riflemen ordered to be raised—Marion in command at Dorchester—At Fort Johnson—Marion promoted to the rank of Major—His excellent discipline—Marion engaged in erecting Fort Sullivan—Arrival of General Lee—His opinion in favor of abandoning Fort Sullivan—Colonel Moultrie's account of the defence of Fort Sullivan.

It would naturally be supposed that, after the seizure of Fort Johnson, actual fighting would immediately commence. But such was not the case. Both parties seemed averse to proceed immediately to the final arbitrement of the sword. The royal governor, Lord William Campbell, who still remained on board the Tamar, was anxious to gain time till a strong British armament should arrive and quell the rebellion; and he was the rallying point of the tory party throughout the province, who communicated with him by means of emissaries, and received from him promises of support in their opposition to the patriots.

On the other hand, the patriots were not yet prepared to drive away the British ships and the governor by open force. They resorted to an indecisive system of annoyance.

The popular leaders issued orders forbidding the king's victuallers to supply the men of war with provisions and water, otherwise than from day to day. After sundry letters and messages had passed on this subject, Captain Thornborough, of the sloop Tamar, gave public notice, "that if his majesty's agents in Charleston were not permitted regularly, and without molestation, to supply the king's ships, Tamar and Cherokee, with such provisions as he thought necessary to demand, he would not from that day, so far as it was in his power, suffer any vessel to enter the harbor of Charleston, or depart from it."

The new provincial congress met, agreeably to their original appointment, on the 1st of November, 1775. On that day, Captain Thornborough sent his menacing letter to the chairman of the general committee. This congress had been chosen subsequent to the late resolution for raising troops, and resisting Great Britain. The royal servants presumed that the people at large would not justify these invasions of their master's prerogative; and, as they had lately had an opportunity given by a general and free election to express their real opinions on the state of the province, that the new congress would reverse the determinations of the former. To the great surprise of the king's officers the new provincial congress, instead of receding from the resolutions of their predecessors, took methods to ward off the injuries that might arise from the execution of the menaces of Captain Thornborough. They sent out two armed pilot boats with orders to cruise near the bar, and to caution all vessels destined for Charleston to steer for some other port.

The late congress in June had agreed to arm the colony; but many still shuddered at the idea of hostile operations against their former friends and fellow-subjects. It was at length, after much debating, resolved by the new congress, on the 9th of November, 1775, to direct the American officer commanding at Fort Johnson, "by every military operation to endeavor to oppose the passage of any British naval armament that might attempt to pass." Though the fort had been in the possession of the Council of Safety for near two months, yet a variety of motives restrained them from issuing orders to fire on the king's ships. When this resolution was adopted, they communicated it to Captain Thornborough, commander of the Tamar sloop of war.

An open passage to the town, without approaching Fort Johnson, was still practicable for the small royal armed vessels Tamar and Cherokee. It was therefore, at the same time, resolved to obstruct the passage through Hog Island channel. Captain Tufts was ordered to cover and protect the sinking of a number of hulks in that narrow strait. While he was engaged in this business on board a coasting schooner, which was armed for the security of the town and called the Defence, the Tamar and Cherokee warped in the night of November 12, 1775, within gun shot of him and began a heavy cannonade. The inhabitants were alarmed, expecting that the town, in its defenceless state, would be fired upon; but about sunrise both vessels dropped down to their moorings on Rebellion Road, without having done any material injury either to the schooner or to any of her crew. The schooner Defence returned a few shot, but they were equally ineffectual. This was the commencement of hostilities in South Carolina.

On the evening of the same day, on which this attack was made, the provincial congress impressed for the public service the ship Prosper; and appointed a committee to fit and arm her as a frigate of war. On the day following they voted that a regiment of artillery should be raised, to consist of three companies with one hundred men in each.

Agreeably to the menaces of Captain Thornborough, the king's ships in the road seized all the vessels within their reach which were either coming to Charleston or going from it. These seizures commenced several weeks prior to the act of parliament for confiscating American property.

After these unauthorized seizures of private property had been continued about six weeks, the Council of Safety took measures to drive the royal armed vessels out of the road of Charleston.* Colonel Moultrie, with a party, took possession of Haddrill's point and mounted a few pieces of heavy artillery on some slight works. A few well directed shots from this post induced the commanders of the Cherokee and Tamar to put out to sea.

---

* An opinion generally prevailed that these small royal armed vessels could at any time destroy Charleston by firing into it. As often as they bent their sails, an alarm was communicated that they were about to commence a bombardment. The inhabitants were for several months kept in daily painful expectation of such an event.

The harbor and road being clear, the Council of Safety proceeded in their plans of defence. They completed the fortifications at Haddrill's point, and at Fort Johnson—continued a chain of fortifications in front of the town, both to the eastward and southward—and erected a new fort on James' Island to the westward of Fort Johnson, and a very strong one on Sullivan's Island. The militia were diligently trained, the provincial troops were disciplined, and every preparation made to defend the colony.

In addition to the four regiments ordered to be raised in the year 1775, two regiments of riflemen were voted in February 1776.

Before the departure of the king's ships, it had been decided to establish a military post at Dorchester; it being supposed that the powder which had been collected in considerable quantities and the other munitions of war would be safer from seizure by the enemy there than in Charleston, the place being situated twenty miles in the interior on Ashley river.

The stores, public records, and munitions of war were accordingly sent to this place, which was occupied by a garrison under the command of Marion. Garrison duty, however, was by no means suited to his taste. There was nothing for him to do at Dorchester but to train the soldiers and keep guard over the stores. He got transferred to Fort Johnson, and here he found more active employment in completing the defences of that place.

Meantime a formidable invasion was preparing for South Carolina. Sir Henry Clinton, the British commander at New York, had determined to make an attempt on the capital of that colony.

Early in the month of April, a letter from the secretary of state to Mr. Eden, the royal governor of Maryland, disclosing the designs of administration against the southern colonies, was intercepted in the Chesapeake; and thus, South Carolina became apprised of the danger which threatened its metropolis. Mr. Rutledge, a gentleman of vigour and talents, who had been chosen president of that province on the dissolution of the regal government, adopted the most energetic means for placing it in a posture of defence.

In the beginning of June, the British fleet came to anchor off the harbor of Charleston. The bar was crossed with some difficulty; after which, it was determined to commence operations by silencing a fort on Sullivan's island.

During the interval between passing the bar and attacking the fort, the continental troops of Virginia and North Carolina arrived in Charleston; and the American force amounted to between five and six thousand men, of whom two thousand five hundred were regulars. This army was commanded by General Lee, whose fortune it had been to meet General Clinton at New York, in Virginia, and in North Carolina. Viewing with a military eye the situation of the post entrusted to his care, Lee was disinclined to hazard his army by engaging it deeply in the defence of the town; but the solicitude of the South Carolinians to preserve their capital, aided by his confidence in his own vigilance, pre-

'vailed over a caution which was thought extreme, and determined him to attempt to maintain the place.

Two regular regiments of South Carolina, commanded by Colonels Gadsden and Moultrie, garrisoned Fort Johnson and Fort Moultrie. About five hundred regulars, and three hundred militia under Colonel Thompson, were stationed in some works which had been thrown up on the northeastern extremity of Sullivan's Island; and the remaining troops were arranged on Haddrill's Point, and along the bay in front of the town. General Lee remained in person with the troops at Haddrill's Point, in the rear of Sullivan's Island. His position was chosen in such a manner as to enable him to observe and support the operations in every quarter, and especially to watch and oppose any attempt of the enemy to pass from Long Island to the continent; a movement of which he seems to have been particularly apprehensive.

From the first, General Lee had been of opinion that Fort Sullivan ought to be abandoned. He did not believe that it could be defended against a powerful British fleet; "But," says Moultrie, "President Rutledge insisted that it should not be given up." * * * * "General Lee," he continues, "one day on a visit to the fort, took me aside and said, 'Colonel Moultrie, do you think you can maintain this post?' I answered him 'Yes, I think I can,' and that was all that passed on the subject between us."

The following is Colonel Moultrie's account of the memorable defence of Fort Sullivan. As he was in command of the fort, and an eye-witness of the whole affair, we give the narrative in his own words:

On the morning of the 28th of June, I paid a visit to our advanced-guard (on horseback three miles to the eastward of our fort); while I was there, I saw a number of the enemy's boats in motion, at the back of Long Island, as if they intended a descent upon our advanced post; at the same time, I saw the men-of-war loose their topsails. I hurried back to the fort as fast as possible; when I got there the ships were already under sail; I immediately ordered the long roll to beat, and officers and men to their posts. We had scarcely manned our guns, when the following ships of war came sailing up, as if in confidence of victory; as soon as they came within the reach of our guns, we began to fire; they were soon abreast of the fort—let go their anchors, with springs upon their cables, and begun their attack most furiously about 10 o'clock, A. M., and continued a brisk fire till about 8 o'clock, P. M.

The ships were, the Bristol, of 50 guns, Commodore Sir Peter Parker. The captain had his arm shot off, 44 men killed and thirty wounded.

The Experiment, 50 guns: the captain lost his arm, 57 men killed, and 30 wounded. The Active, 28 guns: 1 lieutenant killed, 1 man wounded. The Sole-Bay, 28 guns: 2 killed, 3 or 4 wounded. The Syren, 28 guns. The Acteon, 28 guns: burnt; 1 lieutenant killed. The Sphinx, 28 guns: lost her bowsprit. The Friendship, 26 guns: an armed vessel taken into service.*

The Thunder Bomb had the beds of her mortar soon disabled; she threw her shells in a very good direction;

* The killed and wounded on board of the men-of-war was from their own account.

most of them fell within the fort, but we had a morass in the middle, that swallowed them up instantly, and those that fell in the sand in and about the fort, were immediately buried, so that very few of them bursted amongst us. At one time, the Commodore's ship swung round with her stern to the fort, which drew the fire of all the guns that could bear upon her: we supposed she had had the springs of her cables cut away. The words that passed along the platform by officers and men, were, "Mind the Commodore, mind the two fifty gun ships." Most all the attention was paid to the two fifty gun ships, especially the Commodore, who, I dare say, was not at all obliged to us for our particular attention to him; the killed and wounded on board those two fifty gun ships confirms what I say. During the action, General Lee paid us a visit through a heavy line of fire, and pointed two or three guns himself; then said to me, "Colonel, I see you are doing very well here, you have no occasion for me, I will go up to town again," and then left us.

When I received information of General Lee's approach to the fort, I sent Lieutenant Marion, from off the platform, with 8 or 10 men, to unbar the gateway, (our gate not being finished,) the gateway was barricaded with pieces of timber eight or ten inches square, which required three or four men to remove each piece; the men in the ships' tops, seeing those men run from the platform, concluded "we were quitting the fort," as some author mentions. Another says "we hung up a man in the fort, at the time of the action;" that idea was taken from this circumstance; when the action began, (it being a warm day,) some of the men took off their coats and threw them upon the top of the merlons, I saw a shot take one of them and throw it into a small tree behind the platform, it was noticed by the men and they cried out, "Look at the coat." Never did men fight more bravely, and never were men more cool; * their only distress was the want of powder; we had not more than 28 rounds, for 26 guns, 18 and 26 pounders, when we began the action; and a little after, 500 pounds from town, and 200 pounds from Captain Tufft's schooner lying at the back of the fort.

There cannot be a doubt, but that if we had had as much powder as we could have expended in the time, that the men-of-war must have struck their colors, or they would certainly have been sunk, because they could not retreat, as the wind and tide were against them; and if they had proceeded up to town, they would have been in a much worse situation. They could not make any impression on our fort, built of palmetto logs and filled in with earth. Our merlons were 16 feet thick, and high enough to cover the men from the fire of the tops. The men that we had killed and wounded received their shots mostly through the embrasures.†

An author, who published in 1779, says, "The guns

---

* Several of the officers, as well as myself, were smoking our pipes and giving orders at the time of the action; but we laid them down when General Lee came into the fort.

† Twelve men were killed and 24 wounded. When Sergeant M'Donald received his mortal wound, he, addressing his brother soldiers who were carrying him to the doctor, desired them not to give up, that they were fighting for liberty and their country.

were at one time so long silenced, that it was thought the fort was abandoned; it seems extraordinary that a detachment of land forces were not in readiness on board of the transports or boats, to profit of such an occasion."

The guns being so long silent, was owing to the scarcity of powder which we had in the fort, and to a report that was brought me, "that the British troops were landed between the advance guard and the fort;" * it was upon this information, that I ordered the guns to cease firing, or to fire very slow upon the shipping; that we should reserve our powder for the musketry to defend ourselves against the land forces, there being a great scarcity of powder at this time.

At one time, 3 or 4 of the men-of-war's broadsides struck the fort at the same instant, which gave the merlons such a tremor, that I was apprehensive that a few more such would tumble them down. During the action, three of the men-of-war, in going round to our west curtain, got entangled together, by which the Acteon frigate went on shore on the middle ground; the Sphinx lost her bowsprit; and the Syren cleared herself without any damage; had these three ships effected their purpose, they would have enfiladed us in such a manner, as to have driven us from our guns. It being a very hot day, we were served along the platform with grog in fire-buckets, which we partook of very heartily. I never had a more agreeable draught than that which I took out of one of those buckets at the time; it may be very easily

* The advance, is about 3 miles from the fort at the east end of Sullivan's Island.

conceived what heat and thirst a man must feel in this climate, to be upon a platform on the 28th of June, amidst 20 or 30 pieces of cannon,* in one continual blaze and roar; and clouds of smoke curling over his head for hours together; it was a very honorable situation, but a very unpleasant one.

During the action, thousands of our fellow-citizens were looking on with anxious hopes and fears,† some of whom had their fathers, brothers, and husbands, in the battle; whose hearts must have been pierced at every broadside. After some time our flag was shot away; their hopes were then gone, and they gave up all for lost! supposing that we had struck our flag, and had given up the fort. Sergeant Jasper perceiving that the flag was shot away, and had fallen without the fort, jumped from one of the embrasures, and brought it up through a heavy fire, fixed it upon a spunge-staff, and planted it upon the ramparts again. Our flag once more waving in the air, revived the drooping spirits of our friends; and they continued looking on, till night had closed the scene, and hid us from their view; only the appearance of a heavy storm, with continual flashes and peals like thunder; at night when we came to our slow firing (the ammunition being nearly quite gone) we could hear the shot very distinctly strike the ships. At length the British gave up the conflict. The ships slipped their cables, and dropped down with the tide, and out of the reach of our guns. When the firing had ceased, our friends for a time were again in an unhappy suspense,

* 18 and 26 French pounders.

† At about 6 miles distance.

not knowing our fate; till they received an account by a dispatch boat, which I sent up to town, to acquaint them, that the British ships had retired, and that we were victorious.

Early the next morning was presented to our view, the Acteon frigate, hard and fast aground, at about 400 yards distance; we gave her a few shot, which she returned, but they soon set fire to her, and quitted her. Captain Jacob Milligan and others went in some of our boats, boarded her while she was on fire, and pointed 2 or 3 guns at the Commodore, and fired them; then brought off the ship's bell, and other articles, and had scarcely left her, when she blew up, and from the explosion issued a grand pillar of smoke, which soon expanded itself at the top, and to appearance, formed the figure of a palmetto tree; the ship immediately burst into a great blaze that continued till she burnt down to the water's edge.

The other ships lay at the north point of Morris's Island; we could plainly see they had been pretty roughly handled, especially the Commodore.

The same day, a number of our friends and fellow citizens came to congratulate us on our victory, and Governor Rutledge presented Sergeant Jasper with a sword, for his gallant behaviour;* and Mr. William Logan, a hogshead of rum to the garrison, with the following card: "Mr. William Logan presents his compliments to Colonel Moultrie, and the officers and soldiers on Sullivan's Island, and begs their acceptance of a

---

* Governor Rutledge at the same time offered Jasper a commission, which he declined, from his inability to read and write.

hogshead of old Antigua rum, which being scarce in town at this time, will be acceptable." Mr. Logan's present was thankfully received. A few days after the action, we picked up, in and about the fort, 1200 shot of different calibers that was fired at us, and a great number of 13 inch shells.

Mr. Simms says that tradition ascribes to the hand and eye of Marion the terrible effect of the last shot which was fired on that bloody day. It entered the cabin of the Commodore's ship, cut down two officers who were then drinking, and then passing to the main deck killed three sailors, and having gone clear through the ship, fell into the sea.

CHAPTER X.

Effect of the battle of Fort Moultrie—Rewards to the victors—Presentation of flags—Marion promoted to the rank of Lieutenant Colonel—Another Indian war—Marion sent to Georgia with reinforcements—Placed in command of Fort Moultrie—Invasion and subjugation of Georgia—General Lincoln placed in command of the Southern department—Bad state of defence in which he found South Carolina—He advances to Purysburg.

The gallant defence of the Palmetto Fort on Sullivan's Island, was justly regarded as a most important event. It saved the Carolinas from the horrors of war for a period of three years. Great and well merited praise was bestowed on Colonel Moultrie, who commanded the fort, and on the garrison, for the resolution displayed in defending it. Nor was the glory acquired on this occasion confined to them. All the troops that had been stationed on the island partook of it: and the thanks of the United Colonies were voted by Congress to General Lee, Colonel Moultrie, Colonel Thompson, and the officers and men under their command.

Colonel Moultrie was also honoured with the thanks of the Commander-in-chief and of his fellow citizens; and the fortress which he had so nobly defended was thenceforth called Fort Moultrie. The second regiment of South Carolina which had borne so large a share in the defence was particularly distinguished by the praises of the people, and the compliments of Governor Rutledge.

Proud of the encomiums bestowed on their valor, encouraged by the animating address of the governor, to aim at the achievement of new honors, the feelings of the gallant second regiment were still more highly excited, when Mrs. Barnard Elliot, presenting an elegant pair of colors, thus addressed them:

"GENTLEMEN SOLDIERS,—Your gallant behavior, in defence of your country, entitles you to the highest honors! Accept of these two standards as a reward justly due to your regiment; and I make not the least doubt but that, under heaven's protection, you will stand by them as long as they can wave in the air of liberty."*

Moultrie, now advanced to the rank of Brigadier General, in his answer to this address, pledged the honor of the regiment to a compliance with the lady's implied injunction; and this pledge was nobly redeemed at the siege of Savannah.

Marion's share in the glory of this defence of Charleston was publicly acknowledged by Congress, who raised him to the rank of lieutenant colonel.

The effect of the battle of Fort Moultrie was most salutary throughout the whole country. By impressing upon the people a conviction of their ability to maintain the contest, it increased the number of those who resolved to resist British authority, and determined them to stand

* Garden's Anecdotes.

by the declaration of independence, which took place within a week after the battle was fought.

In South Carolina, the government took advantage of the hour of success to conciliate their opponents in the province. The adherents of royal power, who, for a considerable time, had been closely imprisoned, on promising fidelity to their country, were set at liberty, and restored to all the privileges of citizens. The repulse of the British was also attended with another advantage, that of leaving the Americans at liberty to turn their undivided force against the Indians, who had attacked the western frontier of the Southern States with all the fury and carnage of savage warfare.

In 1775, when the breach between Great Britain and her colonies was daily becoming wider, one Stuart, the agent employed in conducting the intercourse between the British authorities and the Cherokees and Creeks, used all his influence to attach the Indians to the royal cause, and to inspire them with jealousy and hatred of the Americans. He found little difficulty in persuading them that the Americans, without provocation, had taken up arms against Britain, and were the means of preventing them from receiving their yearly supplies of arms, ammunition, and clothing from the British government.

The Americans had endeavored to conciliate the good-will of the Indians, but their scanty presents were unsatisfactory, and the savages resolved to take up the hatchet. Deeming the appearance of the British fleet in Charleston Bay a fit opportunity, the Cherokees invaded the western frontier of the province, marking their track with murder and devastation.

The speedy retreat of the British left the savages exposed to the vengeance of the Americans, who, in separate divisions, entered their country at different points, from Virginia and Georgia, defeated their warriors, burned their villages, laid waste their corn-fields, and incapacitated the Cherokees, for a considerable time, from giving the settlers further annoyance. Thus, in the south, the Americans triumphed over the British and Indians.

After the action at Fort Moultrie, the next notice we have of Marion occurs in connection with an abortive invasion of Georgia, by a British force under Colonel Fuser in February 1779. At the approach of the enemy, General Robert Howe, commanding the troops in South Carolina and Georgia, set off for Savannah, and requested that Colonel Moultrie would order a strong detachment in vessels, within land would follow him. Moultrie ordered Lieutenant Colonel Marion to take the command of the required detachment, which consisted of 600 men, in several vessels, with four field pieces, a large quantity of ammunition, stores, intrenching tools, and provisions. This detachment left Charleston on the 20th of February; but before Marion arrived at Savannah the enemy had retreated. They had penetrated as far as Ogechee ferry, but Colonel Elbert, with about 200 men, prevented their crossing, and the advance of Marion precipitated their retreat; the invasion was abandoned, and in March the South Carolina troops were recalled from Georgia. After this affair, Marion was placed in command of a strong garrison at Fort Moultrie, in consequence of apprehensions, which were entertained, that a new expedition from the British main army at New York, was about to be ordered to Charleston. Marion appears to have held this command till the expedition of the British against Savannah, conducted by Lieutenant Colonel Campbell, which arrived on the coast of Georgia in December 1778.

The British force was 4000 men. The fleet consisted of 37 sail. General Robert Howe in command at Savannah had only 600 men, and Savannah speedily fell into the hands of the enemy. Colonel Campbell then proceeded to occupy Ebenezer, Abercorn, and other posts further inland. These operations lasted several months.

The incapacity of General Robert Howe having become apparent, he had as early as September 1778, been ordered to repair to the head quarters of General Washington; and General Lincoln, an excellent officer, was placed in command of the southern department. Sir Henry Clinton had ordered General Prevost to co-operate from East Florida with Colonel Campbell, and he had accordingly advanced into Georgia and captured Sunbury. He then took command of the British forces; and detached Colonel Campbell with 800 regulars and a few tories, who took Augusta without resistance, and thus the whole state of Georgia was reduced.

On his arrival in Charleston, to take command of the southern department, General Lincoln found the military affairs of the country in a state of utter derangement. Congress had established no continental military chest in the southern department. This omission produced a dependence on the government of the state for supplies to move the army on any emergency, and consequent subjection of the troops in continental service to its control. The militia, though taken into continental service, considered themselves as subject only to the military code of the state. These regulations threatened to embarrass all military operations, and to embroil the general with the civil government.

While Lincoln was laboring to make arrangements for the ensuing campaign, he received intelligence of the appearance of the enemy off the coast. The militia of North Carolina, amounting to two thousand men, commanded by Generals Ashe and Rutherford, had already reached Charleston; but were unarmed, and Congress had been unable to provide magazines in this part of the Union. These troops were, therefore, entirely dependent on South Carolina for every military equipment; and arms were not delivered to them until it was too late to save the capital of Georgia.

So soon as it was ascertained that the British fleet had entered the Savannah river, General Lincoln proceeded with the utmost expedition towards the scene of action. On his march, he received intelligence of the victory gained over General Howe; and was soon afterwards joined by the remnant of the defeated army at Purysburgh, a small town on the north side of the Savannah, where he established his head quarters. (Jan. 3. 1779.)

During the period of inaction which now ensued, Sergeant Jasper performed one of those remarkable exploits which have rendered his name so celebrated. Having a brother in the British camp at Ebenezer, he went to pay him a visit, assuming the character of a deserter from the American army, and running the risk of certain death, if his real character of spy should be discovered. Having returned safely, he, some weeks afterwards, made a second visit to Ebenezer, taking Sergeant Newton with him. While in the British camp, they observed some prisoners, handcuffed and guarded, being destined to be sent to Savannah for execution as deserters. One of them named Jones was attended by his wife and child. Jasper and Newton, moved by compassion, determined to attempt their rescue, although they were unarmed, and the prisoners, when sent off for Savannah, were guarded by a sergeant, a corporal, and eight men. By dogging the steps of the guard, to within two miles of Savannah, they finally succeeded in their purpose, while the party were resting at a spring by the roadside. The guard left their muskets leaning against a tree, while they went to drink, and fill the canteens of the prisoners. Jasper and Newton, springing from their ambush, seized the muskets, killed four of the guard, captured the rest, and liberated the prisoners.

CHAPTER XI.

Change in the aspect of affairs—General Pickens defeats Colonel Byrd—General Lincoln sends General Ashe into Georgia—Defeat of Ashe—Its disastrous consequences—Lincoln marches into Georgia—Prevost menaces Charleston—Subsequent operations—Marion at Fort Moultrie—Siege of Savannah—Obstinacy and folly of Count D' Estaing—He grants delay to the garrison till it is reinforced and compels an assault unnecessarily—Marion takes part in the assault—The colors of the Second Regiment planted in the British lines—Several officers killed in defending them—Death of Sergeant Jasper—The siege raised and the expedition totally defeated—Depreciation of the paper currency.

At the time when General Robert Howe was recalled, and General Lincoln was sent to the South to supply his place, Congress had planned the reduction of East Florida, under the direction of the latter officer. But the fall of Savannah and the reduction of Georgia by the British, had totally changed the aspect of affairs. The theatre of war was now to be, not Florida, but Georgia and even South Carolina.

A body of seven hundred tories, who had taken shelter among the Indians, attempted to rejoin the royal army. Being attacked by Colonel Pickens, with a party of militia, Colonel Byrd, their commander, was killed, and only three hundred reached their destination. Several of the prisoners were tried for treason and condemned, but all except the ringleaders were pardoned.

General Lincoln, encouraged by this success, caused General Ashe, with 1400 men, to cross the Savannah, and take post at its junction with Briar Creek, a stream unfordable for some miles up, and appearing completely to secure his front. It was thus hoped to cut off the advance of the British to the upper territories. Colonel Prevost, however, brother to the General, making a circuit of fifty miles, and crossing at fords fifteen miles above, came unexpectedly on the rear of this body, and totally routed them; the regular troops, after attempting resistance, being all either killed or taken.

Moultrie, in his Memoirs, ascribes all the succeeding disasters to this defeat. He says:

This unlucky affair at Briar Creek disconcerted all our plans, and through the misfortune of Generals Howe and Ashe, the war was protracted at least one year longer, for it is not to be doubted that had we crossed the river with our army, and joined General Ashe, which we were preparing to do, we should have had a body of 7,000 men; besides strong reinforcements were marching to us from every quarter sufficient to drive the enemy out of Georgia; and all the wavering, and all the disaffected would have immediately joined us; and it is more than probable that Carolina would not have been invaded, had this event taken place.

Notwithstanding the disastrous effects of Ashe's defeat, General Lincoln, again reinforced, determined to proceed with his main body against Augusta. Prevost, instead of a long and harassing march in that direction, sought to recall him by a movement against Charleston; but intending only a feint, he proceeded with a leisure which he found reason to regret, as it appears had all practicable speed been employed, that capital would have fallen into his hands. The alarm, however, had been given, and such active preparations made, that he did not venture to attack, but distributed his troops in the neighboring island of St. John. Lincoln, who had hastened down, made an attempt to beat up his quarters, without success; and the midsummer heat causing a suspension of military operations, the British troops retired unmolested into Georgia.

While General Prevost was at the island of St. John, in the neighborhood of Charleston, Marion was in command of Fort Moultrie, ready to resit any renewed attempt on Charleston. But he was soon summoned to join the army which was sent to co-operate with the French force under the Count D' Estaing in the attack on Savannah.

The state of affairs in the South had called so imperatively for the attention of Congress, that a portion of Washington's army had been detached to join General Lincoln. Washington solicited more powerful aid from D'Estaing, who then commanded in the West Indies an army sufficiently powerful to crush entirely the English in Georgia. The French admiral received this application just after having fought a hard battle against Commodore Byron without any decisive result, yet such as obliged the latter to go into port to refit. The former, being thus for a time master of the sea, determined at once to comply with the request, took on board six thousand land-troops, and steered direct for Savannah, where, arriving quite unexpectedly, he captured by surprise a fifty-gun ship and three frigates. Prevost, too, was very unprepared, having his force broken up into detachments distributed along the frontier; but these being instantly ordered in, obeyed with such promptitude that before the French had landed and formed a junction with Lincoln, nearly all had arrived. On the 16th of September, D'Estaing appeared before the place and summoned it to surrender. Prevost, under pretext of negotiation, obtained a suspension for twenty-four hours, during which Colonel Maitland entered with the last and largest detachment, eluding the Americans by a route supposed impassable; and the full determination to resist was then announced.

The opinion of all military men now is that D'Estaing was guilty of the most outrageous folly in not marching at once to the attack of the city, without summoning the weakened garrison to surrender at all. The surprise would have then been complete, and the victory sure. If we are to believe Horry, this was the opinion expressed by Marion at the time. He says:

I never beheld Marion in so great a passion. I was actually afraid he would have broke out on General Lincoln. "*My God!*" he exclaimed, "*who ever heard of any thing like this before!—first allow an enemy to entrench, and then fight him!! See the destruction brought upon the British at Bunker's Hill! and yet our troops there were only militia! raw, half-armed clod-hoppers! and not a mortar, nor carronade, nor even a swivel—but only their ducking guns!*

"What then are we to expect from regulars—completely armed with a choice train of artillery, and covered by a breast-work. For my own part, when I look upon my brave fellows around me, it wrings me to the heart, to think how near most of them are to their bloody graves."

A regular siege was now commenced. Heavy ordnance and stores were brought up from the fleet, and the besieging army broke ground. By the first of October they had pushed their sap within 300 yards of the abattis, on the left of the British lines. Several batteries were opened on the besieged which played almost incessantly upon their works, but made no impression on them.

The situation of D'Estaing was becoming critical. More time had already been consumed on the coast of Georgia than he had supposed would be necessary for the destruction of the British force in that State. He became uneasy for the possessions of France in the West Indies, and apprehensive for the safety of the ships under his command. The naval officers remonstrated strenuously against longer exposing his fleet on an insecure coast, at a tempestuous season of the year, and urged the danger of being overtaken by a British squadron, when broken and scattered by a storm, with a degree of persevering earnestness which the Count found himself incapable of resisting.

In a few days the lines of the besiegers might have been carried, by regular approaches, into the works of the besieged, which would have rendered the capture of the town and garrison inevitable. But D'Estaing declared that he could devote no more time to this object;

and it only remained to raise the siege, or to attempt the works by storm. The latter part of the alternative was adopted.

On the left of the allied army, was a swampy hollow way which afforded a cover for troops advancing on the right flank of the besieged, to a point within fifty yards of their principal work. It was determined to march to the main attack along this hollow, and, at the same time, to direct feints against other parts of the lines.

On the morning of the 9th of October, before day, a heavy cannonade and bombardment were commenced from all the batteries as preliminary to the assault. About three thousand five hundred French, and one thousand Americans, of whom between six and seven hundred were regulars, and the residue militia of Charleston, advanced in three columns, led by D'Estaing and Lincoln, aided by the principal officers of both nations, and made a furious assault on the British lines. Their reception was warmer than had been expected. The fire from the batteries of the besieged reached every part of the columns of the assailants which had emerged from the swamp, and did great execution. Yet the allied troops advanced with unabated ardor, passed through the abattis, crossed the ditch, and mounted the parapet. Both the French and Americans planted their standards on the walls, and were killed in great numbers, while endeavoring to force their way into the works. For about fifty minutes, the contest was extremely obstinate. At length, the columns of the assailants began to relax, and a pause was manifested in the assault. In this critical moment, Major Glaziers at the head of a body of grenadiers and marines, rushing suddenly from the lines, threw himself on those who had made their way into the redoubts, and drove them over the ditch and abattis into the hollow through which they had marched to the attack. It became apparent that farther perseverance could produce no advantage, and a retreat was ordered.

In this unsuccessful attempt, the French lost in killed and wounded, about seven hundred men. Among the latter, were the Count D'Estaing himself, Major General De Fontanges, and several other officers of distinction. The continental troops lost two hundred and thirty-four men, and the Charleston militia, who, though associated with them in danger, were more fortunate, had one captain killed, and six privates wounded. Count Pulaski was among the slain.

The loss of the garrison was astonishingly small. In killed and wounded, it amounted only to fifty-five. So great was the advantage of the cover afforded by their works.

Marion, as second in command of the gallant Second South Carolina Regiment, took an active part in the assault. Pressing forward under a heavy fire, upon the Spring Hill redoubt, the Carolinians planted their colors on the berme. But the height of the parapet and the tremendous fire from the besieged prevented their proceeding further, and they were compelled to retreat with the other assailants. In this affair the fate of the two standards presented to the Second Regiment by Mrs. Elliott, is thus minutely described by Mr. Garden :*

"During the assault at Savannah, they were both planted on the British lines. The statement which I am about to give of the event, differs widely from that which has been generally received; but that it is correct, cannot be doubted, as it was afforded me by Lieutenant James Legare, whose services and character entitle him to all credit. He was present in the action, and immediately in front of the colors, at the time that the officers who bore them were killed. Lieutenant Brush, supported by Sergeant Jasper, carried one; Lieutenant Grey, supported by Sergeant McDonald, the other. Brush being wounded early in the action, delivered his standard to Jasper for its better security, who, already wounded, on receiving a second shot, restored it. Brush, at the moment receiving a mortal wound, fell into the ditch, with the colors under him, which occasioned their remaining in the hands of the enemy. Lieutenant Grey received a mortal wound, his colors were seized by McDonald, who planted them on the redoubt, but on hearing an order to retreat, plucked them up again, and carried them off in safety."

The wound which Sergeant Jasper received, in his attempt to save the colors of the Second Regiment, proved mortal. He died in the American camp on the evening of the same day. He was attended in his last moments by Major, afterwards General Peter Horry, and in his last moments retained the noble character for courage

* Anecdotes of the Revolutionary War.

and devotedness to the cause of liberty which he had borne from the commencement of the war.

Count D'Estaing having committed a blunder at the beginning, had committed a worse blunder at the end by insisting on the assault, as unnecessary as it was rash. When the assault failed, he consummated his treachery to the American cause by deserting his allies without effecting the capture of the city, which might still have been done with the aid of the imposing French force. He insisted on raising the siege, and both the French and American armies moved from their ground on the evening of the 18th of October. D'Estaing sailed for the West Indies; and Lincoln recrossed the Savannah at Zubly's Ferry and again encamped in South Carolina.

"This disappointment," says Moultrie, speaking of the result of the siege, " depressed our spirits very much, and we began to be apprehensive for the safety of these two southern states; it also depreciated our money so very low, that it was scarcely worth any thing." He refers to the state currency, the issue of which was commenced by the issue of a million in 1775. Millions were not of much account now. Writing from Charleston to Lincoln (Sep. 26th, 1779), he says, "Yesterday arrived another 500,000 dollars for the State of Georgia. One and a half million more will be in to-morrow, for the purpose of exchanging the two emissions which were stopped in circulation." In a note he adds, "At this time our money was very much depreciated, 1618 for one, and we talked of millions, and in fact it was next to nothing. There was one conveniency in it, which was, that a couple of men on horseback, with their bags, could convey a million of dollars from one end of the continent to the other in a little time, with great facility." This state of the paper currency, on which the gallant colonel jests so pleasantly, was destined to become a matter of very grave importance in the conduct of the war.

CHAPTER XII.

Marion in command at Sheldon—Stationed at Bacon's Bridge—Siege and fall of Charleston—How Marion escaped captivity—His retirement at St. John's—Infamous treatment of the South Carolinians by the British—Defeat of Buford—Clinton's proclamation—Cornwallis left in command—His proceedings.

When General Lincoln had withdrawn from the neighborhood of Savannah to Sheldon, he proceeded to Charleston, leaving Marion in command of the army. In a letter dated at Charleston, January 31st, 1780, Lincoln gives directions to Marion to organize a select body of two hundred of his best men, and to send off the remainder to Charleston. In February following Marion was ordered to Bacon's Bridge on Ashley river, near the capital, where a considerable force was being assembled under the command of Moultrie, destined for the defence of Charleston. While stationed at this post, Marion was actively engaged in disciplining the troops, in which department of military duty he was always remarkably successful.

The danger which now threatened Charleston was by no means an imaginary one. The repulse of the French and American force at Savannah had been considered by the enemy a brilliant triumph.

Clinton, on learning this success, determined finally to begin operations on a great scale in the southern states. Recent information showed them to be more defenceless, and the inhabitants better inclined to the dominion of the parent state, than those on the great northern theatre of war; while their reduction might facilitate that of the others, or at all events preserve for Britain an important portion of her American territory. He had recently obtained a reinforcement from home, and had withdrawn the force hitherto stationed with little advantage upon Rhode Island.

On the 26th of December, 1779, leaving Knyphausen with troops sufficient to defend New York against the ill-organized army of Washington, be sailed with five thousand men for Savannah. The voyage was most tempestuous, and prolonged till the end of January; some of the vessels were wrecked, and nearly all the horses perished. He exerted himself actively to repair these losses; and by the middle of February had re-embarked and landed on St. John's Island, near Charleston. Some time was spent in recruiting and reinforcing his troops and remounting his cavalry; while Lincoln was actively strengthening the garrison, and restoring the works which since the memorable attack in June 1776, had fallen into almost complete decay. He succeeded in assembling above two thousand regulars, one thousand militia, and a great body of armed citizens; but the chief hope, which was soon proved to be fallacious, rested on preventing the British from crossing the bar, as the fleet, under a favorable wind and tide, passed with scarcely any opposition. Lincoln then seriously deliberated on evacuating the place and saving his army; but he dreaded popular reproach, and was buoyed up with promises of reinforcements that never arrived. On the 1st of April, Clinton crossed the Ashley, which, with Cooper River, incloses the peninsula of Charleston, and broke ground before the city. On the 9th, the first parallel was completed, and the maritime blockade rendered very close; yet the garrison still communicated with the country by their cavalry at Monk's Corner, about thirty miles up Cooper River. Colonel Tarleton, by a circuitous route, came upon this body so unexpectedly, that though they held their horses bridled and saddled, they were attacked before they had time to mount, routed, and completely dispersed. The British soon after received a reinforcement of three thousand; when Lincoln seriously proposed an attempt to extricate his army; but the principal inhabitants, entertaining a well founded dread of ill treatment from the captors, prevailed upon him only to offer a capitulation on condition of the garrison being still allowed to serve. This proposal was at once rejected; the siege was steadily pushed; all the outward posts successively fell; two detachments of cavalry which had rallied were by the active movements of Tarleton again dissipated; and the third parallel being completed, preparations were made for a general assault. Lincoln, then seeing his situation hopeless, submitted to the terms proffered by the enemy, that all the military stores should be given up, the regular troops made prisoners of war, while the militia, on giving their parole, might return and remain unmolested at their homes. The prisoners taken were stated by Clinton at five thousand six hundred and eighteen, with one thousand seamen, and three hundred and eleven pieces of ordnance.

Never was success more complete, nor which seemed more to assure the reunion to Britain of at least a large portion of her revolted colonies. With very small exceptions, the whole military force stationed in the southern states, including all its means and implements of war, was at once captured.

Fortunately for his country, Marion was not in the number of those who were made prisoners of war at the fall of Charleston. He was with his regiment in the city in the early part of the siege; and on a certain day was invited to a dinner party, which he perceived was to become at the close a regular debauch, the host having locked the door of the dining-room to prevent any of the guests from withdrawing till a late hour.

Marion, always averse to every species of intemperance, determined not to submit to this tyrannical species of hospitality, and, opening a window, jumped into the street. As the room was on the second floor, the height was considerable, and in coming to the ground he broke his ankle. He was thus totally unfitted for service, and General Lincoln having ordered the departure of "all supernumerary officers, and all officers unfit for duty," Marion was placed on a litter and carried to his plantation on St. John's Island. Here he was compelled to remain inactive, receiving intelligence from time to time of the disastrous progress of events. We may imagine the sorrow and indignation with which he heard of the events which followed the capture of Charleston.

MARION'S ESCAPE FROM A DRINKING PARTY.—PAGE 112.

South Carolina was treated as a conquered country, and not as a province reclaimed by a wise and just government. The terms on which the surrender had been made were grossly and mercilessly violated. The inhabitants were plundered of their property. Their wealth was seized wherever the enemy could lay their hands on it. Thousands of slaves were shipped to the West Indies and sold. The prisoners of war were confined in prison-ships, where in that hot climate they perished by hundreds. Others were sent to the West Indies and compelled to serve in the British regiments stationed there.

Such were the proceedings of which Marion was obliged to hear reports, while suffering with the agony of his wound, which was very slow in healing. The military events which succeeded the fall of Charleston were not more encouraging.

Sir Henry Clinton was aware of the impression his conquest had made, and of the value of the first movements succeeding it. Calculating on the advantages to be derived from showing an irresistible force in various parts of the country at the same time, he made three large detachments from his army;—the first and most considerable, towards the frontiers of North Carolina; the second to pass the Saluda to Ninety-Six; and the third up the Savannah towards Augusta.

Lord Cornwallis, who commanded the northern detachment, received intelligence soon after passing the Santee, that Colonel Buford,* with about four hundred men,

---

* Mr. Simms spells this name Beaufort. Lossing gives his autograph Abm. Buford.

was retreating in perfect security towards North Carolina. He detached Lieutenant Colonel Tarleton with his legion, the infantry being mounted, in pursuit of this party. That officer, by making a movement of near one hundred miles in two days, overtook Buford, in a line of march at the Waxhaws, and demanded a surrender on the terms which had been granted to the garrison of Charleston. This was refused. While the flags were passing, Tarleton continued to make his dispositions for the assault, and, the instant the truce was over, his cavalry made a furious charge on the Americans, who had received no orders to engage, and who seem to have been uncertain whether to defend themselves or not. In this state of dismay and confusion, some fired on the assailants, while others threw down their arms and begged for quarter. None was given. Colonel Buford escaped with a few cavalry; and about one hundred infantry who were in advance saved themselves by flight; but the regiment was almost demolished. Tarleton, in his official report, says that one hundred and thirteen were killed on the spot, one hundred and fifty so badly wounded as to be incapable of being moved, and fifty-three were brought away as prisoners. The loss of the British was five killed and fourteen wounded.

After the defeat of Buford, scarcely the semblance of opposition remained in South Carolina and Georgia. The military force employed by congress was nearly destroyed; the spirit of resistance seemed entirely broken; and a general disposition to submit to the victor displayed itself in almost every part of the country.

The two other detachments saw no appearance of an enemy. They received the submission of the inhabitants, who either became neutral by giving their paroles not to bear arms against his Britannic Majesty, or took the oaths of allegiance, and resumed the character of British subjects.

To keep up this disposition, garrisons were posted in different stations, and a series of measures was pursued for the purpose of settling the civil affairs of the province, and of giving stability to the conquest which had been made.

So entirely did the present aspect of affairs convince Sir Henry Clinton of the complete subjugation of the state, and of the favorable disposition of the people towards the British government, that he ventured to issue a proclamation, (June 3,) in which he discharged the militia who were prisoners from their paroles, with the exception of those who were taken in Charleston and Fort Moultrie, and restored them to all the rights and duties of British subjects; declaring, at the same time, that such of them as should neglect to return to their allegiance, should be considered and treated as enemies and rebels.

This proclamation disclosed to the inhabitants their real situation. It proved that a state of neutrality was not within their reach; that the evils of war were unavoidable; that they must arrange themselves on the one side or the other; and that the only alternative presented to them was, to drive the enemy out of their country, or take up arms against their countrymen.

With the most sanguine hopes that the southern

states would be reunited to the British empire, Sir Henry Clinton embarked, (June 5,) for New York, leaving about four thousand British troops in South Carolina, under the command of Lord Cornwallis.

His lordship found it necessary to suspend the expedition he had meditated against North Carolina. The impossibility of supporting an army in that state before harvest, as well as the intense heat of the season, required this delay. His first care was to distribute his troops through South Carolina and the upper parts of Georgia, so as to promote the great and immediate objects of enlisting the young men who were willing to join his standard, of arranging the plan of a militia, and of collecting magazines at convenient places.

In the meantime he despatched emissaries to his friends in North Carolina, to inform them of the necessary delay of his expedition into their country, and to request them to attend to their harvest, collect provisions, and remain quiet until late in August, or early in September, when the king's troops would be ready to enter the province.

CHAPTER XIII.

Marion leaves St. Johns and takes shelter in the woods and swamps—Joins the Continental army in North Carolina—Appearance of his men—Invited to Williamsburg—Appointed Brigadier General—Starts for Williamsburg—Gates's character—His defeat—Success and subsequent surprise and defeat of Sumter.

THE state of affairs now made it extremely dangerous for Marion to remain at his own plantation in St. Johns. His character for ability and patriotism was well known to both British and tories; and both were on the alert to effect his capture. He was thus compelled to take shelter in the woods and swamps, among the patriotic friends to whom his character and services had endeared him; and for several months he entirely disappeared from the scene of public action.

Meantime a body of regular troops under Baron DeKalb, were on their march from Virginia, and we next hear of Marion with a few followers on his way to join this force. His old friend Colonel Peter Horry joined him on his route. His wound was still so imperfectly healed that he had to be lifted from his horse. But his cheerfulness and his strong hopes of the final triumph of liberty, were by no means abated. When Horry, speaking of the state of affairs lamented that "their happy days were all gone," he replied that on the contrary they were yet to come; that the brutal and oppressive treatment of the Carolinians, by the British and tories, would rouse a spirit of resistance, that would inevitably lead to the final triumph of the American arms. A generous policy, he said, might have bound the conquered states to Great Britain, but their present line of policy would certainly occasion the loss of these colonies to the mother country.

Passing through a region of North Carolina every where infested with tories, Marion and Horry at length succeeded in joining the Continental army, of which General Gates had recently assumed the command, having superseded the Baron DeKalb. In the Continental camp they found General Sumter, who had already assembled a partisan force, and the energetic Governor Rutledge of South Carolina, who had repaired to this part of the country, to reassure the people by his presence and to obtain recruits.

Marion's men, badly equipped and worn out with their long march, made a sorry appearance before the well appointed and handsomely dressed soldiers of the Continental army. Colonel Otho Holland Williams, in a passage of his " Narrative of the Campaign of 1781," quoted by Mr Simms, thus describes the partisan troopers:

He says, " Colonel Marion, a gentleman of South Carolina, had been with the army a few days, attended by a very few followers, distinguished by small leather caps, and the wretchedness of their attire; their number did not exceed twenty men and boys, some white, some black, and all mounted, but most of them miserably equipped; their appearance was in fact so burlesque, that it was with much difficulty the diversion of the regular soldiery was restrained by the officers; and the General himself was glad of an opportunity of detaching Colonel Marion, at his own instance, towards the interior of South Carolina, with orders to watch the motions of the enemy and furnish intelligence."*

It is a curious fact that the officers and soldiers who found so much food for mirth in the appearance of Marion's men, were destined a few days afterwards to suffer the most complete, disastrous, and inglorious defeat, inflicted by the British during the whole war, while the derided soldiers of Marion were to render the most efficient and important aid in recovering the southern states of the Union from the enemy.

The cause of Marion's detachment from the main army, referred to above, was an invitation from the people of Williamsburg to join them and be their leader. This would take him at once into South Carolina in advance of the main army, and open a wide field for his daring spirit of enterprise. Governor Rutledge encouraged his acceptance of the invitation of the people of Williamsburg, and conferred upon him a commission as brigadier general. He accordingly took leave of General Gates and proceeded at once to his destination.

General Gates was so inflated with the victory gained at Saratoga, that he anticipated a speedy and decisive triumphs over any British army which should be bold enough to encounter him. A careful review of the whole career of this officer, leads inevitably to the conclusion

* Narrative of the Campaign of 1781, by Colonel Otho Williams.

that he was a weak and vain man, and a very incapable commander. The noble General Schuyler had paved the way for the defeat of Burgoyne, had in fact insured that defeat, by his able and prudent measures, before Gates assumed the command; and the severe fighting at Stillwater, was directed by the generals who fought under him. He had won at Saratoga splendid laurels which he had never earned. He was now to lose them in a single day.

The expedition for the relief of the southern states had set out in March, under the command of Baron De Kalb. Gates had received his appointment to the command from Congress, on the 3d of June; but want of money, military stores, and provisions, had detained the army so long that though the expedition set out in March, it was the beginning of August before Gates could approach Camden, with about four thousand men, mostly militia. He advanced in the determination to push vigorously offensive operations, hoping to encounter and defeat Lord Rawdon. That officer, however, had given notice to Cornwallis, who hastened to the spot, and though his troops, from disease and other causes, had been reduced to little more than two thousand, he resolved without hesitation to attack. He had set out in the night of the 15th, with a view to surprise the Americans, when, by a singular concurrence, he met Gates in full march with the same design against himself. The advanced guard of the latter was driven in, when both parties thought it advisable to postpone the general action till daylight. In the American line, De Kalb, with most of the regulars, commanded on the right, while the militia of Carolina formed the centre, and that of Virginia the left. The conflict began with the last, who were attacked by the British infantry, under Colonel Webster, with such impetuosity, that they threw down their arms and precipitately fled. The whole of the left and centre were very speedily off the field, few having fired a shot, and still fewer carrying away a musket. Gates was borne along by the torrent, and after vain attempts to rally his men, gave up all for lost, and never stopped until he reached Charlotte, eighty miles distant. Meantime, De Kalb, on the right, opposed to Lord Rawdon, long and firmly maintained his ground, gaining even some advantage; and it was not till the victorious divisions had wheeled round against him, that his corps was broken and dispersed. He himself, covered with wounds, became a captive, and, notwithstanding every care, expired in a few hours. About one thousand prisoners were taken, and the whole army was scattered.

We have already mentioned that Marion on arriving at the continental camp had met General Sumter. This brave partisan had subsequently obtained from Gates a reinforcement to his own corps, of one hundred regular infantry and two brass field pieces, for the purpose of intercepting an escort of clothing, ammunition, and other stores, for the British garrison at Camden, which was on its way to Ninety-six, and must pass the Wateree at a ferry about a mile from Camden, which was covered by a small redoubt on the opposite side of the river.

On his retreat, the day of the battle of Camden, General Gates received information of the complete success of Sumter. That officer had, on the evening that

Lord Cornwallis marched from Camden, reduced the redoubt on the Wateree, captured the guard, and intercepted the escort with the stores.

This gleam of light cheered the dark gloom which enveloped his affairs but for a moment. He was soon informed that this corps also was defeated, and entirely dispersed.

On hearing the disaster which had befallen Gates, Sumter began to retreat up the south side of the Wateree. Believing himself out of danger, he had halted on the twenty-eighth, during the heat of the day, near the Catawba Ford, to give his harassed troops some repose. At that place he was overtaken by Tarleton, who had been detached in pursuit of him on the morning of the 17th, and who, advancing with his accustomed celerity, entered the American camp so suddenly, as in a great measure to cut off the men from their arms. Some slight resistance made from behind the wagons was soon overcome, and the Americans fled precipitately to the river and woods. Between three and four hundred of them were killed and wounded; their baggage, artillery, arms, and ammunition were lost; and the prisoners and stores they had taken were recovered. This advantage was gained with the loss of only nine men killed and six wounded.

Two videttes had been placed by Sumter on the road along which Tarleton had advanced, who fired upon his van and killed one of his dragoons, upon which they were both sabred. We are informed by Colonel Tarleton that the inquiries made by Sumter respecting the two shots, were answered by an assurance from an officer, just returned from the advanced sentries, that the militia were firing at cattle.

Intelligence of this disaster reached Charlotte next day. Generals Smallwood and Gist were then arrived at that place; and about one hundred and fifty straggling, dispirited, half-famished officers and soldiers had also dropped in. It was thought advisable to retreat immediately to Salisbury. From that place, General Gates directed the remnant of the troops to march to Hillsborough, where he was endeavoring to assemble another army which might enable him yet to contend for the southern states.

CHAPTER XIV.

The people of Williamsburg—Their character and proceedings—Mission of Major James to Captain Ardesoif—Bravery and patriotism of James—His report—Formation of Marion's brigade—McCottry and Tarleton—Marion takes the command—His character and appearance at this time—State of the brigade—Arms made of mill-saws—Marion defeats Major Gainey and Captain Barfield—Captures an escort of Maryland prisoners—They refuse to join the brigade—Their reasons—Atrocious instructions of Rawdon and Cornwallis to their officers—Marion's opinion.

The people of Williamsburg, who had sent for Marion to be their leader, were chiefly descendants of Irish emigrants; and consequently earnest haters of British dominion. They lived in the tract of country between the Santee and Pedee, which now forms the district of Williamsburg, and a part of that of Marion. As the British forces had not yet penetrated into this part of the country, the inhabitants were not well informed respecting the treatment of their compatriots in the lower districts, and they had been undecided what part they should take in what seemed to them to be merely a political quarrel. They had received the proclamation of the British commander, claiming only neutrality and peaceable behavior on the part of the non-combatant portion of the people; and they had also received the proclamation issued only twenty days after, requiring the same persons to take up arms in behalf of the British invaders. In an assemblage of citizens called to consider the measures necessary to be adopted for their own security, they determined to solve the doubts raised by these totally inconsistent proclamations, by sending one of their number to the nearest British authority to make inquiries and learn the real state of affairs and their own prospects. The delegate chosen was Major John James, who held his commission in their militia, and had represented the district in the provincial assembly.

Major James repaired to Georgetown, the nearest British post, then under command of Captain Ardesoif. Being admitted to an audience with this officer, Major James inquired what might be the meaning of British protection, and upon what terms the submission of the citizens was to be made. He was haughtily informed that the submission must be unconditional. He next inquired whether the inhabitants were to be permitted to remain on their plantations? The answer of Ardesoif was "No. His Majesty offers you a free pardon, of which you are undeserving; for you all ought to be hanged; but it is only on condition that you take up arms in his cause." Without evincing the slightest intimidation at this ominous announcement, Major James replied that "the people whom he came to represent would scarcely submit on such conditions."

"*Represent!*" exclaimed Ardesoif in a violent rage, "You d——d rebel, if you dare speak in such language, I will have you hung up at the yard arm."

Upon this, Major James seized the chair upon which

he had been sitting, knocked down the insolent official, hurried from the apartment, mounted his horse, and made his way to the secure asylum of the woods before any attempt to capture him could be made.

His report to his constituents decided at once their course of action. Their real situation and prospects were now clearly enough defined, and the insult to their beloved and popular representative set the whole district in a flame. That celebrated corps, "Marion's Brigade," was immediately organized. Four companies, commanded respectively by Captains William McCottry, Henry Mouzon, John James, (cousin to the Major,) and John McCauley.*

As Marion had not at this time arrived in the district, these companies were united under the command of Major James, and hostilities against the British and tories were at once commenced. Captain McCottry's company being sent forward in advance, encountered Colonel Tarleton, who, from hearing an excessive over-statement of McCottry's force, retreated before him, and still further inflamed the district of Williamsburg by the cruelties and plunderings which he committed on his retreat.

Meantime McCottry took post at Lynch's Creek, where he was joined by Marion, on the 14th of August, just four days before Gates's defeat at Camden. By virtue of his commission from Governor Rutledge, General Marion now assumed the command of that "Brigade" which was destined to become so celebrated in the annals of the southern war. Perhaps it will not be

* Simms.

MAJOR JAMES AND CAPTAIN ARDESOIF.—PAGE 126.

inappropriate to insert in this place his character as described by General Henry Lee,* who was subsequently associated with him in command of more than one successful expedition. He says:

Marion was about forty-eight years of age, small in stature, hard in visage, healthy, abstemious, and taciturn. Enthusiastically wedded to the cause of liberty, he deeply deplored the doleful condition of his beloved country. The commonweal was his sole object; nothing selfish, nothing mercenary, soiled his ermine character. Fertile in stratagem, he struck unperceived; and retiring to those hidden retreats, selected by himself, in the morasses of Pedee and Black rivers, he placed his corps not only out of the reach of his foe, but often out of the discovery of his friends.† A rigid disciplinarian, he reduced to practice the justice of his heart; and during the difficult course of warfare, through which he passed, calumny itself never charged him with violating the rights of per-

---

* Memoirs of the War in the Southern Department of the United States.

† Lieutenant Colonel Lee was ordered to join Marion after Greene determined to turn the war back to South Carolina, in 1781. An officer, with a small party, preceded Lee a few days' march to find out Marion, who was known to vary his position in the swamps of Pedee: sometimes in South Carolina, sometimes in North Carolina, and sometimes on the Black River. With the greatest difficulty did this officer learn how to communicate with the brigadier; and that by the accident of hearing among our friends on the north side of the Pedee, of a small provision party of Marion's being on the same side of the river. Making himself known to this party, he was conveyed to the General, who had changed his ground since his party left him, which occasioned many hours' search even before his own men could find him.

son, property, or of humanity. Never avoiding danger, he never rashly sought it; and acting for all around him as he did for himself, he risked the lives of his troops only when it was necessary. Never elated with prosperity, nor depressed by adversity, he preserved an equanimity which won the admiration of his friends, and exacted the respect of his enemies. The country from Camden to the sea-coast, between the Pedee and Santee rivers, was the theatre of his exertions.

And again Lee says:

General Marion was in stature of the smallest size, thin as well as low. His visage was not pleasing, and his manners not captivating. He was reserved and silent, entering into conversation only when necessary, and then with modesty and good sense.

He possessed a strong mind, improved by its own reflections and observations, not by books or travel. His dress was like his address,—plain, regarding comfort and decency only. In his meals he was abstemious, eating generally of one dish, and drinking water mostly.

He was sedulous and constant in his attention to the duties of his station, to which every other consideration yielded. Even the charms of the fair, like the luxuries of the table and the allurements of wealth, seemed to be lost upon him.

The procurement of subsistence for his men, and the contrivance of annoyance to his enemy, engrossed his entire mind. He was virtuous all over; never, even in manner, much less in reality, did he trench upon right. Beloved by his friends, and respected by his enemies, he exhibited a luminous example of the beneficial effects to be produced by an individual, who, with only small means at his command, possesses a virtuous heart, a strong head, and a mind devoted to the common good.

On taking command of the brigade, General Marion found it to be composed of volunteer militia, most of them quite unarmed. To remedy this deficiency, "He took saws from the mills," says Moultrie, "and set smiths to work, to turn them into horsemen's swords." From this expedient, the destitution of the brigade and the desperate means resorted to for arming and supplying them in other respects may be conjectured.

Two days after joining the brigade, Marion surprised and defeated a body of tories commanded by Major Gainey, at Britton's Neck. On this occasion Major James pursuing Gainey in his flight, rode far beyond the support of his men, but extricated himself by turning back on his horse, waving his sword and calling out, as if his men were close behind him, "Come on, boys, here they are," and then dashing in amongst the tories, who speedily resumed their rapid retreat.

The next day after this occurrence, Marion defeated another band of tories under Captain Barfield, having drawn him from a strong position by feigning a retreat.

When Marion heard of the defeat of Gen. Gates, he was on his march to the upper Santee. He concealed the news from his men, lest it should discourage them; and they were unapprized of it until the 20th of August, when Marion fell upon an escort of prisoners bound from Camden to Charleston, when, according to his own despatch,* he "killed and took 22 regulars and two tories prisoners, and retook 150 continentals of the Maryland line, one wagon and a drum; one captain and a subaltern were also captured. Our loss is one killed, and Captain Benson slightly wounded in the head."

Moultrie says, at this time Marion had but thirty militia with him, with these he released the prisoners, and retreated to Britton's Neck, on the Pedee river, to be farther from the enemy, and in hopes of being joined by more of the militia, and to get the released prisoners armed, but they absolutely refused to stay any longer with him: so gloomy were American affairs at this time that very few would join him; and the tories were now gathering from all quarters.

It is not surprising that the continentals of the Maryland line should prefer returning home to joining Marion's brigade; for their own province was comparatively free from annoyance by the enemy, while South Carolina literally afforded no secure shelter to her most peacefully inclined inhabitants. The following letter of Lord Rawdon shows the treatment to which they were naturally subjected as early as July 1780:

LORD RAWDON TO MAJOR RUGELY.

HEAD-QUARTERS, CAMDEN, 1 *July*, 1780.

SIR,—So many deserters from this army have passed with impunity through the districts, which are under your direction, that I must necessarily suspect the inhabitants to have connived at, if not facilitated their escape. If attachment to their sovereign will not move the country

* Simms.

people to check a crime so detrimental to his service, it must be my care to urge them to their duty as good subjects, by using invariable severity towards every one, who shall show so criminal a neglect of the public interest. I am, therefore, Sir, to request of you, that you will signify, to all within the limits of your command, my firm determination in this case. If any person shall meet a soldier straggling without a written pass beyond the pickets, and shall not do his utmost to secure him, or shall not spread an alarm for that purpose, or if any person shall give shelter to soldiers straggling as above mentioned, or shall serve them as a guide, or shall furnish them with horses, or any other assistance, the persons so offending may assure themselves of rigorous punishment, either by whipping, imprisonment, or by being sent to serve his Majesty in the West Indies, according as I shall think the degree of criminality may require. I have ordered, that every soldier who passes the pickets, shall submit himself to be examined by any of the militia, who have any suspicion of him. If a soldier, therefore, attempts to escape when ordered by the militia-man to stop, he is immediately to be fired upon as a deserter. Single men of the light horse need not to be examined, as they may often be sent alone upon expresses. Nor is any party of infantry with a non-commissioned officer at the head of it to be stopped.

I will give the inhabitants ten guineas for the head of any deserter belonging to the volunteers of Ireland; and five guineas only if they bring him in alive. They shall likewise be rewarded, though not to that amount, for such deserters as they may secure belonging to any other regiment. I am confident that you will encourage the country people to be more active in this respect. I am, Sir, with much esteem, &c.

RAWDON.

After Gates's defeat, Cornwallis writes thus:

LORD CORNWALLIS TO LIEUTENANT-COLONEL NESBITT BALFOUR, COMMANDANT AT NINETY-SIX.

August, 1780.

I have given orders, that all the inhabitants of this province, who have subscribed and have taken part in this revolt, should be punished with the greatest rigor, and also those, who will not turn out, that they may be imprisoned, and their whole property taken from them or destroyed. I have likewise ordered, that compensation should be made out of their estates to the persons, who have been injured and oppressed by them. I have ordered in the most positive manner, that every militia-man, who has borne arms with us, and afterwards joined the enemy, shall be immediately hanged. I desire you will take the most rigorous measures to punish the rebels in the district in which you command, and that you will obey, in the strictest manner, the directions I have given in this letter relative to the inhabitants of this country.

CORNWALLIS.

When the reader recollects that these letters represent what was now actually taking place all around him, he will not be surprised at the opinion so often expressed by Marion, that such treatment was more than human nature could bear; and that it would ultimately cause the loss of the southern states by Great Britain. At a little later period even the atrocities authorized in these letters of Rawdon and Cornwallis, were far exceeded by both British and tories. Marion all the while declaring, that although the medicine was harsh, it would ultimately cure the country effectually of all remains of toryism.*

* We have quoted above the whole of Lord Cornwallis's letter, in order that the reader may appreciate the utter baseness of his conduct. Rawdon's letter, written by Cornwallis's orders, had been cruel and oppressive enough; but Cornwallis's letter is still worse—Why? Because he had just defeated Gates; and apparently cut off all hope of succor from the south. The Carolinians were now entirely helpless and entirely in his power. *Therefore, he proceeds to murder, rob, and oppress them to the utmost.* Could human baseness exceed this?

CHAPTER XV.

Marion's activity—Colonel Wemyss sent in pursuit of him—Marion retreats to North Carolina—Cruelties, murders, and burnings by Wemyss—Marion returns to South Carolina—Defeats Captain Ball at Black Mingo—Deliberates on joining General Greene—Surprises Colonel Tynes and captures valuable arms and stores—Cornwallis sends Tarleton to capture Marion—He is foiled, and returns without meeting him—Marion's brother killed by a tory—Marion entertains a British officer at Snow's Island.

MARION'S pursuit of the British and tories was active and incessant. Nothing could discourage him or damp the ardor of his patriotism. Neither was his activity relaxed by the want of ammunition and supplies, nor even by the frequent almost entire dispersion of his force, occasioned by the necessity his men were under to leave him temporarily in order to attend to the wants of their suffering families.

Moultrie says, he frequently engaged when he had only three or four rounds to a man; his little party would sometimes be reduced to five and twenty men—as is common with militia, they grow tired, and have a pretence to go home, or sometimes without any pretence at all; he was very troublesome to Major Wemyss, who had taken post on Pedee, with a detachment of British troops, and had burned a number of the inhabitant's houses on Pedee, Black river, and Lynch's creek, supposing the owners had joined General Marion. The British, by their impolitic conduct, recruited General Marion's little party very fast, who always lay in the woods, in the most unfrequented places, with nothing but their blanket to cover themselves; he had his scouts out constantly, and when they brought him intelligence (which they frequently did) of any small party of the enemy, or any escorts with stores, he sallied out, and was sure to have them. Lord Cornwallis was heard to say, "That he would give a good deal to have him taken." And always praised him as a good partisan officer.*

Major Wemyss, mentioned in the above extract, was sent in pursuit of Marion. Marion had but 150 men, and Wemyss's force was a British regiment, 300 men, and a body of 500 tories. When they approached Marion's position, Major James being sent out to reconnoitre, attacked Wemyss's rear and made some prisoners; but his report of the greatly superior force of the enemy made a retreat indispensable.

Retaining only sixty men and sending the rest home, to be reassembled at a future call, Marion now marched into North Carolina. He thus left the Williamsburg district to be ravaged by Wemyss as mentioned above.

---

* General Marion and myself entered the field of Mars together, in an expedition against the Cherokee Indians, under the command of Colonel James Grant, in 1761; when I had the honor to command a light infantry company, in a provincial regiment; he was my first lieutenant—he was an active, brave, and hardy soldier, and an excellent partisan officer.—*Moultrie's Memoirs.*

It was a hard necessity; but the ultimate effect of the severities practiced by Wemyss, was to confirm the sufferers in their resistance to the British, and to send new recruits to the standard of Marion.

On his march, Marion, finding himself rather encumbered by two field pieces, wheeled them into a swamp, and there left them as totally unsuited to his rapid movements and his quick and decisive methods of attack and retreat. Penetrating into North Carolina, Marion fixed his camp on the east side of the White Marsh, near the head of Waccamaw river. From this position he sent numerous scouts into South Carolina to watch and report the movements of the enemy. Their accounts of the plunderings, burnings, and massacres of Wemyss, of the effect on the inhabitants, and of the desire of the militia of Williamsburg for his presence and aid, decided Marion to return, and he re-entered South Carolina by a forced march.

At Lynch's creek he was reinforced by Captains James and Mouzon, with a considerable body of men. Learning that Wemyss had retired to Georgetown, and that a large body of tories under Captain Ball was at Black Mingo, 15 miles below, he instantly set off to attack them. The attack took place at midnight; but the surprise was not complete. The noise made by his horses in crossing a bridge over the Black Mingo river, alarmed the enemy, and enabled them to form and receive the assailants with a smart fire. But Marion had made his dispositions for surrounding them, and they took flight in the neighboring swamps. In the brief action, Captain Logan was killed and Captain Mouzon and Lieutenant Scott severely wounded. The tories were twice as numerous as Marion's force. After this affair, when he had to cross a bridge by night, he always took care to cover it with blankets. In general he preferred fording the streams to passing over bridges at all.

General Greene having superseded Gates, was now approaching Camden, the chief post of the British in the interior, and Marion deliberated on joining him. Hugh Horry and others of his officers opposed this measure. Just then, new recruits beginning to come, Marion fortunately decided to retain his separate command, and fight the enemy in his own peculiar way.

Marion's next exploit was the surprise and capture of Colonel Tynes at Nelson's plantation on the Black river. By this successful stroke he possessed himself of a large supply of new and excellent arms, provisions, and stores, which Tynes had brought into the country, for the use of the great force of tories which he expected to raise in that part of the province. This was a seasonable and very acceptable acquisition to Marion's men.

Cornwallis, annoyed and alarmed by the bold and successful attacks of Marion on his scattered posts, now sent out his best cavalry officer, Colonel Tarleton, to effect his capture.

Colonel Tarleton, says a late writer, left the room to which he had been confined by sickness in Charleston, and placed himself at the head of his dragoons with the firm resolve not to yield the pursuit until he had secured the enemy. Marion watched his course, and adopted his own with ceaseless caution. At the plantation of General

Richardson, the English partisan believed his triumph complete. Marion was at a wood-yard within a mile of him; but warned by the flames of the general's house that his pursuer was near, he took to flight, and when Tarleton arrived he was filled with rage on finding that the prize was gone. Through forests and swamps, thorny hedges, and tangled undergrowth, he followed the retreating troops, but never came near enough to strike a blow. At length, on arriving at Benbow's ferry on Black River, Marion determined to make a stand. The ferry was rapid and dangerous, and behind him was Ox Swamp, through which only three passes were practicable. His men were perfectly familiar with the localities, and having thrown up a breastwork of logs, and made other defences, they prepared their rifles for the English dragoons. Had Tarleton attempted to carry their position, he would, in the language of Judge James, "have exposed his force to such sharp-shooting as he had not yet experienced, and that in a place where he could not have acted with either his artillery or cavalry." But he prudently turned back; he has himself informed us that his retreat was caused by an order brought by express from Cornwallis; but a well-founded suspicion may be indulged, that he had painful doubts as to the results of a conflict under these circumstances. At the risk of violating the rules of good taste, we will give his own words, stated to have been uttered on reaching the borders of Ox Swamp. "Come, boys," he said, "let us go back. We will soon find the *game cock;** but as for this *swamp fox* the devil himself could not catch him." The devil would certainly have been a very

* General Sumter.

appropriate comrade for Colonel Tarleton in his partisan excursions through the Carolinas.

In addition to the successes of Marion, about this time occurred two battles in which the cause of freedom triumphed. General Sumter, on the banks of Tyger river, defeated a superior force of British troops, killing ninety-two, and wounding one hundred, while only three Americans were slain, and three wounded. But among the latter was Sumter himself, who was long disabled by a severe wound in the breast. At King's Mountain the British under Major Ferguson were totally defeated, and the hopes of America began again to rise. Marion planned an attack upon Georgetown which had long been held by a British garrison; but in consequence of mismanagement on the part of his subordinates, the attempt failed entirely. He now retired to his favourite retreat on Snow's Island, which lay at the point where Lynch's creek and the Pedee river unite. Here the camp of the partisan was regularly established, and it was a spot admirably suited to his purposes. Running water enclosed it on all sides, and the current of Lynch's creek was almost always encumbered by drifting logs and timber. Deep swamps formed the borders of the island, and in the cane-brakes great quantities of game and live-stock might generally be found. The middle part was more elevated, and covered with tall forest trees; here Marion established his stronghold, and increased the natural defences of the island by diligent labor. From this retreat he could sally out in any direction, and by sudden strokes astonish the tories who were gathering in aid of the British power.*

* Washington and the Generals of the Revolution.

It was during his stay at Snow's Island that Marion suffered a domestic calamity of a very trying and afflicting nature. His young brother, Gabriel Marion, was captured and murdered by the tories, while serving on a patrol under Lieutenant Gordon. The murderer was subsequently taken by Horry, and while being brought into camp was shot by a person who escaped detection under cover of the night. Although suffering the severest affliction for the loss of his brother, Marion expressed the strongest indignation at the irregular manner in which his murderer had been punished.

While lying at Snow's Island a mutinous spirit was shown by one of his own officers, but it was promptly suppressed by the decision of Marion. Another incident occurred which has often been recounted, and which has been regarded as worthy to furnish the subject for an historical painting. An exchange of prisoners having been agreed upon, a young English officer was sent from Georgetown to complete the arrangement with Marion. On arriving near the camp, he was carefully blindfolded, and was thus conducted into the presence of the American general. When the bandage was removed, he saw before him a scene for which he was not prepared. Lofty trees surrounded him, casting a sombre shade over all objects beneath them: under these were lying in listless groups the men belonging to the renowned partisan brigade. Active forms and limbs, giving promise of great muscular power, were clad in rude costumes which had already seen much service. Rifles and sabres were seen among the trees, and horses were around ready for instantaneous motion. Before him stood Marion himself, small in

MARION INVITING A BRITISH OFFICER TO DINE WITH HIM.—PAGE 141.

stature, slight in person, dark and swarthy in complexion, with a quiet aspect but a brilliant and searching eye. Scarcely could the officer believe that this was indeed the great man whose name had spread terror among all the enemies of liberty in southern America. After the business before them had been properly arranged, the Englishman was about to retire, but Marion pressed him to stay to dinner. The bewildered officer looked round him in vain for table or plates, knives or forks, roast-meats or savoury vegetables; but his suspense was soon to terminate. Sweet potatoes yet smoking from the ashes were placed upon a piece of bark and set before the American general and his guest. This was the dinner, and while the officer pretended to eat, he asked many questions. "Doubtless this is an accidental meal; you live better in general." "No," was the reply, "we often fare much worse." "Then I hope at least you draw noble pay to compensate?" "Not a cent, sir," replied Marion, "not a cent!" Lost in amazement, the messenger returned to Georgetown, and when questioned as to his seriousness, he declared that he had much cause to be serious, "he had seen an American general and his officers without pay, and almost without clothes, living on roots and drinking water, and all for liberty! What chance have we against such men?" In this rude scene might be found one of the most glorious triumphs of the American Revolution. It is said that this young officer resigned his commission, and never afterwards served during the war.

CHAPTER XVI.

Greene succeeds Gates—Battle of the Cowpens—Lee and Marion attack Georgetown—Escape of Watson—Marion organizes four new companies—Operations of Horry and Postell—Battle of Guilford—Colonels Watson and Doyle sent to drive Marion out of the country—Affair of Peter Horry—Colonel Tynes defeated—Major McIlraith encountered by Marion—Proposal to fight—Backing out—Encounters of Colonel Watson and Marion—Watson driven into Georgetown—Doyle plunders Marion's camp at Snow's Island and escapes to Camden—Marion's council with his officers.

Since the defeat of General Gates, the war in South Carolina had been carried on chiefly by Marion and Sumter, and the vigor and perseverance with which they had proceeded, reanimated the hopes of Washington and the Continental Congress of recovering the provinces of North Carolina and Georgia. General Greene had been appointed to succeed Gates, in the command of the southern continental army; and he had assumed the command at Charlotte, which, since Gates's defeat, had been the head quarters of the army.

Soon after his arrival in camp, he was gratified with the intelligence of a small piece of good fortune obtained by the address of Lieutenant Colonel Washington.

Smallwood, having received information that a body

of royal militia had entered the country in which he foraged, for the purpose of intercepting his wagons, detached Morgan and Washington against them. Intelligence of Morgan's approach being received, the party retreated; but Colonel Washington, being able to move with more celerity than the infantry, resolved to make an attempt on another party, which was stationed at Rugely's farm, within thirteen miles of Camden. He found them posted in a logged barn, strongly secured by abattis, and inaccessible to cavalry. Force being of no avail, he resorted to the following stratagem: Having painted the trunk of a pine, and mounted it on a carriage so as to resemble a field piece, he paraded it in front of the enemy, and demanded a surrender. The whole party, consisting of one hundred and twelve men, with Colonel Rugely at their head, alarmed at the prospect of a cannonade, surrendered themselves prisoners of war.

To narrow the limits of the British army, and to encourage the inhabitants, Greene detached Morgan west of the Catawba, with orders to take a position near the confluence of the Pacolet with the Broad river. His party consisted of rather more than three hundred chosen continental troops, commanded by Lieutenant Colonel Howard, of Maryland, of Washington's regiment of light dragoons, amounting to about eighty men, and of two companies of militia from the northern and western parts of Virginia, commanded by Captains Triplet and Taite, which were composed almost entirely of old continental soldiers. He was also to be joined on Broad river by seven or eight hundred volunteers and militia, commanded by General Davidson, and by Colonels Clarke and Few.

After making this detachment, Greene, for the purpose of entering a more plentiful country, advanced lower down the Pedee, and encamped on its east side, opposite the Cheraw hills. Lord Cornwallis remained at Wynnsborough, preparing to commence active operations, so soon as he should be joined by Leslie.

Supposing Morgan to have designs on Ninety-Six, Cornwallis detached Tarleton with a considerable force to cut him off. Morgan retreated as far as the Cowpens, where he made a stand, and being attacked by Tarleton, inflicted upon him the severest defeat he had yet encountered. (Jan. 17th, 1781.)

Seldom has a battle in which greater numbers were not engaged, been so important in its consequences as that of the Cowpens. Lord Cornwallis was not only deprived of a fifth of his numbers, but lost a most powerful and active part of his army. Unfortunately, Greene was not in a condition to press the advantage. The whole southern army did not much exceed two thousand men, a great part of whom were militia.

After the battle, passing Broad river, Morgan hastened to the Catawba, which he reached on the 23d of January, at Sherald's ford, and encamped on its eastern bank.

While Morgan remained on the Catawba, watching the motions of the British army, and endeavoring to collect the militia, General Greene arrived, and took command of the detachment.

In his camp on the Pedee, opposite the Cheraw hills, Greene had been joined by Lee's legion, amounting to about one hundred cavalry, and one hundred and twenty infantry. The day after his arrival he was ordered to join Marion for the purpose of attempting to carry a British post at Georgetown, distant about seventy-five miles from the American army.

General Greene had commenced a correspondence with Marion on the day of his arrival at Charlotte, and had desired his aid in collecting information respecting the force and positions of the enemy, by means of spies and scouts; a species of service for which Marion was particularly fitted; and Marion had written to him for a reinforcement to enable him to capture the British garrison at Georgetown, a favorite object of his at this time. Moultrie* thus describes the attack on this post:

On January 25th, 1781, General Marion with his brigade of militia, retired to Snow's Island and was there joined by Colonel Lee with his legion. Colonel Lee formed a plan to surprise Georgetown, which was garrisoned with about three hundred regular troops, and some militia, under the command of Colonel Campbell. Captain Carnes and Captain Rudulph, with about ninety (mostly of Lee's infantry) were sent down from Snow's Island, about forty miles from Georgetown, in a large boat, to drop down the river, towards the town, while General Marion and Colonel Lee were to have come down with the main body by land. Just before daybreak, on the second day, Captain Carnes with his party, landed at Mitchell's Point, about a quarter of a

* Memoirs.

mile to the east of the town; they landed and marched on a bank through the rice field, and were in the town a little before daylight. The British knew nothing of them, until they were alarmed by a few popping shots, and then very great confusion ensued; the officers running about for the men, and the men for the officers; in this hurry and confusion, the guides got so alarmed and frightened that they lost their way to the fort, where the main body of the British were quartered, or else the surprise would have been complete. A party went to Col. Campbell's quarters, took him out of bed, and carried him off without any other clothes than his shirt, to about a quarter of a mile on the back of the town, through bushes and briers; he begged and entreated so much that they would allow him to go back and be paroled to Charlestown; after a little time they had compassion upon him, and suffered him to go back upon parole. By this time the enemy began to embody, and the firing was heard from different parts of the town, and General Marion and Colonel Lee not entering the town at the same time, Captains Carnes and Rudulph thought it advisable to retreat. Had the guides not missed their way to the fort, it is more than probable this little detachment would have taken the whole garrison prisoners; some few men were killed on both sides. The cavalry under General Marion and Colonel Lee did not arrive, and as they met with a breast-work not easily to be mounted, they proceeded no further, particularly as the infantry had already retreated.

Although this attack was not successful, its boldness struck terror into the enemy, and prevented the removal of more forces from Charleston into the interior. It was followed by other more successful attacks on the British posts which were established in different parts of South Carolina.

Marion and Lee now proceeded up the Santee towards Nelson's Ferry to surprise Colonel Watson, who had taken post there; but that officer, leaving a garrison of eighty men in Fort Watson, five miles above Nelson's Ferry, retreated to Camden.

Lee being now ordered to join General Greene with his whole legion, Marion was again left to his own resources. This occasioned no diminution in his activity. On the 29th of January he sent out two detachments of only thirty men each, under Colonel and Major Postell, who were very successful in beating up the enemy's quarters, capturing prisoners, and destroying baggage wagons and stores.

For want of ammunition indispensable for infantry operations, Marion now organized four new companies of cavalry, and again had recourse to his old expedient of having broadswords made out of mill-saws. This body he placed under the command of Colonel Peter Horry, who soon after attacked and routed a party of British dragoons under Colonel Campbell, near the great Waccamaw road.

About the same time, Major John Postell with twenty-eight militia surprised and captured Captain Depeyster with twenty-nine grenadiers.

Captain Postell being sent into the British camp with a flag, and detained as a prisoner, upon a charge of breaking his parole, Marion demanded his release and threatened reprisals. He even seized Captain Merritt the bearer of a British flag, and confined him as a security for Postell.

Meantime Greene's celebrated retreat into North Carolina and escape from the superior force of Cornwallis took place, which was followed by the battle of Guilford; (15th March 1781;) on which occasion the British kept the field, but Greene reaped the fruits of victory, as the loss of Cornwallis in the battle was so severe that he was compelled to retreat immediately; and this was the commencement of a series of false moves and disasters which terminated only with his capture at Yorktown.

Meantime, while Cornwallis with the main army of the British was engaged with Greene in North Carolina, Marion's was the only force which was actively operating against the enemy in South Carolina. He cut off detachments and supplies intended for the main army, and scoured the country from the confluence of the Congaree down to Monk's Corner, in the immediate neighborhood of Charleston, and sent terror and dismay into the tory settlements throughout that region.

Marion's active mode of carrying on the war was exceedingly distasteful to Cornwallis, Rawdon, and the other British commanders. It interfered with all their plans for insuring and perpetuating their possession of the southern country. They had military posts established in different parts of North and South Carolina; and Marion's rapid movements and secret expeditions cut off the communication between their posts, and threw their whole system of government and military surveillance into confusion. It therefore became an object with them to capture or expel him from the country at all hazards.

Accordingly Colonel Watson was detached with a body of five hundred men to pursue and destroy or drive him out of the country. In the meantime Colonel Peter Horry, being engaged in beating up the enemy's quarters in the neighborhood of Georgetown, became engaged in a skirmish in which he got separated from his party and narrowly escaped being shot by the Tory captain, Lewis. His life was saved by a boy named Gwin, who shot Lewis as he was taking aim at the Colonel. The enemy was defeated with heavy loss, and the commander Major Gainey, taking flight on horseback, was pursued by Sergeant McDonald, who thrust his bayonet into Gainey's back and left it there, the major escaping into Georgetown, at full speed, with the bayonet still sticking in the hinder part of his person.

Colonel Tynes, who as we have seen had been captured by Marion, had escaped from confinement in North Carolina, raised a small force of tories, and was approaching Marion's camp, when Marion surprised and routed him, taking the whole party prisoners. He was sent again to North Carolina, and again escaped and took the field. Colonel Horry being sent against him, was obliged to abandon the enterprise in consequence of his men being amply supplied with apple-brandy by a cunning tory, and getting incontinently drunk.

In February Marion went in pursuit of a party commanded by Major McIlraith near Nelson's Ferry. He overtook and attacked him near Half-way Swamp. After some skirmishing the major posted himself within an enclosure on the west of the road, and Marion pitched his camp on the edge of a pond on the east side. McIlraith now sent a flag to Marion complaining of his irregular mode of warfare, and challenging him to a fight in the open field. Marion replied that the British practices of burning houses, hanging prisoners, &c., were worse than his shooting piquets; and that he should continue to retaliate. Meantime he had no objection to a contest between twenty pitched men of his party opposed to the same number of British.

The challenge was accepted and the men paraded ready for the fight, when the British champions were suddenly recalled to the main body. The Americans gave them three cheers as they retired, but not a shot was fired. McIlraith, on the night succeeding this inglorious affair, secretly decamped and made his escape to a stronghold at Singleton's Mill. Marion was not very anxious to capture him, as he had learnt that he was the most humane of all the British commanders, treating the people with forbearance, and committing no unnecessary destruction of property or life.

On the first of March Colonel Watson left Fort Watson with five hundred regulars and a formidable force of tory auxiliaries, determined to capture or destroy or drive out of the country, the most troublesome enemies in it—Marion and his men. He marched down the Santee towards Marion's stronghold on Snow's Island. At the same time Colonel Doyle with another British regiment marched for McCallum's Ferry on his way down Jeffers' Creek to the Pedee, where he was to unite his force with Watson's.

Every thing promised well for the success of this enterprise, so far as the great force of the British was concerned. Marion's handful of troopers could not meet them in a pitched battle, of course. They numbered but three hundred, and their enemies were not less than five times that number, all told. But Marion, far from being discouraged at this great superiority, took the initiative in the contest. Constantly apprised, by his numerous scouts, of Watson's movements, he chose his own time and place for assailing him in his own fashion. He first attacked him at Wiboo swamp between Nelson's and Murray's ferries. The contest with the tories who were in the advance was severe and protracted, ending in the total dispersion of these irregular troops, who sought shelter with the main body of regulars.

This answered Marion's purpose for the present. He drew off on the approach of the main body, and retired to a safe distance. On the next day he retreated, and Watson pursued. At Mount Hope Watson had a similar affair with a detachment of Marion's men, under Colonel Horry; and again his attempt to pass a bridge over the Santee, was successfully resisted by Major James with a detachment of McCottry's rifles, notwithstanding Watson's artillery and his greatly superior force. The sharpshooting of Marion's men was terrifying, Watson declared that "he never had seen such shooting in his life."

He wrote to Marion, bitterly complaining of his mode of warfare, and daring him to come out and fight him like a gentleman and a Christian. As he called Marion's men, "banditti and murderers," in this missive, he got no answer to it. But Sergeant McDonald, whose clothes had been taken by the enemy, sent a message by Watson's flag that if they were not returned he would kill eight of his men. The clothes were forthwith returned. When McDonald received them, he said to the bearer, "Tell Colonel Watson, I will now kill but four of his men." He began with Lieutenant Torriano whom he shot through the knee two days after, at the distance of three hundred yards.

Marion's rifles still deterred Watson from crossing the river; but he sent over detachments of light troops who drove Watson to Blakeley's plantation, where he formed a camp, and remained for ten days in a state of siege, Marion's detachment harassing him continually, cutting off his supplies, and giving him no repose by day or by night.

Watson now wrote again to Marion; but took care not to insult him. He wanted a pass for Torriano and other wounded men, to go to Charleston, which Marion courteously granted. Finally the situation of Watson had become so intolerable that by a desperate effort he effected his retreat to Georgetown, harassed and cut up all the way by his indefatigable enemy, having his horse killed in the last skirmish, and coming very near a total defeat at the hands of the partisan whom he had gone forth to capture, destroy, or drive out of the country.

Meantime Colonel Doyle had succeeded in reaching Marion's stronghold on Snow's Island, and capturing the stores, arms, and ammunition, which had hitherto been considered safe in that place. On learning this disaster, Marion set off in pursuit of Doyle and encountered him at Witherspoon's Ferry, on Lynch's Creek, so posted that it was impossible to cross the river in that place; while he made a detour and swam the river five miles higher up, Doyle decamped and joined Lord Rawdon at Camden. "Thus," says Moultrie, "the scene was reversed: instead of Watson and Doyle pushing Marion out of the country, he faces about and pursues them towards Camden; their marches were too rapid for them to be overtaken."

It was about this time that Marion called his officers together to make known to them the perilous condition in which he was placed from being almost the only opponent of the British in South Carolina. Mr. Simms places this incident after the retreat of Doyle and Watson. Moultrie says it was when these officers were first sent out in pursuit of him. His account of the affair is as follows:

General Marion retired to Lynch's creek, and was soon informed that Colonel Watson and a party of tories were advancing fast upon him, the first in his rear, the second on his right, and that Colonel Doyle from Camden was in his front, three detachments from different directions, and all pointed towards Marion, with an intention to drive him out of the country. They knew he could get no support or assistance, and that he had but very few men with him. General Marion made known his situation to Colonel Peter Horry, and said if the enemy did drive him out of the country, he was determined to retire over the mountains, with as many as would follow him, and from time to time would gather a party and sally down the country, and do them as much injury as he could, until he was killed or they had left the country, he would not leave off warring against them: he said he was afraid that, if he should be hard pushed, many of his men would not leave their families and fly with him. General Marion desired Colonel Peter Horry to call the field-officers together privately, and lay the circumstances of their situation fully before them; to acquaint them of his determination, and to have theirs, in order that he might know how far he could rely on them: he recommended that the officers should unite with him as a band of brother officers; and that each should most solemnly pledge to the other his sacred word and honor, to be faithful, and never submit to the enemy but with their lives.

The field-officers then in camp, were Colonels Peter Horry, Hugh Horry, James Postell, and Irvin; Majors James Baxter and Swinton; these met and resolved according to the wishes of the general, and without hesitation, said they were bound in honor to adhere to his fortune, whether good or bad; and they all declared they would be faithful to each other, and would carry on the war as the general should direct: these determinations being made at a time when there was the greatest prospect of distress, were truly honorable to themselves and to their country.

On General Marion's being acquainted with their resolutions, he said "he was satisfied, and that one of the enemy's detachments should feel his force."

The reader has already been made acquainted with the manner in which they were made to "*feel his force.*"

CHAPTER XVII.

Retreat of Watson—Siege and capture of Fort Watson by Marion and Lee—Battle of Hobkirk's Hill—Watson escapes to Camden—Siege of Fort Motte—Noble conduct of Mrs. Motte—Marion rescues a prisoner from assassination.

AFTER the retreat of Doyle, Marion again turned his attention to Watson, who had a force double his own, and was now pushing on for the Pedee. Marion encamped at the Wahees within five miles of the enemy. But he was nearly destitute of powder for his rifles, and could only watch his opponent without venturing to attack. The approach of General Greene's army drew off Watson who made a hasty retreat towards Camden, while Lieutenant Colonel Lee again joined Marion; and on the fifteenth of April their united force appeared before Fort Watson.

Determined, says Lee,* to carry this post without delay, Marion and Lee sat down before it early in the evening, not doubting, from the information received, that the garrison must soon be compelled to surrender, for want of water, with which it was supplied from an adjacent lake, and from which the garrison might be readily and effectually secluded. In a very few hours

* Memoirs.

the customary mode of supplying the post with water was completely stopped; and had the information received been correct, a surrender of the garrison could not have been long delayed.

The ground selected by Colonel Watson for his small stockade, was an Indian mount, generally conceived to be the cemetery of the tribe inhabiting the circumjacent region: it was at least thirty feet high, and surrounded by table land. Captain M'Koy, the commandant, saw at once his inevitable fate, unless he could devise some other mode of procuring water, for which purpose he immediately cut a trench from his fosse (secured by abattis) to the river, which passed close to the Indian mount.

Baffled in their expectation, and destitute both of artillery and intrenching tools, Marion and Lee despaired of success; when Major Mayham, of South Carolina, accompanying the brigadier, suggested a plan, which was no sooner communicated than gratefully adopted. He proposed to cut down a number of suitable trees in the nearest wood, and with them to erect a large strong oblong pen, to be covered on the top with a floor of logs, and protected on the side opposite to the fort with a breastwork of light timber. To the adjacent farms dragoons were despatched for axes, the only necessary tool, of which a sufficient number being soon collected, relays of working parties were allotted for the labor; some to cut, some to convey, and some to erect.

Major Mayham undertook the execution of his plan, which was completely finished before the morning of the 23d, effective as to the object, and honorable to the genius of the inventor. The besieged was, like the besieger, unprovided with artillery, and could not interrupt the progress of a work, the completion of which must produce immediate submission.

A party of riflemen, being ready, took post in the Mayham tower the moment it was completed; and a detachment of musketry, under cover of the riflemen, moved to make a lodgment in the enemy's ditch, supported by the legion infantry with fixed bayonets. Such was the effect of the fire from the riflemen, having thorough command of every part of the fort, from the relative supereminence of the tower, that every attempt to resist the lodgment was crushed.

The commandant, finding every resource cut off, hung out the white flag. It was followed by a proposal to surrender, which issued in a capitulation. This incipient operation having been happily effected by the novel and effectual device of Major Mayham, to whom the commandants very gratefully expressed their acknowledgment, Marion and Lee, preceded by the legion cavalry under Major Rudulph, who had been detached on the day subsequent to the investiture of the fort, turned their attention to Lieutenant Colonel Watson, now advancing from below to relieve his garrison. Knowing that the fall of Camden was closely connected with the destruction of Watson, the American commandants viewed with delight his approach; and having disposed of the prisoners, moved to join the cavalry, now retiring in front of the enemy.

As soon as the capitulation for the surrender of Fort Watson was signed, Lee followed by his infantry hastened to the cavalry, who had been sent to the front of Watson; and on the subsequent morning was joined by

Marion, who had been necessarily delayed until the prisoners and stores were disposed of. Watson, seeing that the passes on his route were occupied, and knowing that the advantages possessed by his enemy would be strenuously maintained, relinquished his project of gaining Camden on the direct route, and determined, by passing the Santee, to interpose it between himself and the corps opposed to him; presuming that he might with facility make his way good to Camden, by recrossing the Santee above; or, by taking the route by Fort Motte, pass first the Congaree, and then the Wateree, which unite some small distance below the post at Motte's.

Drawing off in the night, he placed himself at a considerable distance from his enemy before his change of plan was discovered. Nevertheless he would have been pursued, with the expectation of falling upon him before he could make good his passage of the river, had not the general's orders directing the junction of the corps under Lee arrived, which necessarily arrested the proposed attempt upon Watson. With all possible despatch Lee set out for the army; and, in the course of the day and a small part of the night, marched thirty-two miles.

But before he could rejoin Greene, the order was countermanded, and Captain Finley of the artillery with a six pounder was sent to join him. Lee then rejoined Marion.

Meantime during the siege of Fort Watson, the indecisive battle of Hobkirk's Hill had taken place, in which, as in other instances, General Greene, although suffering a repulse by Lord Rawdon, still reaped the fruits of victory. After the battle he sat down in a strong position near Camden, depriving Rawdon of his supplies from Charleston, and preventing Colonel Watson's approach to Camden on the southern route. At the same time he sent orders to Marion and Lee to intercept Watson in his attempts to reach Camden.

Marion and Lee lost not a moment after their union in taking measures to execute the command of their general, well apprised of the vast importance attached to the interception of Watson. Marion, being perfectly acquainted with the country, guided the measures adopted. He well knew that, although General Greene's position would stop Watson on the usual route from Motte's post to Camden, it would not stop him from passing the Wateree at or below the high hills of Santee; and that Watson, to avoid the corps destined to strike him, would probably, notwithstanding the judicious position taken by Greene, pass the Congaree at Motte's, and afterwards pass the Wateree below the high hills.

If Watson should not deem it eligible to pass the Congaree, but one way was left for him, and that was to recross the Santee at the confluence of the two rivers just mentioned.

Whether to sit down on the north side of the Santee, prepared to fall upon Watson in the act of passing the river, or to cross it and strike at him on the southern banks, was the alternative presented to the American commandants.

Well informed of every step taken by Watson after he reached the southern side of the Santee, no doubt remained but that he would pass either the Congaree or the Santee on the ensuing morning. It was now decided to cross to his side of the river, from a conviction that we should reach him on its southern banks, which ever course of the two before him he might select. The indefatigable Marion, seconded by his zealous associates, foreseeing the probable necessity of a quick passage over the Santee, had provided the means of transportation, which was effected in the course of the night, and, with the dawn of day, the troops moved with celerity up the Santee. It was now ascertained that Watson had taken the route leading over that river where its two branches unite—the very spot which had so forcibly attracted the attention of Marion and Lee, and would have been selected by them, had it not been apprehended that Watson might have preferred the route across the Congaree.

Had they confined their attention entirely to the north side of the river, the much desired interception would have been effected: for with horse, foot, and artillery, it was not to be expected that a corps of infantry only could have made good its landing in the face of an equal foe, and secured its arrival into Camden.

Mortified with the result of their unceasing exertions, the deranging information was immediately forwarded to General Greene, and the disappointed commandants moved upon Fort Motte.*

The following account of the siege of Fort Motte we transcribe from Lee's Memoirs:

On the 10th of May the evacuation of Camden took place, and Lord Rawdon proceeded to Nelson's ferry with the expectation of crossing the Santee in time to dislodge Marion and Lee, still prosecuting the siege of

* Lee's Memoirs.

Fort Motte. Previous to his lordship's departure he burnt the jail, the mills, and some private houses, and destroyed all the stores which he could not take with him. He carried off four or five hundred negroes, and all the most obnoxious loyalists accompanied him.

As soon as Greene was informed of the retreat of the enemy, persuaded that Rawdon's first effort would be directed to relieve Fort Motte, he advanced towards the Congaree, determined to pass that river, if necessary, and to cover the operations of the besieging corps.

This post was the principal depot of the convoys from Charleston to Camden, and sometimes of those destined for Fort Granby and Ninety-six. A large new mansion house, belonging to Mrs. Motte, situated on a high and commanding hill, had been selected for this establishment. It was surrounded with a deep trench, along the interior margin of which was raised a strong and lofty parapet. To this post had been regularly assigned an adequate garrison of about one hundred and fifty men, which was now accidentally increased by a small detachment of dragoons,—which had arrived from Charleston, a few hours before the appearance of the American troops, on its way to Camden with despatches for Lord Rawdon. Captain M'Pherson commanded, an officer highly and deservedly respected.

Opposite Fort Motte, to the north, stood another hill, where Mrs. Motte, having been dismissed from her mansion, resided, in the old farmhouse. On this height Lieutenant Colonel Lee with his corps took post, while Brigadier Marion occupied the eastern declivity of the ridge on which the fort stood.

Very soon the fort was completely invested; and the six pounder was mounted on a battery erected in Marion's quarter for the purpose of raking the northern face of the enemy's parapet, against which Lee was preparing to advance. M'Pherson was unprovided with artillery, and depended for safety upon timely relief, not doubting its arrival before the assailant could push his preparations to maturity.

The vale which runs between the two hills admitted our safe approach within four hundred yards of the fort. This place was selected by Lee to break ground. Relays of working parties being provided for every four hours, and some of the negroes from the neighboring plantations being brought, by the influence of Marion, to our assistance, the works advanced with rapidity. Such was their forwardness on the 10th, that it was determined to summon the commandant.

A flag was accordingly despatched to Captain M'Pherson, stating to him with truth our relative situation, expressing with decision the fate which awaited him, and admonishing him to avoid the disagreeable consequences of an arrogant temerity. To this the captain replied, that, disregarding consequences, he should continue to resist to the last moment in his power. The retreat of Rawdon was known in the evening to the besiegers; and in the course of the night a courier arrived from General Greene confirming that event, urging redoubled activity, and communicating his determination to hasten to their support. Urged by these strong considerations, Marion and Lee persevered throughout the night in pressing the completion of their works. On the next day, Rawdon reached the country opposite to Fort Motte; and in the succeeding night encamping on the highest ground in his route, the illumination of his fires gave the joyful annunciation of his approach to the despairing garrison. But the hour was close at hand, when this fallacious joy was to be converted into sadness.

The large mansion in the centre of the encircling trench, left but a few yards of the ground within the enemy's works uncovered: burning the house must force their surrender.

Persuaded that our ditch would be within arrow shot before noon of the next day, Marion and Lee determined to adopt this speedy mode of effecting their object. Orders were instantly issued to prepare bows and arrows, with missive combustible matter. This measure was reluctantly adopted; for the destruction of private property was repugnant to the principles which swayed the two commandants, and upon this occasion was peculiarly distressing. The devoted house was a large, pleasant edifice, intended for the summer residence of the respectable owner, whose deceased husband had been a firm friend to his oppressed country, and whose only marriageable daughter was the wife of Major Pinckney, an officer in the South Carolina line, who had fought and bled in his country's cause, and was now a prisoner with the enemy. These considerations powerfully forbade the execution of the proposed measure; but there were others of much cogency, which applied personally to Lieutenant Colonel Lee, and gave a new edge to the bitterness of the scene.

Encamping contiguous to Mrs. Motte's dwelling, this

officer had, upon his arrival, been requested in the most pressing terms to make her house his quarters. The invitation was accordingly accepted; and not only the lieutenant colonel, but every officer of his corps, off duty, daily experienced her liberal hospitality, politely proffered and as politely administered. Nor was the attention of this amiable lady confined to that class of war which never fail to attract attention. While her richly spread table presented with taste and fashion all the luxuries of her opulent country, and her sideboard offered without reserve the best wines of Europe,—antiquated relics of happier days,—her active benevolence found its way to the sick and to the wounded; cherishing with softest kindness infirmity and misfortune, converting despair into hope, and nursing debility into strength. Nevertheless the imperative obligations of duty must be obeyed; the house must burn; and a respectful communication to the lady of her destined loss must be made. Taking the first opportunity which offered, the next morning, Lieutenant Colonel Lee imparted to Mrs. Motte the intended measure; lamenting the sad necessity, and assuring her of the deep regret which the unavoidable act excited in his and every breast.

With the smile of complacency this exemplary lady listened to the embarrassed officer, and gave instant relief to his agitated feelings, by declaring, that she was gratified with the opportunity of contributing to the good of her country, and that she should view the approaching scene with delight. Shortly after, seeing accidentally the bow and arrows which had been prepared, she sent for Lee, and presenting him with a bow and its apparatus

MRS. MOTTE PRESENTING THE BOW AND ARROWS TO DESTROY HER OWN DWELLING.—PAGE 164.

imported from India, she requested his substitution of these, as probably better adapted for the object than those we had provided.

Receiving with silent delight this opportune present, Lee rejoined his troops, now making ready for the concluding scene. The lines were manned, and an additional force stationed at the battery, lest the enemy, perceiving his fate, might determine to risk a desperate assault, as offering the only chance of relief. As soon as the troops reached their several points, a flag was again sent to M'Pherson, for the purpose of inducing him to prevent the conflagration and the slaughter which might ensue, by a second representation of his actual condition.

Doctor Irwin, of the legion cavalry, was charged with the flag, and instructed to communicate faithfully the inevitable destruction impending, and the impracticability of relief, as Lord Rawdon had not yet passed the Santee; with an assurance that longer perseverance in vain resistance would place the garrison at the mercy of the conqueror; who was not regardless of the policy of preventing the waste of time, by inflicting exemplary punishment, where resistance was maintained only to produce such waste. The British captain received the flag with his usual politeness, and heard patiently Irvin's explanations; but he remained immovable; repeating his determination of holding out to the last.

It was now about noon, and the rays of the scorching sun had prepared the shingle roof for the projected conflagration. The return of Irwin was immediately followed by the application of the bow and arrows. The first arrow struck, and communicated its fire; a second was shot at another quarter of the roof, and a third at a third quarter; this last also took effect, and, like the first, soon kindled a blaze. M'Pherson ordered a party to repair to the loft of the house, and by knocking off the shingles to stop the flames. This was soon perceived, and Captain Finley was directed to open his battery, raking the loft from end to end.

The fire of our six pounder, posted close to one of the gable ends of the house, soon drove the soldiers down; and no other effort to stop the flames being practicable, M'Pherson hung out the white flag. Mercy was extended, although policy commanded death, and the obstinacy of M'Pherson warranted it. The commandant, with the regulars, of which the garrison was chiefly composed, were taken possession of by Lee; while the loyalists were delivered to Marion. Among the latter was a Mr. Smith, who had been charged with burning the houses of his neighbors friendly to their country. This man consequently became very obnoxious, and his punishment was loudly demanded by many of the militia serving under the brigadier; but the humanity of Marion could not be overcome. Smith was secured from his surrounding enemies, ready to devote him, and taken under the general's protection.

M'Pherson was charged with having subjected himself to punishment, by his idle waste of his antagonists' time; and reminded as well of the opportunities which had been presented to him of saving himself and garrison from unconditional submission, as of the cogent considerations, growing out of the posture of affairs, which urged the prevention of future useless resistance by present exemplary punishment. The British officer frankly acknowledged his dependent situation, and declared his readiness to meet any consequence which the discharge of duty, conformably to his own conviction of right, might produce. Powerfully as the present occasion called for punishment, and rightfully as it might have been inflicted, not a drop of blood was shed, nor any part of the enemy's baggage taken. M'Pherson and his officers accompanied their captors to Mrs. Motte's, and partook with them in a sumptuous dinner;* soothing in the sweets of social intercourse the ire which the preceding conflict had engendered. Requesting to be permitted to return to Charleston on parole, they were accordingly paroled and sent off in the evening to Lord Rawdon, now engaged in passing the Santee at Nelson's ferry. Soon after, General Greene, anxious for the success of his detachment against Fort Motte, attended by an escort of cavalry, reached us, for the purpose of knowing precisely our situation, and the progress of the British general, who he expected would hasten to the relief of M'Pherson, as soon as he should gain the southern banks of the Santee; to counteract which the American general had resolved, and was then engaged in preparing boats, to transport his army over the Congaree. Finding the

---

* The deportment and demeanor of Mrs. Motte gave a zest to the pleasures of the table. She did its honors with that unaffected politeness, which ever excites esteem mingled with admiration. Conversing with ease, vivacity, and good sense, she obliterated our recollection of the injury she had received; and though warmly attached to the defenders of her country, the engaging amiability of her manners left it doubtful which set of officers constituted these defenders.

siege prosperously concluded, he returned to camp; having directed Marion, after placing the prisoners in security, to proceed against Georgetown, and ordering Lee to advance without delay upon Fort Granby, to which place the American army would now move.

Mr. Simms, in his life of Marion, gives the following account of Marion's interposition in behalf of the tory prisoners:

While at the hospitable table of Mrs. Motte, it was whispered in Marion's ears, that Col. Lee's men were even then engaged in hanging certain of the tory prisoners. Marion instantly hurried from the table, seized his sword, and running with all haste, reached the place of execution in time to rescue one poor wretch from the gallows. Two were already beyond rescue or recovery. With drawn sword and a degree of indignation in his countenance that spoke more than words, Marion threatened to kill the first man that made any further attempt in such diabolical proceedings.

The reader will perceive how totally at variance this is with Col. Lee's account quoted above. (See page 166.)

Mr. Simms gives no author for his statement; but on the other hand we have the authority of Col. Lee himself. Moreover, it is not probable that Lee's soldiers would meddle with the tories after they had become the prisoners of Marion.

CHAPTER XVIII.

General Greene's opinion of Gen. Marion—Misunderstanding between Marion and Greene—Reconciled—Lord Rawdon evacuates Camden—General Sumter takes Orangeburg—Lee captures Fort Granby—Siege of Ninety Six—Greene pursues Rawdon to Orangeburg and offers battle—The British garrison evacuates Ninety-Six, and joins Rawdon at Orangeburg—Operations of Greene to cause the evacuation of Orangeburg—Sumter and Marion sent to the posts at Monk's Corner and Dorchester—Colonel Wade Hampton's exploits—Attack on Col. Coates at Shubrick's plantation—Effect of these operations on the country—Lord Rawdon sails for Europe.

From the time when General Greene, having taken command of the army of the southern department, entered into correspondence with Marion, and sent Lee, with his legion, to act in conjunction with Marion's brigade, Marion had been acting under Greene's orders, instead of conducting the war in South Carolina as an independent partisan leader. His subsequent operations were consequently all more or less connected with the movements of the main army.

How much Greene depended on his support, and how highly he estimated his past services, may be seen by the following letter from Greene to Marion, dated at the camp before Camden, April 24, 1781:*

* Quoted by Simms, p. 244.

"When I consider," writes Greene, "how much you have done and suffered, and under what disadvantage you have maintained your ground, I am at a loss which to admire most, your courage and fortitude, or your address and management. Certain it is, no man has a better claim to the public thanks than you. History affords no instance wherein an officer has kept possession of a country under so many disadvantages as you have. Surrounded on every side with a superior force, hunted from every quarter with veteran troops, you have found means to elude their attempts, and to keep alive the expiring hopes of an oppressed militia, when all succor seemed to be cut off. *To fight the enemy bravely with the prospect of victory, is nothing; but to fight with intrepidity under the constant impression of defeat, and inspire irregular troops to do it, is a talent peculiar to yourself.* Nothing will give me greater pleasure than to do justice to your merit, and I shall miss no opportunity of declaring to Congress, to the commander-in-chief of the American army, and to the world, the great sense I have of your merit and your services."

To operate successfully in the plain level country of Carolina, an efficient body of cavalry was indispensable; and General Greene was anxious to increase this species of force in the main army. But there was great difficulty in obtaining horses. The British had robbed the stables pretty generally, and few horses fit for service could be found. Colonel Lee writing to Greene (May 23, 1781) had said that General Marion could supply him with 150 good dragoon horses, if he would. This was a great mistake of Lee's, and led to a very unpleasant correspondence between Greene and Marion, the former supposing that the latter had not duly regarded his pressing demands for horses, and the latter repelling the charge and finally offering his resignation.

Greene on learning the real state of affairs, and that he had done Marion great injustice in supposing that he was unnecessarily withholding supplies for the public service, when in point of fact it was utterly out of his power to furnish them, wrote to Marion very earnestly dissuading him from resigning his command, and using his utmost powers of conciliation. Fortunately he was successful, and this unfortunate misunderstanding between two of the most illustrious heroes of the revolution was satisfactorily adjusted. Its effects, however, in one respect were injurious, as many of Marion's men, supposing that they were about to be dismounted, and their horses given to the troopers of the main army, left the service and returned to their homes. The terms which they served under Marion, were not, as we have already seen, incompatible with this proceeding. They were always *volunteers*, in the widest sense of the word.

After the battle of Hobkirk's Hill, (April 25th, 1781,) as we have already related, General Greene had taken a position to cut off the advance of Colonel Watson towards Camden. At the same time (May 3d) he sent a reinforcement to General Marion, who was to co-operate with him in the same object. But Watson eluded them, by a circuitous route, and entered Camden on the 7th of May, bringing a considerable reinforcement to the army under Lord Rawdon's command, the main body of the British force in the south.

With this increase of force Lord Rawdon attempted, on the day following, to compel General Greene to another action; but soon found that this was impracticable. Failing in his design, he returned to Camden, and on the tenth burned the gaol, mills, many private houses, and a great deal of his own baggage—evacuated the post—and retired with his whole army to the south of the Santee; leaving about thirty of his own sick and wounded, and as many of the Americans, who, on the 25th of April, had fallen into his hands.

Lord Rawdon discovered as great prudence in this evacuation of Camden as he had shown bravery in its defence. The fall of Fort Watson broke the chain of communication with Charleston, and the positions of the American army intercepted all supplies from the country. The return of Greene to the southward being unexpected, the stores of the garrison were not provided for a siege.

Lord Rawdon had the honor of saving his men, though he lost the post, the country, and the confidence of the tories. He offered every assistance in his power to the friends of British government who would accompany him; but it was a hard alternative to the new-made subjects to be obliged to abandon their property, or to be left at the mercy of their exasperated countrymen. Several families nevertheless accompanied his lordship. These were cruelly neglected after their arrival in Charleston. They built themselves huts without the works. Their settlement was called Rawdon Town; which from its poverty and wretchedness, became a term of reproach. Many women and children, who lived comfortably on their farms near Camden, soon died of want in these their new habitations.

This evacuation animated the friends of congress, and gave a very general alarm to the British. The former had been called upon for their personal services, to assist in regaining the country, but were disheartened by the repulse of General Greene from before Camden; but from the moment that Lord Rawdon evacuated that post their numbers daily increased, and the British posts fell in quick succession. On the day after the evacuation of Camden, the garrison of Orangeburg, consisting of seventy British militia and twelve regulars, surrendered to General Sumter.

Two days after the surrender of Fort Motte, the British evacuated their post at Nelson's ferry—blew up their fortifications—and destroyed a great part of their stores. The day following, Fort Granby, near Friday's ferry, about thirty miles to the westward of Fort Motte, surrendered by capitulation. Very advantageous terms were given by the assailants in consequence of information that Lord Rawdon was marching to its relief. This was a post of more consequence than the others, and might have been better defended; but the offer of security to the baggage of the garrison, in which was included an immense quantity of plunder, hastened the surrender. For some time before, it had been greatly harassed by Colonel Taylor's regiment of militia, and had also been invested by General Sumter. On the night of the 14th of May, Lieutenant Colonel Lee erected a battery within six hundred yards of its outworks, on which he mounted a six-pounder. After the third discharge of this field-piece, Major Maxwell capitulated. His force consisted of three hundred and fifty-two men, a great part of whom were royal militia.

While these operations were carrying on against the small posts, General Greene proceeded with the main army to Ninety-Six. This place being of great consequence was defended by a considerable force. Lieutenant Colonel Cruger conducted the defence with great bravery and judgment. Major Green, in particular, acquired distinguished reputation by his spirited and judicious conduct in defending the redoubt against which the Americans made their principal efforts.

The siege was protracted from the 23d of May to the 18th of June, when it was abandoned in consequence of the approach of Lord Rawdon with a large and powerful reinforcement. Colonel Lee won great honor by his gallant conduct in the final assault which was made before the siege was abandoned. While the siege was in progress, Marion and Sumter were engaged in watching, and impeding as far as was practicable, the advance of Lord Rawdon to the relief of the garrison.

The arrival of the British reinforcement, and the subsequent retreat from Ninety-Six, induced a general apprehension that the British would soon re-establish the posts they had lost to the southward of Santee. The destination of the main army under Lord Cornwallis having been for some time known, the British commanders in South Carolina had contracted their boundaries to that extent of country which is in a great measure inclosed by the Santee, the Congaree, and the Edisto. Within these rivers Lord Rawdon intended to confine his future operations, and to canton his forces in the most eligible positions. His lordship, taking it for granted that the Americans had abandoned South Carolina, resolved, upon his return from pursuing General Greene, to divide his army, with the intention of fixing a detachment at the Congaree; but he soon found that his adversaries were not disposed to give up the prize for which they had so long contended.

Greene, on hearing that Lord Rawdon had marched with a part of his force to Congaree, faced about to give him battle. Lord Rawdon, no less surprised than alarmed at this unexpected movement of his lately retreating foe, abandoned the Congaree in two days after his arrival there, and retreated expeditiously to Orangeburg. In this position he was secured on one side with a river, and on the other with strong buildings little inferior to redoubts. Greene pursued—encamped within five miles of this post, and offered him battle. His lordship, secure in his stronghold, would not venture out; and General Greene was too weak to attack him in his works with any prospect of success. In the course of these movements, on the second of July, Captain Eggleston of Lee's legion, fell in with forty-nine British horse, near the Saluda, and took forty-eight of them prisoners.

Whilst the American army lay near Orangeburg, advice was received that Lieutenant Colonel Cruger had evacuated Ninety-Six, and was marching with the troops of that garrison through the forks of Edisto to join Lord Rawdon at Orangeburg. As the north fork of Edisto is not passable by an army, without boats, for thirty miles above or below the British encampments, General Greene could not throw himself between with any prospect of preventing the junction; he therefore retired to the high hills of Santee, and Lord Rawdon and Lieutenant Col. Cruger the day after made a junction.

The evacuation of Camden having been effected by striking at the posts below it, the same manœuvre was now attempted to induce the British to leave Orangeburg. With this view, on the day that the main American army retired from before that post, Generals Sumter and Marion, with their brigades and the legion cavalry, were detached to Monk's Corner and Dorchester. They moved down by different roads, and in three days commenced their operations. Lieutenant Colonel Lee took all the wagons and wagon horses belonging to a convoy of provisions.

Colonel Wade Hampton charged a party of British dragoons within five miles of Charleston. He also took fifty prisoners at Strawberry ferry, and burned four vessels loaded with valuable stores for the British army.

General Sumter appeared before the garrison at Biggin's church, which consisted of five hundred infantry, and upwards of one hundred cavalry. Lieutenant Col. Coates, who commanded there, after having repulsed the advanced party of General Sumter, on the next evening destroyed his stores and retreated towards Charleston.

He was closely pursued by Lieutenant Colonel Lee with the legion, and Lieutenant Colonel Hampton with the state cavalry. The legion came up with them near Shubrick's plantation, took their rear guard and all their baggage. Captain Armstrong, of Lee's legion, at the head only of five men, charged through a considerable part of their lines and escaped with the loss of two men.

Generals Sumter and Marion, after some hours, came up with the main body; but by this time the British had secured themselves by taking an advantageous post in a range of houses. An attack was however made, and continued with spirit till upwards of fifty of Marion's men were killed or wounded by the fire from the houses. The British lost in these different engagements one hundred and forty prisoners, besides several killed and wounded, all the baggage of the nineteenth regiment, and above one hundred horses and several wagons.

Thus was the war carried on. While the British kept their forces compact, they could not cover the country, and the American general had the precaution to avoid fighting. When they divided their army, their detachments were separately and successfully attacked. While they were in force in the upper country, light parties of Americans were annoying their small posts in the low country near Charleston. The people soon found that the late conquerors were not able to afford them their promised protection. The spirit of revolt became general, and the British interest daily declined.

Soon after these events Lord Rawdon, driven from almost the whole of his posts—baffled in all his schemes, and overwhelmed with vexation, sailed for Europe. In the course of his command he aggravated the unavoidable calamities of war by many acts of severity, which admit of no other apology than that they were supposed to be useful to the interest of his royal master.

About the same time that Generals Sumter and Marion were detached to the lower parts of the state, the main American army retired to the high hills of Santee, and the British returned to their former station near the junction of the Wateree and the Congaree.

CHAPTER XIX.

State of the southern country—Bitter hostility between the contending parties—Cruel excesses—Moderation of General Greene—Rawdon succeeded by Stewart—Greene prepares to attack Stewart—Secret expedition of Marion—He defeats the British force under Major Frazer, and relieves Colonel Harden—Receives the thanks of Congress—Battle of Eutaw Springs.

The spirit in which the war was carried on at this this time is thus described by Marshall.*

The suffering sustained in this ardent struggle for the southern states was not confined to the armies. The inhabitants of the country felt all the miseries which are inflicted by war in its most savage form. Being almost equally divided between the two contending parties, reciprocal injuries had gradually sharpened their resentments against each other, and had armed neighbor against neighbor, until it became a war of extermination. As the parties alternately triumphed, opportunities were alternately given for the exercise of their vindictive passions. They derived additional virulence from the examples occasionally afforded by the commanders of the British forces. After overrunning Georgia and South Carolina, they seem to have considered those states as completely reannexed to the British empire;

* Life of Washington.

and they manifested a disposition to treat those as rebels, who had once submitted and again taken up arms, although the temporary ascendancy of the continental troops should have induced the measure. One of these executions, that of Colonel Hayne, took place on the 3d of August, while Lord Rawdon* was in Charleston, preparing to sail for Europe. The American army being at this time in possession of great part of the country, the punishment inflicted on this gentleman was taken up very seriously by General Greene, and was near producing a system of retaliation. The British officers, pursuing this policy, are stated to have executed several of the zealous partisans of the revolution who fell into their hands. These examples had unquestionably some influence in unbridling the revengeful passions of the royalists, and letting loose the spirit of slaughter which was brooding in their bosoms. The disposition to retaliate to the full extent of their power, if not to commit original injury, was equally strong in the opposite party. When Fort Granby surrendered, the militia attached to the legion manifested so strong a disposition to break the capitulation, and to murder the most obnoxious among the prisoners who were inhabitants of the country, as to

---

* The execution of Colonel Hayne has been generally ascribed to Lord Rawdon, and he has been censured throughout America for an act which has been universally execrated. A letter addressed by him to the late General Lee, on receiving the memoirs of the southern war, written by that gentleman, which has been published in the "View of the Campaign of 1781, in the Carolinas, by H. Lee," gives the British view of that transaction, and exonerates Lord Rawdon from all blame. Lieutenant Colonel Balfour commanded, and Lord Rawdon sought to save Colonel Hayne.—*Marshall.*

produce a solemn declaration from General Greene, that any man guilty of so atrocious an act, should be executed. When Fort Cornwallis surrendered, no exertions could have saved Colonel Brown, had he not been sent to Savannah, protected by a guard of continental troops. Lieutenant Colonel Grierson, of the royal militia, was shot by unknown marksmen, and, although a reward of one hundred guineas was offered to any person who would inform against the perpetrator of the crime, he could never be discovered. "The whole country," said General Greene in one of his letters, "is one continued scene of blood and slaughter."

Greene was too humane, as well as too judicious, not to discourage this exterminating spirit. Perceiving in it the total destruction of the country, he sought to appease it by restraining the excesses of those who were attached to the American cause.

On the departure of Lord Rawdon for Europe, Lieut. Colonel Stewart was left in command at Orangeburg. Leaving this post, he encamped near McCord's Ferry, on the Congaree. General Greene's army was encamped on the opposite side of the river, and the fires of the two armies were visible to each other. While the armies were thus situated, Colonel Lee was sent up the north bank of the Congaree, Colonel Washington down the country across the Santee to cut off the communication of the enemy with Charleston, and to co-operate with General Marion in covering the lower Santee, while Col. Harden was sent to the Edisto with a body of mounted militia to harass the outposts of the enemy in that quarter.

On the 22nd of August Greene broke up his camp at the high hills of Santee, and proceeded to Howell's Ferry, on the Congaree, intending to cross it and advance upon Stewart, who, on learning this movement, took post in a strong position at Eutaw Springs.

While these operations were going on, General Marion, learning that Colonel Harden was closely pressed by a British force of five hundred men, in the neighborhood of the Pon Pon, secretly marched to his relief, a distance of 200 miles, ambushed, and defeated the British under Major Frazer, killing a great number of his cavalry, and rescued Colonel Harden without loss to himself. (Aug. 31, 1781.) After this, being recalled by General Greene, he returned to a position on the Santee, in the track of Greene's advance. This brilliant expedition for which Marion received the thanks of Congress, occupied him but six days. He joined Greene at Laurens's plantation, seventeen miles from Eutaw Springs, when he was still advancing to attack Stewart.

It was on the 8th of September, 1781, that the celebrated battle of Eutaw Springs took place. Greene drew up his little force, consisting of about two thousand men, in two lines. The front consisted of the militia from North and South Carolina, and was commanded by Generals Marion and Pickens, and by Colonel De Malmedy. The second consisted of the continental troops from North Carolina, Virginia, and Maryland, and was led on by General Sumner, Lieutenant Colonel Campbell, and Colonel Williams. Lieutenant Colonel Lee, with his legion, covered the right flank; Lieutenant

Colonel Henderson, with the state troops, covered the left. Lieutenant Colonel Washington, with his cavalry, and Captain Kirkwood with the Delaware troops, formed a corps of reserve.

As the Americans advanced to the attack, they fell in with two advanced parties of the British, three or four miles ahead of the main army. These, being briskly charged by the legion and state troops, soon retired. The front line continued to fire and advance on the British till the action became general, and till they, in their turn, were obliged to give way. They were well supported by General Sumner's North Carolina brigade of continentals, though they had been under discipline only for a few weeks, and were chiefly composed of militia men, who had been transferred to the continental service to make reparation for their precipitate flight in former actions.

In the hottest of the engagement, when great execution was doing on both sides, Colonel Williams and Lieutenant Colonel Campbell, with the Maryland and Virginia continentals, were ordered by General Greene to charge with trailed arms. Nothing could surpass the intrepidity of both officers and men on this occasion—they rushed on, in good order, through a heavy cannonade and a shower of musketry, with such unshaken resolution that they bore down all before them.

The state troops of South Carolina were deprived of their gallant leader, Lieutenant Colonel Henderson, who was wounded very early in the action; but they were nevertheless boldly led on by the second in command, Lieutenant Colonel Hampton, to a very spirited and successful charge, in which they took upwards of a hundred prisoners.

Lieutenant Colonel Washington brought up the corps-de-reserve on the left, and charged so briskly with his cavalry and Captain Kirkwood's light infantry, as gave them no time to rally or form. The British were closely pursued, and upwards of five hundred prisoners were taken. On their retreat they took their posts in a strong brick house and in impenetrable shrubs and a picquetted garden. From these advantageous positions they renewed the action.

Lieutenant Colonel Washington made every possible exertion to dislodge them from the thickets, but failed in the attempt; had his horse shot under him—was wounded and taken prisoner. Four six-pounders were ordered up before the house from which the British were firing under cover. These pieces finally fell into their hands, and the Americans retired out of the reach of their fire. They left a strong picquet on the field of battle, and retreated to the nearest water in their rear.

In the evening of the next day, Lieutenant Colonel Stewart destroyed a great quantity of his stores, abandoned Eutaw, and moved towards Charleston, leaving upwards of seventy of his wounded, and a thousand stand of arms. He was pursued for several miles, but without effect. The loss of the British amounted to upwards of eleven hundred men. That of the Americans was about five hundred, in which number were sixty officers. Among the killed of Greene's army, the brave Lieutenant Colonel Campbell of the Virginia line was the theme of universal lamentation. While with great firmness he was leading on his brigade to that charge which determined the fate of the day, he received a mortal wound. After his fall he inquired who gave way; and being informed the British were fleeing in all quarters, he added, "I die contented," and immediately expired.

Congress honored General Greene, for his decisive conduct in this action, with a British standard and a golden medal; and they also voted their thanks to the different corps and their commanders.

After the action at Eutaw the Americans retired to their former position on the high hills of Santee, and the British took post in the vicinity of Monk's Corner. While they lay there, a small party of American cavalry, commanded by Colonel Mayham, took upwards of eighty prisoners within sight of their main army. The British no more acted with their usual vigor. On the slightest appearance of danger, they discovered a disposition to flee scarcely inferior to what was exhibited the year before by the American militia

CHAPTER XX.

Events succeeding the battle of Eutaw—Marion chosen to a seat in the Assembly of South Carolina—Laws passed by the Assembly—Marion's brigade suffers a severe defeat in his absence—He returns to the brigade and restores order and reinspires confidence—Greene takes post at Bacon's bridge.—Mutiny in his army.

At the battle of Eutaw each party had pretensions to the victory, and each claimed the merit of having gained it with inferior numbers. The truth probably is that their numbers were nearly equal.

Nor can the claim of either to the victory be pronounced unequivocal. Unconnected with its consequences, the fortune of the day was nearly balanced. But if the consequences be taken into the account, the victory unquestionably belonged to Greene. The result of this, as of the two preceding battles fought by him in the Carolinas, was the expulsion of the hostile army from the territory which was the immediate object of contest.

Four six-pounders, two of which had been taken in the early part of the day, were brought to play upon the house, and, being pushed so near as to be within the command of its fire, were unavoidably abandoned; but a three-pounder which had been also taken, was brought off by Captain Lieutenant Gaines, whose conduct was mentioned with distinction by General Greene. Thus the trophies of victory were divided.

On the day succeeding the action, Nov. 9, Lieutenant Col. Stewart marched from Eutaw to meet Major McArthur, who was conducting a body of troops from Charleston. The junction was effected about fourteen miles from Eutaw; and this movement saved McArthur from Marion and Lee, who had been detached on the morning of the same day to intercept any reinforcement which might be coming from below. Stewart continued his retreat to Monk's Corner, to which place he was followed by Greene, Nov. 15, who, on finding that the numbers and position of the British army were such as to render an attack unadvisable, returned to the high hills of Santee.

The ravages of disease were added to the loss sustained in battle, and the army remained for some time in too feeble a condition for active enterprise.

The capitulation at Yorktown was soon followed by the evacuation of Wilmington, in North Carolina, and the British seemed to limit their views in the south to the country adjacent to the sea coast. As the cool season approached, (Nov. 18,) the diseases of the American army abated; and Greene, desirous of partaking in the abundance of the lower country, marched from the high hills of Santee towards the Four Holes, a branch of the Edisto. Leaving the army to be conducted by Colonel Williams, he proceeded in person at the head of his cavalry, supported by about two hundred infantry, towards the British post at Dorchester, where six hundred and fifty regular troops and two hundred royal militia were understood to be stationed.

Though his march was conducted with the utmost secrecy, the country through which he passed contained so many disaffected, that it was impossible to conceal this movement, and intelligence of his approach was communicated to the officer commanding in Dorchester, the night before he reached that place. The advance, commanded by Lieutenant Colonel Hampton, met a small party, which he instantly charged, and, after killing and taking several, drove the residue over the bridge under cover of their works. In the course of the following night, the stores at Dorchester were burnt, and the garrison retired to the Quarter House, where their principal force was encamped. Greene returned to the army at the Round O, at which place he purposed to await the arrival of the reinforcements marching from the north under the command of General St. Clair. In the meantime, General Marion and Lieutenant Col. Lee were stationed on each side of Ashley, so as to cover the country between the Cooper and the Edisto; thus confining the influence of the British arms to Charleston neck, and the adjacent islands.*

* During this campaign a very effective expedition against the Cherokees was conducted by General Pickens. When the struggle for South Carolina recommenced, those savages were stimulated to renew their incursions into the settlements of the whites. At the head of about four hundred mounted militia, Pickens penetrated into their country, burned thirteen of their villages, killed upwards of forty Indians, and took a number of prisoners, without the loss of a single man. On this occasion a new and formidable mode of attack was introduced. The militia horse rushed upon the Indians, and charged

While in his camp at the Round O, General Greene was informed that large reinforcements from Ireland and New York, were expected by the army in Charleston. This intelligence excited the more alarm, because the term of service for which the levies from Virginia were engaged was about expiring, and no adequate measures had been taken for supplying their places. It proved untrue; but such was its impression, that the general addressed a letter to the governor of South Carolina, in which, after taking a serious view of the state of his army, he recommended that it should be recruited from the slaves. The governor thought the proposition of sufficient importance to be laid before the legislature, which was soon afterwards convened; but the measure was not adopted.

On the 4th of January, 1782, General St. Clair, who conducted the reinforcement from the north, arrived in camp, and, five days afterward, General Wayne,* with them sword in hand. Terrified at the rapidity of the pursuit, the Cherokees humbly sued for peace, which was granted on terms calculated to restrain depredations in future.

* In the judicious orders given to Wayne, Greene endeavored to impress on that officer the importance of a course of conduct, always observed by himself, which might tend to conciliate parties. "Try," says he, "by every means in your power, to soften the malignity and dreadful resentments subsisting between Whig and Tory; and put a stop as much as possible to that cruel custom of putting men to death after they surrender themselves prisoners. The practice of plundering you will endeavor to check as much as possible; and point out to the militia the ruinous consequences of the policy. Let your discipline be as regular and as rigid as the nature and constitution of your troops will admit."—2 *Johnson*, 277.

his brigade, and the remnant of the third regiment of dragoons, commanded by Colonel White, was detached over the Savannah for the recovery of Georgia.

General Greene crossed the Edisto and took post, Jan. 16, six miles in advance of Jacksonborough, on the road leading to Charleston, for the purpose of covering the state legislature, which assembled at that place on the 18th. Thus was civil government re-established in South Carolina, and that state restored to the union.

Governor Rutledge, being persuaded that the happy period had at length arrived for the restoration of the government, had issued a proclamation in a few weeks after the battle of Eutaw, convening the general assembly at Jacksonborough, a small village upon the Edisto river, about thirty-five miles from Charleston. Invested with dictatorial powers, the governor not only issued writs for the intervening elections, but also prescribed the qualifications of the electors.

The right of suffrage was restricted to those inhabitants who had uniformly resisted the invader; and to such who, having accepted British protection, had afterwards united with their countrymen in opposition to the royal authority before the 27th day of September; in the early part of which month the battle of Eutaw had been fought. The exchange of prisoners which had previously taken place, liberated many respectable and influential characters too long lost to the state.

These citizens had now returned, and were ready to assist with their counsel in repairing the desolation of war. This period presents an interesting epoch in the annals of the South. From all quarters were flocking home our unfortunate maltreated prisoners. The old and the young, the rich and the poor, hastened to their native soil; burying their particular griefs in the joy universally felt in consequence of the liberation of their country.

They found their houses burnt, their plantations laid waste, their herds and flocks destroyed, and the rich rewards of a life of industry and economy dissipated. Without money, without credit, with debilitated constitutions, with scars and aches, this brave and patriotic groupe gloried in the adversity they had experienced, because the price of their personal liberty and of national independence. They had lost their wealth, they had lost their health, and had lost the props of their declining years in the field of battle; but they had established the independence of their country; they had secured to themselves and posterity the birth-right of Americans. They forgot past agony in the delight of present enjoyment, and in the prospect of happiness to ages yet unborn. From this class of citizens the senators lately chosen were chiefly selected.

In addition to this class of citizens there were many officers of the army, chosen as representatives in the Assembly. Among them were Sumter and Marion. The latter was returned by the district of St. John Berkley, which he had represented, as already related, on a previous occasion. The assembly passed a number of important laws. One was for the subsistence of the army by civil authority. Another law was passed for regulating the militia, and another for raising the State quota of the Continental troops; and still another for amercing and confiscating the estates of certain loyalists, and for banishing some of the most criminal among them. With respect to the last of these laws, which may seem severe, it must be recollected that the loyalists thus punished had been offered pardon and immunity in a proclamation of the governor issued some time before; and that their proceedings with respect to the property and even the lives of the patriots had been such as to justify severe reprisals.

Marion's absence from his brigade during the session of the legislature appears to have nearly occasioned its destruction. He would not have left it if a quorum could have been assured without his presence.

Before he set out for Jacksonborough, he had selected a station for his militia near the Santee river, remote from Charleston. His absence from his command, notwithstanding the distance of the selected position, inspired the enemy with the hope that a corps which had heretofore been invulnerable might now be struck. A detachment of cavalry was accordingly prepared for the meditated enterprise, and placed under the orders of Lieutenant Colonel Thompson. This officer having passed the Cooper river near Charleston, late in the evening, proceeded towards the Santee. Observing the greatest secrecy, and pushing his march with diligence, he fell upon the militia camp before the dawn of day, and completely routed the corps. Some were killed, some wounded, and the rest dispersed, with little or no loss on the part of the British. Major Benson, an active officer, was among the killed.

Thompson hastened back to Charleston with his detachment; and Marion, returning from Jacksonborough, reassembled his militia.

He arrived at the scene of the disaster in season to engage in an action with the triumphant enemy and hold him in check, while the brigade recovered its wonted state of effectiveness.

After the adjournment of the Assembly at Jacksonborough, General Greene with the main army took post at Bacon's Bridge at the head of Ashley river.

During the stay of the army in this place, General Greene had to call in the faithful brigade of Marion, to aid in repressing a mutiny which threatened to spread through his ranks. This affair is thus noticed by Colonel Lee in his Memoirs:

At this juncture treason had found its way into our camp. The inactivity which had succeeded the preceding series of bold and vigorous service was a fit season for recollection of grievances long endured, and which, being severely felt, began to rankle in every breast. Hunger sometimes pinched, at other times cold oppressed, and always want of pay reminded us as well of the injustice of our government as of our pressing demands upon it. The Pennsylvania line had joined the army; the soldiers of which being chiefly foreigners, were not so disposed to forget and to forgive as were our native troops. Even heretofore this line had pushed their insubordination so far as to abandon in a body the commander in chief, to drive off their officers, to commit the eagles to base hands, and to march under the orders of leaders elected by themselves.

They justified this daring mutiny by referring to their

contract of enlistment, which they alleged had been violated; and it must be admitted that this allegation was too well founded. Soldiers who had enlisted for three years had been detained after the period of their service expired, under the pretext that they had enlisted for the war. As soon as this injustice was redressed, and some pecuniary accommodation rendered, all not entitled to their discharge returned to their duty.

The violation of contract is always morally wrong; and however it may sometimes yield present good, it is generally overbalanced by the subsequent injury. The government which is under the necessity of resorting to armed men, enlisted for a term of service, to protect its rights, ought to take care that the contract of enlistment is fair as well as legal, and that it be justly executed; or they afford a pretext for incalculable ills, which, though often avoided from the force of circumstances, is sometimes productive of irreparable misfortunes to the nation. Every effort was made at the time by the enemy to turn this menacing occurrence into the deepest injury; but the fidelity of the revolting troops remained invulnerable; the best possible apology for their previous conduct.

The present mutiny was marked by a very different character. It was grounded on the breach of allegiance, and reared in all the foulness of perfidy. Greene himself was to be seized and delivered to the enemy. How could treason ascend higher?

A serjeant in the Pennsylvania line took the lead in this daring conspiracy; a soldier heretofore much esteemed, and possessing talents adapted to the enterprise.

No doubt exists but that he and his associates held continual correspondence with the enemy, and that an arranged plan had been concerted for the protection of the mutineers by the co-operating movements of the British force.

The vigilance and penetration of Greene could neither be eluded nor overreached. He well knew that the soldiers were discontented; nor was he insensible to the cause of their complaints. But he confided in the rectitude of congress, and in the well tried fidelity of that portion of the army which had so often fought by his side. He nevertheless dreaded the effects of the wiles of the artful and wicked when applied to the inflammable mass around him.

To the enemy's camp and to that section of his troops most likely to forget self-respect and patriotism, he directed his close and vigorous attention. From both he drew information which convinced him that his apprehensions were not groundless. Redoubling his exertions, as well to discover the plan and progress of the conspirators as to thwart their designs, he learnt that the serjeant, supposed to be the leader, had, by indulging unwarily the free declaration of his sentiments, subjected himself to martial law, and alarmed all the faithful soldiers, who, though prone to unite in the declarations of the wrongs they had suffered, and of their determination to obtain redress, had never entertained a thought of executing their views by the prostitution of military subordination, much less by the perpetration of the blackest treason, of the basest ingratitude. Greene, acting with his usual decision, ordered the arrest and trial of the serjeant.

This order was immediately executed; and the prisoner being by the court martial condemned to die, the sentence of the court was forthwith carried into effect. (22d April.)

Some others, believed to be associates with the serjeant, (among whom were Peters and Owens,) domestics in the general's family, were also tried; but the testimony was not deemed conclusive by the court. Twelve others deserted in the course of the night and got safe to Charleston.

Thus the decisive conduct of the general crushed instantly this daring conspiracy; and the result proved, as often happens, that although the temper of complaint and of discontent pervaded the army, but few of the soldiers were in reality guilty of the criminal intentions which were believed at first to have spread far through the ranks.

While the arrests and trials were progressing in our camp, and while General Greene continued to watch the movements of the enemy, they disclosed a spirit of adventure, which had been for some months dormant. Large bodies of horse and foot were put in motion; some of which, in the course of the night, approached us with unusual confidence. The boldness tended to confirm the suspicions before entertained that the enemy was not only apprized of the intentions of our mutineers, but had prepared to second their designs. General Greene, feeling his critical situation, contented himself for the present with detaching select parties to hover around the enemy for the purpose of observing his motions, with the determination to strike his adversary as soon as he should find his army restored to its pristine discipline and character. On the morning (24th) after the execution of the traitor, Captain O'Neal of the legion cavalry fell in with a body of the enemy's horse under Major Frazer.

O'Neal, being very inferior in strength to his antagonist, retired, and was vigorously pursued by Frazer. During his flight he perceived a second body of the enemy in possession of his line of retreat. He was now compelled to change his course; and with the utmost difficulty escaped himself, after losing ten of his dragoons. Frazer had advanced as high as Stan's bridge, the place assigned for the reception of that portion of the conspirators who had undertaken to betray the person of their general. On his return he was met by O'Neal, not far from Dorchester. This was the sole adventure resulting to the enemy in a conjuncture from which he expected to derive signal benefits.

CHAPTER XXI.

Marion takes post at Sinkler's plantation—Suppresses an insurrection in North Carolina—Second treaty with Gainey—Rescues Butler—Affair of Fanning—Marion defeats Frazer—General Leslie seeks an armistice, which Greene refuses—Leslie's incursions into the country to obtain provisions—Resisted by Gist's detachment—Colonel Laurens killed—Evacuation of Charleston by the British army.

GENERAL GREENE had summoned Marion to the camp on the occurrence of the mutiny; and his advance towards Greene with the brigade, had overawed the mutineers and discouraged the advance of the British, who were to co-operate with the mutineers in the destruction of the American army.

Marion's next movement, when the mutiny had been suppressed, was to protect Georgetown against an apprehended attack of the British from Charleston. He marched 160 miles to White's bridge, where the alarm was discovered to be unfounded, (April 1782). With a force of 200 militia and 120 horse, he took post at Sinkler's plantation, on the Santee. While he was posted here, a messenger was sent to North Carolina to stir up a new insurrection among the loyalists in order to draw Marion from the protection of the country in the neighborhood of the Santee. Having succeeded in this object, the messenger was intercepted by Marion on his return and summarily executed.

Marion being now summoned to the camp of Greene, had only reached Dorchester, when he learnt that Major Gainey was at the head of an insurrection on the banks of the Pedee. He turned about and succeeded in surprising Gainey, and bringing him to terms of submission, which proved more lasting than those which Horry had, a year before, compelled him to subscribe. On the occasion of the new treaty, 500 tories laid down their arms at Burch's mill, on the 8th of June. Instead of becoming prisoners of war, they agreed to remain peaceable, to deliver up all property which they had plundered, and to sign a declaration of allegiance to the United States. For this they received a full pardon for past treasons, and all who declined to accept these terms were allowed to retire to the British lines. Gainey, by permission of Marion, went to Charleston, surrendered his commission to Colonel Balfour, and returning, joined the American army, in which he afterwards did good service. Many of his men followed his example. A notorious offender named Butler, seeking the benefit of this treaty, had a narrow escape from the death which he richly deserved. Marion had to protect him by taking him to his own tent, and resisting the attemps of his own followers to destroy him.

A ruffian named Fanning sought to renew hostilities; but being baffled by Marion, he sent a flag of truce, requesting a safe conduct for his wife to Charleston. This was instantly granted, and Fanning, as Marion had foreseen, abandoned his followers and fled to Charleston himself.

Leaving the neighborhood of the Pedee under the protection of Colonel Baxter with 150 men, Marion now returned (July 1782) to the Santee. By the union of a new corps under Major Conyers, and the corps of horse under Mayham, with his own militia, he was now at the head of a force of 300 dismounted infantry and a respectable body of cavalry.

With these he took post on the Wassamasaw, for the purpose of covering the country and protecting it from the marauding incursions of the enemy.

The British were now tired of the war, and they were preparing to evacuate the country. They were in want of provisions, and sent expeditions from Charleston into the interior to obtain them. With one of these marauding parties under Major Frazer, Marion had a brisk encounter at Watboo, in which the enemy suffered a signal repulse. In this affair Major Gainey and a considerable body of new converts signalized their fidelity to the patriot cause.

The officer now in command of the British garrison at Charleston, General Leslie, had proposed a cessation of hostilities, and that his troops might be supplied with fresh provisions, in exchange for articles of the last necessity in the American camp. The policy of government being adverse to this proposition, General Greene was under the necessity of refusing his assent to it.

Foiled in accomplishing his object in the way desired, the British general prepared to resume his suspended incursions into the country, determined to effect by force the procurement of those supplies which he had flattered himself with obtaining by purchase. Supported by marine co-operation applicable with readiness to all the circumjacent country by the facilities of its interior navigation, and possessing the contiguous islands, with strong detachments from his army, General Leslie proceeded to the execution of his determination, fearless of consequences, but lamenting the necessity of wasting human life in useless battle.

A detachment of light infantry, attended by armed vessels, passed along the interior navigation, and having reached Combahee river, began to collect and convey provisions to the transports which accompanied the expedition for the purpose of transporting to Charleston whatever might be procured. General Greene, never doubting Leslie's execution of his menace, held his light corps ready to counteract any attempt he might make. As soon, therefore, as he became apprised of the movement of the British detachment, he directed Brigadier Gist to advance in pursuit. Gist was soon in motion, and after a long and rapid march, gained the neighborhood of the enemy, then at Page's point, on the Combahee. At this moment, Lieut. Col. Laurens, commanding the infantry under Gist, joined, having, as soon as informed of the march of the light troops, left his sick bed to hasten to the field of battle. Laurens no sooner overtook the corps than, by permission of the brigadier, he put himself at the head of the American van. Discovering that the enemy were preparing to retire, he determined, with his inferior force, though out of supporting distance, to commence the attack. This bold decision was gallantly executed; but incapable of making any serious impresssion from the inadequacy of his force, he fell in the vain attempt at the head of his intrepid band, closing his short and splendid life in the lustre of heroism. Gist now got up with the main body, and took one of the vessels from the enemy returning to Charleston.

The British general, finding himself foiled in his expectations, henceforward discontinued these predatory inroads, and confined his exertions in the collection of provisions to the islands along the coast, and to the country contiguous to the interior navigation, remote from the American camp.

General Leslie had declared, in his orders of the 7th of August, his intention of withdrawing his army; but September had passed away, and Charleston still remained in possession of the enemy.

In the course of the preceding month, Governor Matthews had contrived, through his influence with some of the royalists in Charleston, who had resolved to throw themselves on the mercy of their country, to procure a small quantity of the most necessary articles of clothing. This fortunate acquisition, added to a supply forwarded from Philadelphia by means of the superintendent of finance, enabled the general to cover the most naked of his army; and the unceasing exertions of the state commissary, aided by the co-operation of the quartermaster general, produced an agreeable change in the quantity and quality of provisions. Still the situation of the army was deplorable, and much remained to be done to give durable comfort to the troops, whose past distress is thus described by General Greene in an official letter written on the thirteenth of August. "For upwards of of two months more than one third of our army was naked, with nothing but a breech cloth about them, and never came out of their tents; and the rest were as ragged as wolves. Our condition was little better in the articles of provision. Our beef was perfect carrion; and even bad as it was, we were frequently without any. An army thus clothed and thus fed, may be considered in a desperate situation."

The delay and uncertainty in evacuating Charleston, however productive of gloomy forebodings in the American camp, did not stop the enterprise of adventurous individuals, who, believing the event at hand, seized, as they presumed, the sure opportunity of advancing their fortunes. Many of these procured admittance into Charleston, and entered into contracts with the British merchants, whom they found as desirous of selling their stock on hand, as they were eager to buy it.

Among the adventurers who, about the end of August, or beginning of September, made their way into Charleston, was Mr. John Banks from Virginia. This gentleman, (no doubt with permission,) after a short stay in town, visited the American army. Here he was introduced to General Greene. Well knowing the naked condition of his countrymen in arms, and convinced of the general's solicitude to relieve their sufferings, he offered to procure and deliver whatever might be wanted. Greene having been, as before mentioned, authorized by the superintendance of finance to enter into contracts for supplying his army, did not hesitate in accepting Banks' proposal, and a contract was arranged with him for the requisite clothing to be delivered on the evacuation of Charleston. This was the first opportunity which had presented of effecting the long wished and much desired object. It was embraced with avidity, and Mr. Banks completely executed his contract at the designated period, to the great joy of the general and army.

The preparations for evacuating Charleston began now to assume a determinate character; and the doubts heretofore entertained on that subject dissipated. The American general held a position at Ashley hill, shutting up every avenue to intercourse between town and country. The enemy no longer attempted to interrupt this operation, but fixed in his design of withdrawing from South Carolina, he avoided unavailing conflict. Thus passed the autumn, and General Leslie, although never intermitting his preparations to retire, still continued with his army in Charleston. At length, early in December, the embarkation of the military stores, ordnance, and baggage, commenced. When this was completed, the troops followed, and on the 14th, the embarkation was finished. General Wayne, with the legion and light infantry, had, for some days previous, by order of Greene, placed himself near to the quarter house for the purpose of entering the town as soon as it should be evacuated. To this officer, Leslie informally intimated his wish to prevent injury to the town, in which he presumed on cordial coincidence from the American general, and which he insinuated was only to be effected by prohibiting every attempt to interrupt the embarkation of the retiring army.

Wayne communicated to the general the intimation he had received from Leslie, who directed him to conform to the same.

Accordingly no effort was made to disturb the enemy's embarkation, which took place without the smallest confusion or disorder: the light troops under Wayne entering into town close after the retirement of the British rear.

Thus was the metropolis of South Carolina restored to the United States, after having been in possession of the enemy from its surrender to Sir Henry Clinton on the 12th of May, 1780.

The governor with his suite was escorted into the capital on the same day. On the next the civil authority resumed its former functions, and the din of arms yielded to the innocent and pleasing occupations of peace.

CHAPTER XXII.

Marion's parting with the Brigade—His resemblance to Washington—He retires to his plantation—Finds it desolated—Resumes his agricultural pursuits—Is elected Senator—The Confiscation act—Anecdote of his magnanimity—Voted thanks and a medal by the senate—Appointed to command Fort Johnson—Marion's marriage—His death—His character.

AFTER the evacuation of Charleston by the British army, Marion assembled his brigade at Walboo and took an affectionate leave of them. His address on this occasion was characterized by his peculiar modesty and simplicity. He called to their recollection the scenes of their past services in the war of the Revolution, thanked them for their services, and bade them farewell.

In reviewing his career as a commander, we are struck with its resemblance to that of Washington. It was the characteristic merit of both these illustrious men to accomplish almost without means what other men can hardly accomplish with all the means and appliances they could desire. By dint of their own force of character, Washington and Marion were both able to keep together and command the efficient services of men, who were without pay, often without ammunition, with imperfect arms, almost destitute of clothing, and frequently quite destitute of provisions. Yet these soldiers remained in each case entirely devoted to their respective commanders and ever ready to do battle at their command. Each accomplished his objects not by brilliant and imposing victories over the enemy, but by patiently and unweariedly opposing him, avoiding pitched battles, wearing him out by persevering hostility and unceasing vigilance. Although both Washington and Marion were held in high estimation by their cotemporaries, their peculiar merits are better understood now than they were in their own time, and their glory will go on increasing in brilliancy for ages to come.

After taking leave of his companions in arms, the immortal "Brigade," Marion retired to his plantation in St. John's Berkley. He found it literally desolated by the ravages of war. Being within a mile of one of the ordinary routes of the British army, it had been exposed to repeated depredations. Half of his negroes had been removed. The remainder had escaped capture by secreting themselves on the approach of the enemy, in order to save their future services for their master, who had won their strong personal attachment; so that on his return to the plantation he had still ten workers left. But this was all except the land and the buildings. Stock, utensils, furniture, subsistence for his servants—all were to be purchased. He had received no pay for the invaluable services which he had rendered the state, and even the promised half pay of the retiring officer was withheld. But he nevertheless went to work cheerfully to repair, in part, the losses he had sustained, his only dependence being his own industry and economy.

But the public still required his services and he once more responded to the call of his country.

Accordingly we find him again taking his place in the Senate of South Carolina as the member from St. John's. The "Confiscation act" at first received his sanction. It passed originally in January, 1782, and devoted the property of tories to meet the public wants. But when peace was fully restored, Marion could no longer approve of this policy, and his voice was raised against it with such effect that it could not long be preserved. We have at this time an incident illustrating the lofty independence of character which distinguished him. A bill was introduced exempting from legal responsibility many American officers and soldiers, who had been active partisans, and who had often been compelled to use private property in securing their ends. The name of Marion was included, but when it was announced he rose, and with a brow flushed with generous shame he insisted that his name should be stricken off. "If," he said, "I have given any occasion for complaint, I am ready to answer in property and person. If I have wronged any man, I am willing to make him restitution." It is not wonderful that such a man should have been honored by all who knew him.

On the 26th of February, 1783, the following resolutions were unanimously adopted by the Senate of South Carolina:—"Resolved, That the thanks of this House be given to Brigadier General Marion in his place, as a member of this House, for his eminent and conspicuous services to his country. Resolved, That a gold medal be given to Brigadier General Marion, as a mark of public approbation for his great, glorious, and meritorious conduct."

In 1784, it was judged expedient by the legislature to fortify anew Fort Johnson, in Charleston harbor, and Marion was appointed to its command, with a salary of five hundred pounds. The duties were almost nominal, and it is probable that the salary was intended rather to pay a past debt of gratitude than to compensate for present services. It was afterwards considerably reduced, and the brave soldier of the Revolution might have suffered want, but for an unexpected change in the even tenor of his way. Among his acquaintances was Miss Mary Videau, a maiden lady of the Huguenot descent, of considerable wealth, and of most estimable character. She admired Marion so much that her feelings for him assumed a more tender character, and when their friends discovered this, it was not long ere they secured an interchange of views on the subject. When they were united in marriage, Marion was more than fifty years of age, and we have reason to believe that the lady was not much his junior. They were not blessed with children, but they lived together in tranquil content. She was always his companion in his excursions through the country, and tradition has preserved many proofs of the mutual affection they cherished for each other, even to the end of life.

Thus peaceful and happy were the closing years of a career which had once been one of excitement and bloody conflict. On the 27th day of February, 1795, at his home in St. John's parish, Francis Marion breathed his last. He had reached his sixty-third year. In the hour of death he was composed, and was comforted by the hope of future happiness. "Thank God," he exclaimed, "I can lay my hand on my heart and say that since I came to man's estate I have never intentionally done wrong to any."

In the life of this brave man, says a late writer, we see disclosed the true secret of American independence. We do not find in his course those exploits which dazzle the eyes of the soul, and fill us with admiration even for a polluted character; but we find patient courage, firmness in danger, resolution in adversity, hardy endurance amid suffering and want. In hunger, and nakedness, and toil, he lived, and seemed to live, only that liberty might not die. While the names of many of the greatest conquerors shall be remembered only to serve as beacons to posterity, the name of Marion will grow dearer to every patriot with each succeeding age of the land that has had the privilege of giving him birth.*

* Washington and the Generals of the Revolution.

MAJOR GENERAL WILLIAM MOULTRIE.

LIFE OF

MAJOR GENERAL WILLIAM MOULTRIE.

CHAPTER I.

Family and birth of Moultrie—His services in the war with the Cherokees—Returns to his plantation—Condition of South Carolina—Moultrie takes an active part at the opening of the Revolution—Member of Provincial Congress—Chosen Colonel of the famous Second Regiment of South Carolina—Seizes the king's stores of arms and ammunition—Devises the flag—Drives the British ships out of Charleston harbor.

GENERAL William Moultrie was descended from distinguished Scottish ancestry, and was born in South Carolina, in 1730. His education was respectable for the time and country in which he was reared; but, although he has given to the world two octavo volumes of "*Memoirs of the American Revolution, as far as it related to the States of North and South Carolina and Georgia,*" he has left no memoir of himself, excepting an incidental account of his services in the revolutionary war. Of his early life we have consequently no record.

He appears, however, on the theatre of public life, when quite a young man, and, as he always played a conspicuous part, the history of his time furnishes a satisfactory account of his life.

The first military service of Moultrie of which we find any record is in the campaign against the Cherokee Indians, in which he served as captain, having Marion for lieutenant. A full account of this campaign will be found in Chapter V. of the Life of Marion, in the preceding part of this volume. It took place in 1761, when Moultrie was thirty-one years of age, and in the full vigor of manhood. The service was extremely arduous and perilous, imposing on the army very long and laborious marches through dreary wastes and deep forests and swamps, and exposing the officers and men to the ambushes of savage foes. It terminated in the utter defeat of the Indians, who were compelled to sue for peace.

Moultrie profited well by his training in this hardy school of warfare, and he was ever afterwards distinguished not only by the most unblenching courage, but by a degree of coolness and composure in the most perilous emergencies of war, which attracted the admiration of all his cotemporaries.

After the conclusion of the Cherokee war, Moultrie returned to his plantation, in the district of St. Helena, and resumed the quiet pursuits of a southern planter. South Carolina, in the period which ensued between the Cherokee war (1761) and the breaking out of the revolution, was in a highly prosperous state. The planters accumulated property rapidly, and Charleston, the capital of the colony, was one of the greatest emporiums of trade in North America. The wealth of her citizens, their high intellectual cultivation and refinement, and the noble and liberal spirit which had grown up among them are disclosed incidentally by many of the incidents of the revolutionary war. Indeed, it might be a matter of surprise, that a colony so highly favored, and which had apparently so little to gain by taking part in the Revolution, should not have imitated the example of Canada, and adhered to the royal cause; more especially as the principal theatre of the political debates which preceded open hostilities was so remote from her borders.

But the Carolinians were as generous and brave as they were rich and prosperous. They sympathized in all the feelings of the Massachusetts and Virginia patriots who led the contest; and when the tocsin of war sounded from the plains of Lexington and Concord, they instantly buckled on their armor and prepared for the battle field.

But many preliminary steps had already been taken previous to this period; and in these Moultrie took a leading part. He was one of the noble and generous spirits who periled all, and sacrificed nearly all in the great contest. At the time when the war broke out, his agricultural labors had prospered so well that he had a fine plantation and two hundred negroes; so that he was no mere military adventurer, but a gentleman of position and substance, who had a large interest in the welfare of the country.

In the list of members of the first Provincial Congress,

held at Charleston, January 11th, 1775, we find the name of Col. William Moultrie, as delegate from St. Helena. "The acts of this Congress furnish an honorable record of the spirit and the wisdom of the time and people. The progress of events kept him active. Britain, rashly resolving to coerce rather than conciliate, the colonists began to look around them for weapons of defence. The South Carolinians were greatly deficient in supplies of this nature. But the king's stores were tolerably well provided, and Moultrie was one of a party of patriotic citizens to apply the wrench to bolt and bar, at midnight, when it became necessary to relieve the public arsenals of their hoarded arms and ammunition. The king's stores were disburdened, by this bold proceeding, of twelve hundred stand of arms, and some three thousand pounds of powder. 'Fairly entered upon the business,' says Moultrie himself, in his Memoirs, 'we could not step back, and not break open the magazines.' The news of the battle of Lexington led to the organization of the militia as regular troops, and Moultrie was elected to the colonelcy of the Second Regiment of South Carolina. He designed the temporary flag of the colony, under whose folds its first victory was gained. This was a single field of blue, with a silver crescent in the dexter corner, the design suggested by the uniform of the state troops, which was blue, and by the silver ornament upon their caps. Two British sloops-of-war occupied the harbor of Charleston, and daily, by their threats, kept the citizens in alarm, lest the town should be bombarded. It was necessary to curb this insolence; and Moultrie was despatched, under cover of a stormy night, with a select body of troops, and a few pieces of artillery, to Haddrill's Point, from which these vessels might be commanded. A rude breastwork was rapidly thrown up, the guns mounted, and at daylight, opening with long shot upon the enemy, they were compelled to haul off to a more respectful distance."*

The details of these proceedings in which Marion also took an active part as a captain in the Second regiment, will be found in his "Life," in the preceding part of the volume.

* Washington and the Generals of the Revolution.

CHAPTER II.

Invasion of South Carolina by the fleet and army under Gen. Clinton—Defence of Sullivan's Island by Colonel Moultrie—Opinions of General Lee and Governor Rutledge—Presentation of colors to the Second Regiment—Officers who were in Fort Sullivan on the 28th of June—Vote of thanks by Congress—Declaration of Independence read to the army—Lee's expedition to Florida—Moultrie predicts its failure—It fails—Lee's thanks to the troops—General Moultrie's brigade placed on the continental establishment—General Lee goes to the north—Moore succeeds him—Moultrie stationed at Haddrill's Point—Nash succeeds Moore.

THE well known wealth of South Carolina, and the spirit of opposition to the British government which had been so openly manifested in that province, had determined the government to attempt its conquest. A formidable armament was accordingly fitted out from New York and placed under the command of Sir Henry Clinton, who arrived with a fleet of fifty sail, with several thousand troops, and came to anchor off the harbour of Charleston, in the beginning of June, 1776. The bar was crossed on the 10th of June, and preparations commenced for capturing the fort on Sullivan's Island. This fort was under the command of Colonel Moultrie, and his gallant defence of it saved South Carolina from British conquest for the time.

DESCRIPTION OF FORT SULLIVAN. 219

"Sullivan's Island," says a late writer,* "was regarded as the key to the harbor. Lying within point-blank shot of the channel, it was particularly susceptible of employment in retarding or harassing an enemy's fleet; and the difficulties of the bar, which was unfavorable to the passage of very large vessels of war, increased the value of the position as a key to the entrance. Hither, accordingly, he proceeded early in March, 1776. The island, which is now occupied by a pleasing summer village, was then a wilderness, having in its bosom, upon the spot subsequently covered in a great part by the fortress, a deep morass, which was sheltered by massive live-oaks, and by a dense covert of myrtle, sprinkled with palmetto trees. The palmettos were soon hewn down, and made to serve as the outer wall of the fortress, which was rendered dense and massive by sand and earth thrown into the spaces between the logs. These were fastened together in alternate layers, rudely notched at the extremities, and secured by pegs of wood. Upon its density, and the soft porous character of the palmetto timber, which did not fracture when wounded by shot, rather than the strength of the works, did the garrison rely for safety. It was at best a cover, rather than a shelter. The common opinion was, that a British frigate would knock it about the ears of the defenders in half an hour. To one who uttered this opinion in the ears of Moultrie, he answered, that he 'could still fight the enemy, and prevent their landing, from behind the ruins.' His coolness during all this time, and when all other persons were excited, led to suspicions of his

* Washington and the Generals of the Revolution.

energy. He was somewhat phlegmatic in his moods, and was thought to take things quite too easily. Indeed, it must be admitted that his good temper was sometimes too indulgent. He was not sufficiently the disciplinarian, and did not succeed in extorting and extracting from those about him, what they might have done, and what the emergency seems to have required. But his coolness and fortitude amply compensated for this deficiency, and had the happiest effect in inspiring his men with confidence. 'General Lee thinks me quite too easy,' says Moultrie himself, good-naturedly enough;—'for my own part, I never was uneasy.' In this respect he certainly was a philosopher. Charles Lee would have had the post abandoned without an effort. He had a profound faith in British frigates, to do anything; and pronounced the fort on Sullivan's Island to be a mere slaughter-pen. To his exhortations that the place should be abandoned, Governor Rutledge opposed a steady refusal. He had asked Moultrie if he could defend it. The reply was affirmative. 'General Lee wishes you to evacuate the fort. You will not do so without an order from me; I will sooner cut off my hand than write one.' He knew Moultrie. Lee was particularly anxious, finding that he could not effect this object, that the means of retreat should be furnished for the garrison. Moultrie never gave himself any concern on this account; and this led to Lee's impatience with him. 'I never was uneasy,' says he, 'at having no retreat, as I never imagined that the enemy could force me to this necessity. I always considered myself able to defend the post.' Lee thought otherwise; and, even had the post been defensible, did not conceive Moultrie to be the man for such a trust. His phlegm and coolness annoyed the impetuous and restless spirit of this mercurial soldier. Moultrie says—' General Lee does not like my having command of this important post. He does not doubt my courage, but says I am "too easy in command."' A little of that calm temper, which was so conspicuous in Moultrie, might have saved Lee himself from all his mortifications."

Moultrie's own graphic description of the battle of Fort Sullivan, which took place on the 28th of June, will be found in the ninth chapter of the Life of Marion, in the preceding part of this volume.

The following extracts from Moultrie's Memoirs, will be read with interest, as furnishing some additional particulars respecting the presentation of the flags by Mrs. Elliott, and other incidents which followed the battle of the 28th of June. The first is a note from Governor Rutledge to Colonel Moultrie:

"*June* 30*th*, 1776.

"His excellency, the president, desires his very particular thanks to the brave officers and men of this garrison, for their gallant behavior in the engagement of the 28th of June last. General Lee says no men ever did, and it is impossible that any can behave better: and that he will do us justice in his letters to the Continental Congress. His excellency has sent a hogshead of rum to the garrison."

JULY 1. Yesterday, the lady of Major Bernard Elliott presented an elegant pair of colors to the 2nd regiment, with these words:

"The gallant behavior in defence of liberty and your country, entitles you to the highest honors; accept of these two standards as a reward justly due to your regiment; and I make not the least doubt, under heaven's protection, you will stand by them as long as they can wave in the air of liberty."

The colors were presented by her own hands to the Colonel and Lieutenant Colonel; she was thanked and promised "that they should be honorably supported, and never should be tarnished by the 2nd regiment."

There were never colors more honorably supported, and never were colors better disposed of; they were planted on the British lines at Savannah; one by Lieut. Bush, who was immediately shot down; Lieut. Hume going to plant his, who was also shot down; and Lieut. Gray, in supporting them, received his mortal wound; and the gallant Jasper, who was with them, seeing Lieut. Hume shot down, took up the color and planted it; he also received his death wound, however he brought off his color with him, which was taken at the fall of Charleston; they were very elegant, one of a fine blue silk, the other a fine red silk richly embroidered: I am told they are now in the tower of London.

After this the legislature did me the honor to call the fort, Fort Moultrie.

Officers who were in the fort on 28th June.

William Moultrie, Col. Isaac Motte, Lieut. Col. Francis Marion, Maj. Andrew Dellient, Adj.

Captains Peter Horry, Nicholas Eveleigh, James Mc-

Donald, Isaac Harleston, Charles Motte, Francis Huger, Richard Ashby, Richard Shubrick, William Oliphant, John Blake.

Lieutenants William Charnock, Thomas Lessesne, Daniel Mazyck, Jacob Shubrick, Thomas Dunbar, William Moultrie, jr., Thomas Hall, Henry Gray, Isaac Dubose, Richard B. Baker, Adrian Proveaux, Richard Mayson, Peter Gray, Basil Jackson, Gad Marion.

"PHILADELPHIA, *July* 20*th* 1776.
"IN CONGRESS.

"Resolved, That the thanks of the United States of America be given to Maj. Gen. Lee, Col. William Moultrie, Col. William Thompson, and the officers and soldiers under their commands; who, on the 28th of June last, repulsed, with so much valor, the attack which was made on the State of South Carolina, by the fleet and army of his Britannic majesty.

"That Mr. President transmit the foregoing resolution to Maj. Gen. Lee, Col. Moultrie, and Col. Thompson.

"By order of the Congress.
"JOHN HANCOCK, President."

The latter end of July, the Declaration of Independence arrived in Charleston, and was read at the head of the troops, in the field, by Major Bernard Elliott; after which an oration was delivered by the Rev. Mr. Pearcy.

JULY. About this time, Mr. Jonathan Bryan arrived in Charleston, from Georgia, and informed General

Lee that if he would send a detachment of troops to East Florida, he could easily take the town of St. Augustine, as there were but very few men in that garrison; upon which Gen. Lee hastily marches off the Virginia and North Carolina troops, at this inclement season of the year, (leaving Gen. James Moore to command in Charleston,) without one necessary article, nor a field-piece, nor even a medicine chest; he was followed by General, Howe and myself.

As soon as the British had retreated after the battle of Sullivan's Island, the state was left tranquil, and free from any apprehension of another attack soon, an expedition was planned against the Cherokee Indians, (who began to be troublesome,) and carried on by Col. Andrew Williamson, and a strong body from North Carolina, under General Rutherford, who came upon them through the mountains, and a body of men from Virginia, under Col. Christie, and another body from Georgia, under Col. Jacks. The detachment under Col. Williamson had several skirmishes with them, before the other detachments came up. The Indians being attacked on all sides, sued for peace, which was granted them, upon their giving up all the lands to the eastward of the Oconee Mountains. If the British had set their Indian allies upon us a few months before Sir Henry Clinton and Sir Peter Parker made their descent on South Carolina, they would have disconcerted us very much, by keeping thousands of our back country people from coming down; because they must have staid at home to protect their families from the savages.

August 11th, a detachment of South Carolina troops

was sent off for Georgia, with two field pieces; when we got to Savannah, in Georgia, Gen. Lee proposed to me to take the command of the expedition against St. Augustine, and asked me whether my brother being there as governor, would not be an obstacle in the way. I told him my brother being there would be no objection with me; but with respect to other matters, I did not see one thing in the place that we could get to aid such an expedition; that if I undertook the expedition, I must have eight hundred men, and many things else; and, at his request, I gave a list of such articles as I thought would be wanted. I told him I knew what it was to march an army through the wilderness: that I had been warring against Indians, that I had seen an army of 3000 men reduced to only one day's provision, and that, in an Indian enemy's country. General Lee immediately sent to Augusta to have the articles got agreeably to the list I gave in; and we were preparing for the march, when an express, in September, arrived from Congress, calling Gen. Lee immediately to the northward; in two days after, he left Savannah, and ordered the Virginia and North Carolina troops to follow him. This put an end to the East Florida expedition.

The troops that went to Georgia, suffered exceedingly by sickness; at Sunberry, 14 or 15 were buried every day, till they were sent to the sea islands, where they recruited a little.

On the 8th of September, Gen. Lee arrived in Charleston, and the governor and council prevailed upon him to leave the North Carolinians in this province, as a great part of the South Carolina troops were in Georgia, and we should be left, with very few men, quite defenceless. He consented to leave the North Carolina troops; and before his departure, he issued the following orders:

"ORDERS, *September 9th.*

"Gen. Lee thinks it his duty, before his departure, to express the high sense he entertains of the conduct and behavior of the colonels and officers of the several battalions of South Carolina, both as gentlemen and soldiers; and begs leave to assure them, that he thinks himself obliged to report their merit to the Continental Congress."

Hitherto the South Carolina battalions were upon the establishment of the colony; but it was found very inconvenient to the service, that troops doing duty together, should be governed by different laws; it was recommended by Congress to have the colony troops put upon continental establishment, which was agreed to.

"IN GENERAL ASSEMBLY, *Sept. 20th,* 1776.

"RESOLVED, That this house do acquiesce in the resolution of the Continental Congress of the 18th of June, and the 24th of July last, relative to the putting the two regiments of infantry, the regiment of rangers, the regiment of artillery, and the two regiments of riflemen, in the service of this State, upon the continental establishment."

By this resolve, the South Carolina officers came into the continental line as youngest officers of their different ranks.

Gen. Lee left the southern states, and went to the

northward; upon which the command of the southern troops devolved upon Gen. James Moore.

"ORDERS BY GEN. MOORE, *Jan. 9th*, 1777.

"The detached situation of Fort Moultrie, Haddrill's Point, this town, and Fort Johnson, from each other, making it necessary that the command of the troops be divided: Gen. Howe will command in town and Fort Johnson; Gen. Gadsden, at Fort Moultrie and Sullivan's Island; and Gen. Moultrie to command the North Carolinians, at Haddrill's Point."

Gen. Moore returned to North Carolina, and left the command of the troops of that State to Gen. Nash.

An express arrived with orders for the North Carolina troops to march to the northward.

CHAPTER III.

Moultrie attached to Lincoln's army—Moultrie's account of the fall of Savannah, and the succeeding events—Moultrie at Purysburg—Ordered to Port Royal Island—Defeats the British there—Lincoln marches into Georgia—General Prevost enters South Carolina and marches for Charleston—His march retarded by Moultrie—Moultrie defends Charleston against Prevost and prevents its capture—Prevost returns to Georgia.

GENERAL MOULTRIE was now placed under the command of General Lincoln, who had been ordered to the southern department by Congress, with the intention of invading and conquering the province of Florida which still remained loyal to the British crown. But on Lincoln's arrival, he learnt that Savannah had been taken by the British Colonel Campbell, who, with 2000 men, had defeated General Robert Howe, on the 29th of December, 1778. Moultrie, in his Memoirs, thus comments upon this affair, and narrates the events connected with it:

When Gen. Howe perceived that the British, by their movements, intended a descent upon Savannah, he called a council of war of his field officers, to advise with them, whether he should retreat from Savannah, or stay and defend the town with his troops. The majority of the council were of opinion that he should remain in Savannah, and defend it to the last. This was the most ill-advised, rash opinion, that possibly could be given; it was absurd to suppose that six or seven hundred men, and some of them very raw troops, could stand against two or three thousand as good troops as any the British had, and headed by Colonel Campbell, an active, brave, experienced officer.

From every information which Gen. Howe received, he was well assured that the British troops were at least that number. Gen. Howe should have retreated with his six or seven hundred men, up the country, especially as he had certain information that Gen. Lincoln was marching with a body of men to join him, and did actually arrive at Purysburg on the 3d day of January, only four days after his defeat, (which happened a few minutes after the action began.) It was a total rout, and the whole had nearly been cut off from their retreat; the 2nd brigade was entirely so, those of them who made their escape, were obliged to file off to the right, and cross the Spring Hill causeway, and some were obliged to swim Yamacraw creek, leaving their arms behind; those who could not swim were either killed or taken. The loss of the arms to us was a very serious consideration. On this attack, the British landed about 2000 men.

On the 6th December, Gen. Lincoln arrives from the northward, and issues the following order:

"GENERAL ORDERS, BY GEN. LINCOLN.
"*December 7th*, 1778.

"The honorable, the Continental Congress, have been pleased to pass the following resolve

"IN CONGRESS, *September 26th*, 1778.

"RESOLVED, That Major General Lincoln take the command in the southern department, and repair immediately to Charleston, South Carolina."

General Lincoln, immediately after his arrival, began to prepare the troops to march to the southward, to the relief of Georgia; knowing that the British had arrived there in force, and informed of the very weak state of Georgia. On the 24th instant, some reinforcements came in from North Carolina, and on the 25th, General Lincoln issued the following order:

"The Colonel or commanding officer of the regiment of new raised levies and militia, lately arrived from North Carolina, will immediately call on the deputy quartermaster general, for such number of arms as are wanting in their respective regiments."

This order shows the want of arms in the states, even at this time, four years after the beginning of our Revolution. South Carolina was better supplied with arms and ammunition, than any State in the union; their situation being at one end of the continent, they were more out of the way of the British cruisers, and nearer to the islands from whence they drew their supplies, and the Carolinians spared no pains or cost, and ran every risk to procure these necessaries. On the 26th instant, the following orders were issued:

"General Orders.

"The first and second regiments will hold themselves in readiness to march at 6 o'clock to-morrow morning."

On the 27th of December, we marched off the North and South Carolina troops, amounting to about 1200, and arrived at Purysburg on 3d January, 1779.

"General Orders by Gen. Lincoln at Headquarters, at Purysburg.

"*January 3d*, 1779.

"The troops will, immediately after dinner, remove to the right, near the river, at the lower end of the town, where they will take possession of the camp marked out by the deputy quartermaster general."

This evening, Gen. Howe joined us with his suite, and gave us a particular account of his unfortunate affair in Savannah; he left the remains of his troops on the other side of the river, at the Two Sisters, under the command of Col. Isaac Huger; the next day they were ordered to join us at this place.

Had Gen. Howe retired from Savannah and gone up the country, we should soon have joined him, and made a body of 2000 men; besides, such reinforcements were marching to us from Augusta, Ninety-Six, and many other parts of Georgia and Carolina, that in a short time we should have had an army of four or five thousand men; with them we could have marched down to Savannah before the British could have had time to fortify, and before they were reinforced by the troops under Gen. Prevost from Florida, and obliged them to leave the town and take to their shipping again. The loss of Savannah was not the only misfortune we met with in Gen. Howe's defeat, we lost the aid of almost all the citizens of that State, as the British immediately encamped the troops along the Savannah river up to Augusta, and it also damped the ardor of the well affected in our State for a time, and I believe continued the war one year longer. Sometimes the most trifling circumstance of error in war, brings about great events; and the loss of Savannah was the occasion of the fall of Charleston. On Gen. Lincoln's taking the command in the southern department, Gen. Howe was ordered to join the northern army."

In the latter part of January, 1779, General Moultrie was with the main army of General Lincoln, at Purysburg. At this time Lincoln was severely tried by the misconduct of the militia who composed a part of his army. In a letter to Col. Charles C. Pinckney, president of the Senate of South Carolina, dated Jan. 26th, Moultrie gives a particular account of an instance of insubordination in a soldier, whom Lincoln attempted to have tried by a court martial, when it was ascertained that by the laws of South Carolina, the militia were not subject to the continental martial law. Commenting on his own letter, Moultrie says:

This letter shows what difficulties Gen. Lincoln had to encounter, with having such an army, mostly composed of militia, who were governed by such a public law, that for the greatest military crime they could be guilty of, they were only punishable by a small pecuniary fine; with such an army, what anxiety, perplexity, and difficulties must a general be put to; how uneasy must he feel when his military reputation was at stake, with such odds against him, at a time when his camp was three miles from an enemy, superior in force to him, and veteran troops. It was fortunate that a river and a large swamp was between us: a militia army should be brought into action immediately as they take the field: they do not want for spirit; but they soon tire of a camp life—they then get home-sick, and off they go, without giving the least notice, or obtaining leave, because they know that the fine for their disobedience is so trifling that they care not about it. It was very fortunate for us, and impolitic in Lord Cornwallis, to withdraw the paroles from the militia, and to order them to take arms against their country that being the case, they soon determined on which side to fight, they then joined their countrymen; whereas, had they been suffered to remain upon parole, I believe many of them would have been very well pleased to have staid at home quietly; but when once they had taken arms again in favor of their country, they were then obliged to keep the field as a place of security from being made prisoners, and perhaps hanged. I believe one half of the militia of the State were upon parole at that time.

By order of General Lincoln, Moultrie was sent with a detachment to dislodge the enemy from Beaufort on Port Royal Island. At Port Royal Ferry he was joined by General Ash, with 1157 men, of which 234 were continentals. On his preparing to cross the Savannah, the enemy spiked their cannon and retreated. Moultrie crossed and took possession of Beaufort; when he was viewing the fort which they had deserted, his spies brought intelligence that the British under Major Gardner were returning to attack him. He put his troops in order, marched out, and encountering them, inflicted a severe defeat upon them and drove them from the Island. In his report (Feb. 4th, 1779) to General Lincoln, Moultrie says: " This action was reversed from the usual way of fighting between the British and Americans; they taking to the bushes, and we remaining upon the open ground. After some little time, finding our men too much exposed to the enemy's fire, I ordered them to take trees; about three quarters of an hour after the action began, I heard a general cry through the line, of 'no more cartridges;' and was also informed by Captains Heyward and Rutledge, that the ammunition for the field pieces was almost expended, after firing about forty rounds from each piece; upon this I ordered the field pieces to be drawn off very slowly: and their right and left wings to keep pace with the artillery to cover their flanks, which was done in tolerable order for undisciplined troops. The enemy had beat their retreat before we began to move, but we had little or no ammunition, and could not of consequence pursue. They retreated so hastily as to leave an officer, one sergeant, and three privates, wounded, in a house near the action, and their dead lying on the field."

Savannah having, as we have seen, been captured by the British in 1778, was still in their possession, and from this point they now determined to penetrate Carolina in force.

"Lincoln," says a late writer,* " at the same time, passed

* Washington and the Generals of the Revolution.

into Georgia, with the view of diverting the enemy from his objects; and, if possible, of confining his operations to the sea-coast of Georgia only. One of his detached bodies, however, under General Ash, suffered a surprise, which greatly enfeebled his strength, and encouraged his opponent.

"General Prevost, the active commander of the British, aware of Lincoln's absence with the great body of the American force, in the interior, suddenly resolved upon throwing himself between him and the seaboard, and pressing forward to Charleston. His object was a *coup de main.* But Moultrie lay in his path with a thousand militia. He succeeded in retarding the advance which he could not resist, and thus gained time for the citizens to put themselves in trim for the reception of the foe. His despatches apprized Lincoln of the British enterprise, and summoned to his assistance Governor Rutledge, at the head of the country militia. Five large bodies of men were accordingly in motion at the same moment, all striving for the same point.

"The British, amounting to three thousand men, pressed rapidly upon the heels of Moultrie. One or two skirmishes, which took place between small parties, soon satisfied the latter that it would not be prudent, with his inferior force, wholly of militia, to attempt a stand short of Charleston. He had prepared to try the strength of the enemy at Tulifinall, but was discouraged by the result of a skirmish between his own and the British light troops. He has been censured for not having done so, and it has been suggested, that in the frequent swamps and dense forests through which his progress lay, there were adequate covers and fastnesses, in which to baffle and arrest an enemy. But the routes were various. His opposition might have been turned, and the prize was quite too important—the safety of Charleston—to peril by any rash confidence in the coolness and temper of an inexperienced militia. He reached Charleston but a little while before Prevost appeared in sight. He found the citizens in great consternation, and proceeded to reassure them, and put the town in a posture of defence.

"On the 11th of May, the advance of the British army crossed Ashley river. Their cavalry was encountered in a spirited skirmish by the legion of Count Pulaski. Unprepared for a siege, the hope of Prevost was in the vigor of a prompt assault. To meet this, the garrison stood to their arms all night. The next day the place was formally summoned. In the panic of the citizens, the proposition of surrender was really entertained.

"Fortunately, the negotiation was left to Moultrie. Prior to this, all things were in confusion. A question as to the proper authority arose in the minds of many. Orders were brought to the military, equally from the governor, the privy council, and the brigadier.

"Moultrie gave a proof of his decision at this moment. 'Obey no orders from the privy council,' was his stern command, as he rode along the lines. 'It will never do,' were his words to the governor and council, 'we shall be ruined and undone, if we have so many commanders. It is absolutely necessary to choose one commander, and leave all military affairs to him.' He was unanimously appointed to the station, and soon closed the negotiations with the enemy, by a stern and laconic answer, which silenced all the arguments of the timid. 'We will fight it out!'

"The resolution was, in fact, victory! Prevost had no time for fighting. Lincoln was rapidly approaching with four thousand men; and, fearful of a foe so powerful in his rear, and with no longer a hope of effecting anything by a *coup de main*, the British general suddenly recrossed the Ashley in the night. He retired to James's Island, where he was watched closely by the Americans under Lincoln. An attempt made upon his intrenchments at Stono Ferry, in which Moultrie attempted to co-operate, but failed to reach the field in due season, was creditable to the spirit of the American troops, but did not realize the wished-for consequences. It sufficed, however, with the vigilant watch maintained upon the British, to discourage their enterprise; and they gradually drew off, by way of the Sea Island, to their *point d'appui*, in Georgia. And thus ended the second expedition against the metropolis of Carolina.

"In the whole anxious period in which the presence of the enemy was either felt or feared, Moultrie exhibited the cool, steadfast courage by which he was distinguished, with all the unremitted vigilance and activity which characterized the zeal of one having deeply at heart the great interests which are confided to his hands."

CHAPTER IV.

General Moultrie appointed commander in chief of the Southern army, to take the place of Lincoln, who has permission to retire on the plea of ill health—Lincoln however remains with the army—His dissatisfaction at the criticisms on his campaign in Georgia—The correspondence between Jay and Moultrie respecting his appointment—General Moultrie attends the legislature as Senator—His notice of the siege of Savannah.

AFTER the retreat of General Prevost from Charleston, and before his final retirement to Georgia, he continued for some time among the Islands, watched by Lincoln and Moultrie, and once attacked at Stono, as related in the last chapter. It was during this period that General Lincoln, pleading ill health, requested leave to go to the north. On the 11th of May 1779, Congress passed a resolution granting the desired permission, and appointing General Moultrie commander in chief of the Southern army during Lincoln's absence.

By the correspondence in Moultrie's Memoirs, it would seem that Lincoln's real reason for wishing to retire from his command, was a series of ill natured comments on his campaign in Georgia. Moultrie makes the following remarks on this subject:

"About this time, General Lincoln was very much displeased, because some ill natured persons had been casting reflections on him, for his having marched up to Augusta with the main body of his army, and leaving the low country exposed to the enemy, and putting Charleston in such imminent danger: these reflections were thrown out by persons who were not acquainted with General Lincoln's motives for taking that step, in which he was perfectly justifiable; as the council of general officers, held at Black-swamp on the 19th of April, advised the measures as being rational and proper. General Lincoln was a brave, active, and very vigilant officer; and always so very cautious, that he would take no step of any consequence, without first calling a council of officers, to advise with them on the measures."

It does not appear that Lincoln actually availed himself of the permission of Congress to leave his command; and although Moultrie wrote to John Jay, the President of Congress, accepting his appointment, it was only conditionally, in case of Lincoln's actual retirement. We insert the correspondence, because it is highly creditable to General Moultrie's modesty as well as his merit.

Letter from the President of Congress, with Resolves.

"Philadelphia, *May* 15*th*, 1779.

"Major General Lincoln's ill state of health has induced Congress to permit him to retire from a climate and service unfriendly to its recovery.

"I have now the honor of transmitting to you, a copy of an act of the 13th instant, appointing you commander in his absence, during the continuance of the Southern army to the southward of North Carolina; and until the further order of Congress.

"Accept my best wishes, that this appointment may be productive of fresh laurels, and that you may again be the instrument of increasing the honors and security of your country.

"I have the honor to be, &c.

"JOHN JAY, President.

"Brig. Gen. MOULTRIE."

"IN CONGRESS, *May* 13*th*, 1779.

"Resolved that Brigadier General Moultrie, be commander, in the absence of Major General Lincoln, of the Southern army, during its continuance to the southward of North Carolina; with the allowance of a Major General, on a separate command, until the further order of Congress.

"Extract from the Minutes.

"CHARLES THOMSON, Sec'ry."

ANSWER TO THE PRESIDENT OF CONGRESS.

"CHARLESTON, *June* 7*th*, 1779.

"SIR,—I have been honored with yours of 15th May, inclosing the copy of a resolution of Congress; by which I am, in the absence of General Lincoln, appointed commander in chief of the Southern army, during its continuance to the southward of North Carolina: the present posture of affairs will, I trust, prevent General Lincoln from availing himself of the permission granted him by Congress; but should the state of his health require, at any future time, his return to the northward, and deprive us of an officer to whom the country is so much indebted, be assured, sir, that my ambition will be to supply so great a loss, to the best of my abilities; and that my utmost endeavors will be exerted for the welfare of this state, and in defence of our common cause: permit me, in the mean time, to make, through you, my most sincere acknowledgments to Congress, for this proof of the confidence they are pleased to honor me with.

"I have the honor to be, &c.
"WM. MOULTRIE.
"His Excellency JOHN JAY, ESQ.,
"President of Congress."

General Lincoln's reason for remaining at his post of duty, was probably the menacing state of affairs in the south. There was every reason to apprehend that Prevost would renew his attack on Charleston. He was still in the neighborhood of that place when the above correspondence took place, and might be waiting for reinforcements to renew his attack. At such a critical moment, Lincoln was not the man to leave his post. He remained with the army, and on the 20th of June made his attack on Prevost at Stono Ferry. After that battle, as we have already seen, Prevost retired to Georgia and took post at Savannah, leaving Colonel Maitland at Beaufort on Port Royal Island. He was closely watched by Moultrie who was posted at Sheldon (July 20th).

As the legislature was now in session in Charleston, Moultrie had permission to attend to his duty as Senator. He says:

"General Lincoln wished all the officers of the army that were members of the general assembly, to attend at the meeting, that they might be upon the spot, to inform the Representatives with the difficulty there was in this State to keep an army together; that it was a folly to depend upon the militia; that it was impossible to keep them in the field: therefore some other method must be fallen upon to raise an army, or else the country must be given up."

General Moultrie was not present at the siege of Savannah which occurred in the ensuing autumn. He was left, by General Lincoln, in command of the army at Charleston. As we have noticed the siege of Savannah particularly in the former part of this volume, we shall here only insert the following characteristic notice of the affair in Moultrie's journal:

JULY 20th. At this time, nothing material was done; the legislature was in session; and our little army remained at Sheldon, waiting upon the British, who had taken post at Beaufort, under the command of Colonel Maitland. About the 4th of September, an officer came to town, from Count D'Estaing's fleet, then off our bar, consisting of twenty sail of the line, two 50 gun ships, and eleven frigates, to acquaint General Lincoln that the Count D'Estaing was ready to co-operate with him in the reduction of Savannah, and at the same time, to urge the necessity of dispatch; as he could not remain long upon our coast, at this season of the year. This information put us all in high spirits: the legislature adjourned: the governor and council, and the military joined heartily in expediting every thing that was necessary: boats were sent to Count D'Estaing's fleet, to assist in taking the cannon and stores on shore: every one cheerful, as if we were sure of success; and no one doubted but that we had nothing more to do, than to march up to Savannah, and demand a surrender. The militia were draughted; and a great number of volunteers joined readily, to be present at the surrender, and in hopes to have the pleasure of seeing the British march out, and deliver up their arms; but, alas! it turned out a bloody affair; and we were repulsed from the lines, with the loss of eight or nine hundred men killed and wounded: and I think I may say, that the militia volunteers were much disappointed; as I suppose they did not go with the expectation of storming lines. I was pleased, when I was informed that in general they behaved well; and they could truly say, they had been in very severe fire.

CHAPTER V.

Moultrie stationed at Bacon's Bridge—His force there—Leaves his command and goes to Charleston—Siege of Charleston—Surrender—Coolness of Moultrie—His account of the surrender and the explosion of the magazine—Moultrie sent to Haddrill's Point.

IN anticipation of a renewed attack upon Charleston, General Lincoln ordered General Moultrie (Feb. 19, 1780) to proceed to Bacon's Bridge, and form a camp of the militia of that neighborhood, and of those who had been ordered to the city. Marion's brigade was also placed under his command, for the purpose of hanging on the enemy's flanks and opposing him at every advantageous pass. The following directions were given in General Lincoln's orders:

"You will cause to be removed all the horses, beeves, sheep, swine, carriages, boats, and indeed everything which may comfort the enemy, or facilitate their march, saving such as may be necessary for the support of families left. You will throw up a work on the rising ground, on this side of Bacon's Bridge, to command it. You will, on approach of the enemy, previous to your leaving your post, effectually destroy the bridge. You will please to examine Stan's Bridge, and the swamp above it, and report your opinion of the practicability of passing it with heavy cannon. You will keep a small guard at Dorchester Bridge, and one on your right at Stan's Bridge. You will advise me daily of your situation and strength, and of the state of the enemy."

This order is dated at Charleston. A body of the enemy was stationed at Stono, at this time, and Sir Henry Clinton's grand expedition had landed troops on St. John's Island. On the 23d of February, the force under General Moultrie's command, at Bacon's Bridge, was 379 cavalry of all ranks, and 227 infantry under Colonel Marion. "My being so strong in cavalry," says Moultrie, "kept the enemy pretty close to their lines."

On the 9th of March, Moultrie left his command at Bacon's Bridge to General Huger, and came to Charleston, where he was confined to the house for several days, owing to weakness from a recent illness. He was a great sufferer from the gout, and it appears from his correspondence that he was afflicted with this disorder at the time of the defence of Fort Moultrie.

General Moultrie was now to enter upon the tour of duty, which, unfortunately for his country, was to close his active military service. The enemy were already approaching Charleston in great force. On the 11th of February, 1780, the British force under Sir Henry Clinton, "amounting to more than ten thousand men, were within thirty miles of Charleston.* Their fleet, availing themselves of favorable winds and tides, hurried past Fort Moultrie without repeating the error of Sir Peter Parker, in stopping to engage it. Their ships suffered

* Washington and the Generals of the Revolution.

considerably from its fire, and one was destroyed; but the mischief done was not such as to embarrass or retard their progress. The British army, occupying a neck of land lying above the city, and between the rivers Ashley and Cooper, opened their batteries on the 12th of April. To oppose their formidable armament, the Charlestonians could bring into the field but five thousand men. The approach of summer, with the appearance of small-pox in the capital, effectually discouraged the militia of the interior from hastening to the defence. The garrison was accordingly composed wholly of citizen militia, including a force of less than a thousand men from Virginia and North Carolina. Lincoln was still first in command; Moultrie second, but enjoying, perhaps, something more than a secondary influence. Sir Henry Clinton was a slow and cautious commander. The fortifications of Charleston were field-works only. A force so powerful as that of the British should have overrun them in a single night. Yet the siege continued for six weeks. The city was finally reduced by famine; but not until the works were completely overawed by the besiegers, and their artillery rendered almost useless. General Moultrie was conspicuously active during the siege. Philip Neyle, one of his aids, was slain; and he lost a brother, Thomas Moultrie, the only victim in one of the most successful sorties which were made by the garrison. He himself had a narrow escape on one occasion, having just left his bed, when it was traversed and torn asunder by a cannon shot. This was not his only escape. His coolness and phlegm did not desert him, as he walked the ramparts, or passed from them to the city, not heeding the covered way, though the route which he took was one which was completely commanded by the bullets of the Hessian yagers. It was thought miraculous that he should have escaped their aim.*

The following were the terms of the surrender of Charleston:

The town, and all public stores were surrendered.

---

* The following note in Moultrie's Memoirs relates the incident above referred to :

"Mr. Lord and Mr. Basquin, two volunteers, were sleeping upon a mattress together, when Mr. Lord was killed by a shell falling upon him, and Mr. Basquin at the same time, had the hair of his head burnt, and did not wake until he was called upon. The fatigue in that advance redoubt was so great for want of sleep, that many faces were so swelled they could scarcely see out of their eyes. I was obliged to relieve Major Mitchell, the commanding officer : they were constantly upon the look-out for the shells that were continually falling among them, it was by far the most dangerous post on the lines. On my visit to this battery, not having been there for a day or two, I took the usual way of going in, which was a bridge that crossed our ditch, quite exposed to the enemy ; in the meantime, they had advanced their works within seventy or eighty yards of the bridge, which I did not know of. As soon as I had stepped upon the bridge, an uncommon number of bullets whistled about me; on looking to my right, I could just see the heads of about twelve or fifteen men firing upon me from behind a breastwork ; I moved on and got in. When Major Mitchell saw me, he asked me which way I came in ; I told him over the bridge, he was astonished, and said, 'Sir, it is a thousand to one that you were not killed,' and told me, 'that we had a covered way to go out and in,' which he conducted me through on my return. I stayed in this battery about a quarter of an hour, to give the necessary orders, in which time we were constantly skipping about to get out of the way of the shells thrown from their howitzers, they were not more than one hundred yards from our works, and throwing their shells in bushels on our front and left flanks."

The garrison, as well the citizens who had borne arms as the continental troops, militia, and sailors, were to be prisoners of war. The garrison were to march out of town, and to deposite their arms in front of their works; but their drums were not to beat a British march, nor their colours to be reversed. The militia were to retire to their homes on parole, and their persons and property, as well as the persons and property of the inhabitants of the town, to be secure while they adhered to their paroles.

These terms being agreed on, the garrison laid down their arms, and General Leslie was appointed to take possession of the town.

The defence of Charleston was obstinate, but not bloody. The besiegers conducted their approaches with great caution; and the besieged, too weak to hazard repeated sorties, kept within their lines. The loss on both sides was nearly equal. That of the British was seventy-six killed and one hundred and eighty-nine wounded; and that of the Americans, excluding the inhabitants of the town not bearing arms, was ninety-two killed, and one hundred and forty-eight wounded.

From the official returns made to Sir Henry Clinton by his deputy adjutant general, the number of prisoners, exclusive of sailors, amounted to five thousand six hundred and eighteen men. This report, however, presents a very incorrect view of the real strength of the garrison. It includes every male adult inhabitant of the town. The precise number of privates in the continental regiments, according to the report made to Congress by General

Lincoln, was one thousand nine hundred and seventy-seven; of whom five hundred were in the hospital.

The following is Moultrie's own account of the surrender, and of the thrilling incidents which took place on that occasion:

About eleven o'clock, A. M. on the twelfth of May, we marched out between 1500 and 1600 continental troops, (leaving five or six hundred sick and wounded in the hospitals,) without the horn-work, on the left, and piled our arms; the officers marched the men back to the barracks, where a British guard was placed over them; the British then asked where our second division was? they were told these were all the continentals we had, except the sick and wounded; they were astonished, and said we had made a gallant defence.

Captain Rochfort had marched in with a detachment of the artillery to receive the returns of our artillery stores: while we were in the horn-work together in conversation, he said, "Sir, you have made a gallant defence, but you had a great many rascals among you," (and mentioned names,) "who came out every night and gave us information of what was passing in your garrison."

The militia marched out the same day and delivered up their arms at the same place; the continental officers went into town to their quarters, where they remained a few days to collect their baggage, and signed their paroles, then were sent over to Haddrill's point.

The militia remained in Charleston. The next day the militia were ordered to parade near Lynch's pasture,* and to bring all their arms with them, guns, swords,

* Where the spring pump now stands.

pistols, &c.; and those that did not strictly comply, were threatened with having the grenadiers turned in among them; this threat brought out the aged, the timid, the disaffected, and the infirm, many of them who had never appeared during the whole siege, which swelled the number of militia prisoners to, at least, three times the number of men we ever had upon duty: I saw the column march out, and was surprised to see it so large; but many of them we had excused, from age and infirmities; however, they would do to enrol on a conqueror's list.

When the British received their arms, they put them in wagons, and carried them to a store-house, where we had deposited our fixed ammunition (about 4,000 pounds); and although they were informed by some of our officers that the arms were loaded, and several of them went off before the explosion took place, yet in taking them out of the wagons they threw them so carelessly into the store, that some at last set fire to the powder, which blew up the whole guard of fifty men, and many others that were standing by; their carcasses, legs, and arms were seen in the air, and scattered over several parts of the town.

One man was dashed with violence against the steeple of the new Independent church, which was at a great distance from the explosion, and left the marks of his body there for several days. The houses in the town received a great shock, and the window sashes rattled as if they would tumble out of the frames.

Most of our militia were still together; after delivering up their arms, they went in a body to assist in extinguishing the fire, that had communicated itself to the neighboring houses; and while they were working they were under the dreadful apprehension lest the magazine should take fire, as the work-house and others that were next to it were in a blaze; at last some timid person called out, that "the magazine was on fire," this gave the alarm; every one took fright, both British and Americans, and instantly broke off from work, and run away as fast as possible through the streets, throwing down and tumbling over each other, and others coming, after tumbling over them, in endeavoring to get as far from the expected explosion, as possible. I have heard some of them say, that although they were so confoundedly frightened at the time, they could not keep from laughing, to see the confusion and tumbling over each other: the alarm was soon brought into the town.

I was then in a house, joining St. Michael's church, with some company; I advised the going out of the house, and walking to South-bay, because I was apprehensive, from the great shock which was felt in the houses, from the explosion of 4,000 pounds of powder, that, should the magazine blow up, which had 10,000 pounds of powder in it, many of the houses in town would be thrown down: on my way thither, I met a British officer, who asked me how much powder was in the magazine; I told him 10,000 pounds: "Sir," said he, "if it takes fire, it will blow your town to hell!" I replied, "I expected it would give a hell of a blast!"

The British were very much alarmed at the explosion; all the troops were turned out under arms, and formed: they could not tell what was the matter: some of the British and Hessian officers supposed it was designed by us: I was abused, and taken up by a Hessian officer, (whose guard was at Broughton's-battery,) he was very angry, and said to me, "You, General Moultrie, you rebels have done this on purpose, as they did at New York;" and ordered his guard to take me a prisoner, into a house near, and placed a sentry at the door, where a number of us were confined; but I soon got a note over a back way, to General Leslie, acquainting him of my situation, upon which he immediately sent one of his aides to me, with an apology, that my confinement was contrary to orders, and ordered the sentry from the door. After a little time, the alarm subsided; they went back, and stopped the progress of the fire: and if they had considered for a moment, they would have found that it was almost impossible for the magazine to take fire from the adjacent houses, because it was inclosed with a high brick wall, and the magazine itself was built of brick, and bomb proof.

After the surrender, the officers were sent to Haddrill's point, and Moultrie being the senior was placed at their head by General Lincoln, who directed him to arrange the barracks and see that justice was done to all the officers in respect to the rooms.

"When we got to Haddrill's-point," says Moultrie, "it was very difficult to get quarters in barracks, for the number of officers that were sent over; they went to the neighboring houses, within the limits of their paroles;* and many of them built huts about in the woods, and in a very little time, were comfortably settled with little gardens about them: the number of officers (prisoners)

* I was, at this time, allowed to come to town when I pleased.

at Haddrill's-point, and the adjacent houses, were two hundred and seventy-four; Colonel Pinckney and myself were in excellent quarters, at Mr. Pinckney's place, called Snee-farm."

General Lincoln was furnished with a vessel, to carry him and his suite to Philadelphia.

CHAPTER VI.

Moultrie a prisoner at Charleston—Attempt of Colonel Balfour and Lord Montague to gain him over to the British side—Balfour's letter to Moultrie's son—Lord Montague's letter to Moultrie, and his noble answer—Moultrie's important services while a prisoner in Charleston—Exchange of prisoners—Moultrie goes to Philadelphia on parole—Is exchanged—Returns to his plantation in South Carolina—Is present at the evacuation of Charleston by the British—His description of the scene—Moultrie elected Governor of South Carolina—Close of his life.

GEN. MOULTRIE remained a captive with the British, at Charleston, till May, 1781. His ability as a commander was well known to them, and they were extremely anxious to engage his services in the royal cause. Colonel Balfour first applied to his son in the following letter:

"MR. MOULTRIE: Your father's character and your own have been represented to me in such a light that I wish to serve you both. What I have to say, I will sum up in few words. I wish you to propose to your father to relinquish the cause he is now engaged in, which he may do without the least dishonor to himself. He has only to enclose his commission to the first general (General Greene, for instance)—the command will devolve on the next officer. This is often done in our service. Any officer may resign his commission in the field, if he chooses. If your father will do this, he may rely on me. He shall have his estate restored, and all damages paid. I believe you are the only heir of your father. For you, sir, if he continues firm, I shall never ask you to bear arms against him. These favors you may depend I shall be able to obtain from my Lord Cornwallis. You may rely upon my honor—this matter shall never be divulged by me."

Young Moultrie declined to make this proposal to his father, saying that he was sure his father would not listen to it. But the attempt was renewed by Lord Charles Montague, formerly governor of South Carolina, and a personal friend of General Moultrie. He wrote to the general as follows:

"*March* 11*th*, 1781.

" SIR :—" A sincere wish to promote what may be to your advantage, induces me now to write ; and the freedom with which we have often conversed, makes me hope you will not take amiss what I say. My own principles, respecting the commencement of this unfortunate war, are well known to you, and, of course, you can conceive what I mention is out of friendship: you have now fought bravely in the cause of your country for many years, and, in my opinion, fulfilled the duty every individual owes to it. You have had your share of hardships and difficulties, and if the contest is still to be continued, younger hands should now take the toil from you. You have now a fair opening of quitting that service, with honor and reputation to yourself, by going to Jamaica with me. The world will readily attribute it to the known friendship that has subsisted between us: and by quitting this country for a short time, you would avoid any disagreeable conversations, and might return at leisure, to take possession of your estates for yourself and family.

"The regiment I am going to command, the only proof I can give you of my sincerity is, that I will quit that command to you with pleasure, and serve under you. I earnestly wish I could be the instrument to effect what I propose, as I think it would be a great means towards promoting that reconciliation we all wish for. A thousand circumstances concur to make this a proper period for you to embrace: our old acquaintance: my having been formerly governor in this province: the interest I have with the present commanders.

"I give you my honor, what I write is entirely unknown to the commandant, or to any one else; so shall your answer be, if you favor me with one. Think well of me.

"Yours sincerely,
"CHARLES MONTAGUE.
"GEN. MOULTRIE."

The following is Moultrie's noble answer:

"HADDRILL'S POINT, *March* 12*th*, 1781.

"MY LORD:—"I received yours this morning, by Fisher; I thank you for your wish to promote my advantage, but am much surprised at your proposition; I flattered myself I stood in a more favorable light with you: I shall write with the same freedom with which we used to converse, and doubt not you will receive it with the same candor. I have often heard you express your sentiments respecting this unfortunate war, when you thought the Americans injured; but am now astonished to find you taking an active part against them; though not fighting particularly on the continent, yet seducing their soldiers away, to enlist in the British service, is nearly similar.

"My lord, you are pleased to compliment me with having fought bravely in my country's cause for many years, and, in your opinion, fulfilled the duty every individual owes to it; but I differ very widely with you in thinking that I have discharged my duty to my country, while it is still deluged with blood, and overrun with British troops, who exercise the most savage cruelties. When I entered into this contest, I did it with the most mature deliberation, and with a determined resolution to risk my life and fortune in the cause. The hardships I have gone through I look back upon with the greatest pleasure and honor to myself: I shall continue to go on as I have begun, that my example may encourage the youths of America to stand forth in defence of their rights and liberties. You call upon me now, and tell me I have a fair opening of quitting that service with honor and reputation to myself by going with you to Jamaica. Good God! is it possible that such an idea could arise in the breast of a man of honor? I am sorry you should imagine I have so little regard for my own reputation as to listen to such dishonorable proposals; would you wish to have that man whom you have honored with your friendship play the traitor? Surely not. You say, by quitting this country for a short time, I might avoid disagreeable conversations, and might return at my own leisure, and take possession of my estates for myself and family; but you have forgot to tell me how I am to get rid of the feelings of an injured honest heart,

17

and where to hide from myself; could I be guilty of so much baseness I should hate myself and shun mankind. This would be a fatal exchange from my present situation, with an easy and approved conscience of having done my duty, and conducted myself as a man of honor.

"My lord, I am sorry to observe, that I feel your friendship much abated, or you would not endeavor to prevail upon me to act so base a part. You earnestly wish you could bring it about, as you think it will be the means of bringing about that reconciliation we all wish for. I wish for a reconciliation as much as any man, but only upon honorable terms. The repossessing my estates, the offer of the command of your regiment, and the honor you propose of serving under me, are paltry considerations to the loss of my reputation: no, not the fee simple of that valuable island of Jamaica should induce me to part with my integrity.

"My lord, as you have made one proposal, give me leave to make another, which will be more honorable to us both; as you have an interest with your commanders, I would have you propose the withdrawing the British troops from the continent of America, allow the independence, and propose a peace: this being done, I will use my interest with my commanders to accept the terms, and allow Great Britain a free trade with America.

"My lord, I could make one proposal,* but my situation as a prisoner circumscribes me within certain bounds;

---

*Which was to advise him to come over to the Americans: this proposal I could not make when on parole.

I must therefore conclude with allowing you the free liberty to make what use of this you may think proper. Think better of me.

"I am, my lord, your lordship's most obedient humble servant,

WM. MOULTRIE.

Both these letters and the note, we copy from Moultrie's Memoirs.

The answer of Moultrie, of course, put an end to the tempting solicitations of the British officers. Among all the documents relating to the history of the Revolution there is none more creditable to the writer than this. Written off hand on the day after he had received Lord Montague's letter, it is hardly less remarkable for its dignified and elevated style than for the noble sentiments which actuated the writer. It well deserves the admiration and the remembrance of every American.

The period during which Moultrie remained a captive at Charleston was one of ceaseless activity and vigilance. As senior officer it was his duty to defend the American prisoners as best he could from the constant oppressions of the British, and to remonstrate against their frequent infractions of the terms of the capitulation. His Memoirs contain many letters addressed to the British officers on this subject, and they evince not only his vigilance and zeal in the defence of his countrymen, but a determination to exact from the haughty officials of the enemy the respect which was due to himself.

At length, on the 3d of May 1781, a cartel for the exchange and relief of prisoners was agreed to between

Captain Cornwallis on the part of Lord Cornwallis, and Lieutenant Colonel Carrington on the part of General Greene.

"This cartel being agreed upon," says Moultrie, "Major Hyrne, the American commissary of prisoners, came to Charleston and proceeded upon the exchange of prisoners, and where similar ranks could not apply, the officers were paroled; some went to Philadelphia, others to Virginia with what soldiers were left, and the sick to the hospital.

"I was allowed a small brig for myself and family, and such others as I chose to take on board; in consequence of which, by applications and intreaties of my friends, we had upwards of ninety souls on board that small brig; we sailed some time in June, and after a pleasant passage, arrived safe in Philadelphia; the other vessels all arrived in Virginia."

Although Moultrie was allowed by the terms of the cartel to go to Philadelphia, his final release from his parole did not take place till February 1782, when an exchange of the prisoners captured with Burgoyne took place. He was promoted by Congress to the rank of Major General, but was not again called into active service, as his health was still infirm and the war was now virtually closed. The exciting events which took place during the period of his captivity will be found in the Life of Marion, in the preceding part of this volume.

The following extract from Moultrie's Memoirs presents an affecting picture of his return to his home in South Carolina:

General Burgoyne's exchange released almost a whole

brigade of American officers, prisoners of war. Only two of the South Carolina line were included in this exchange, which were Colonel C. Pinckney* and myself.

Soon after my being exchanged, I prepared to set off with my family for South Carolina, and early in April left Philadelphia, and arrived at Waccamaw in South Carolina in June, where I was informed that General Greene's army lay at Ashley River, quite inactive, and no military operations going on. I remained at Winyaw till late in September, at which time I paid a visit to General Greene. It was the most dull, melancholy, dreary ride that any one could possibly take, of about one hundred miles through the woods of that country; what I had been accustomed to see abound with live-stock and wild fowl of every kind, was now destitute of all. It had been so completely checquered by the different parties, that not one part of it had been left unexplored; consequently, not the vestige of horses, cattle, hogs, or deer, &c. was to be found. The squirrels and birds of every kind were totally destroyed. The dragoons told me, that on their scouts, no living creature was to be seen, except now and then a few camp scavengers,† picking the bones of some unfortunate fellows, who had been shot or cut down, and left in the wood above ground. In my visit to General Greene's camp, as there was some danger from the enemy, I made a circuitous route to General Marion's camp, then on Santee-river, to get an escort, which he gave me, of twenty infantry and twenty cavalry: those, with the volunteers that attended me from Georgetown, made us pretty strong. On

* General Pinckney. † Turkey Buzzards.

my way from General Marion's to General Greene's camp, my plantation was in the direct road, where I called and stayed a night. On my entering the place, as soon as the negroes discovered that I was of the party, there was immediately a general alarm, and an outcry through the plantation, that "Massa was come! Massa was come!" and they were running from every part with great joy to see me. I stood in the piazza to receive them: they gazed at me with astonishment, and every one came and took me by the hand, saying, "God bless you, massa! we glad for see you, massa!" and every now and then some one or other would come out with a "ky!" And the old Africans joined in a war-song in their own language, of "welcome the war home." It was an affecting meeting between the slaves and the master: the tears stole from my eyes and run down my cheeks. A number of gentlemen that were with me, could not help being affected at the scene. Many are still alive, and remember the circumstance. I then possessed about two hundred slaves, and not one of them left me during the war, although they had had great offers, nay, some were carried down to work on the British lines, yet they always contrived to make their escape and return home. My plantation I found to be a desolate place; stock of every kind taken off; the furniture carried away, and my estate had been under sequestration. The next day we arrived at General Greene's camp; on our near approach, the air was so infected with the stench of the camp, that we could scarcely bear the smell; which shows the necessity of moving camp often in the summer, in these hot climates. General Greene, expecting the evacuation to take place every week, from the month of August, was the reason he remained so long on the same ground.

Before I conclude my memoirs, I must make my last tribute of thanks to the patriotic fair of South Carolina and Georgia, for their heroism and virtue in those dreadful and dangerous times whilst we were struggling for our liberties. Their conduct deserves the highest applause; and a pillar ought to be raised to their memory: their fortitude was such as gave examples, even to the men, to stand firm; and they despised those who were not enthusiasts in their country's cause. The hardships and difficulties they experienced were too much for their delicate frames to bear; yet they submitted to them with a heroism and virtue that never has been excelled by the ladies of any country; and I can with safety say, that their conduct during the war contributed much to the independence of America.

Soon after this General Moultrie was gratified by being present at the surrender of Charleston. The following is his characteristic description of this scene:

On Saturday, the fourteenth day of December, 1782, the British troops evacuated Charleston, after having possession two years, seven months, and two days.

The evacuation took place in the following manner: Brigadier General Wayne was ordered to cross Ashley River,* with three hundred light-infantry, eighty of Lee's cavalry, and twenty artillery, with two six pouders, to move down towards the British lines, which was near Colonel Shubrick's, and consisted of three redoubts.

* General Greene's army lay on the west side of Ashley River, above the ferry.

General Leslie who commanded in town, sent a message to General Wayne, informing him, that he would next day leave the town, and for the peace and security of the inhabitants, and of the town, would propose to leave their advanced works next day at the firing of the morning gun; at which time, General Wayne should move on slowly, and take possession; and from thence to follow the British troops into town, keeping at a respectful distance (say about two hundred yards); and when the British troops after passing through the town gates, should file off to Gadsden's Wharf, General Wayne was to proceed into town; which was done with great order and regularity, except now and then the British called to General Wayne that he was too fast upon them, which occasioned him to halt a little. About 11 o'clock, A. M. the American troops marched into town and took post at the State-house.

At 3 o'clock, P. M., General Greene conducted Governor Mathews, and the council, with some other of the citizens, into town; we marched in, in the following order: an advance of an officer and thirty of Lee's dragoons; then followed the governor and General Greene; the next two were General Gist and myself; after us followed the council, citizens, and officers, making altogether about fifty: one hundred and eighty cavalry brought up the rear: we halted in Broad street, opposite where the South Carolina Bank now stands; there we alighted, and the cavalry discharged to quarters: afterwards, every one went where they pleased; some in viewing the town, others in visiting their friends. It was a grand and pleasing sight, to see the enemy's fleet (upwards of three hundred sail) lying at anchor from Fort Johnson to Five-fathom hole, in a curve line, as the current runs; and what made it more agreeable, they were ready to depart from the port. The great joy that was felt on this day, by the citizens and soldiers, was inexpressible: the widows, the orphans, the aged men and others, who, from their particular situations, were obliged to remain in Charleston, many of whom had been cooped up in one room of their own elegant houses for upwards of two years, whilst the other parts were occupied by the British officers, many of whom were a rude, uncivil set of gentlemen; their situations, and the many mortifying circumstances occurred to them in that time, must have been truly distressing. I cannot forget that happy day when we marched into Charleston with the American troops; it was a proud day to me, and I felt myself much elated, at seeing the balconies, the doors, and windows crowded with the patriotic fair, the aged citizens and others, congratulating us on our return home, saying, "God bless you, gentlemen! you are welcome home, gentlemen!" Both citizens and soldiers shed mutual tears of joy.

It was an ample reward for the triumphant soldier, after all the hazards and fatigues of war, which he had gone through, to be the instrument of releasing his friends and fellow citizens from captivity, and restoring to them their liberties and possession of their city and country again.

This fourteenth day of December, 1782, ought never to be forgotten by the Carolinians; it ought to be a day of festivity with them, as it was the real day of their deliverance and independence.

"The close of the Revolutionary war," says the excellent writer whom we have repeatedly quoted, "did not close the public career of Moultrie. The establishment of a new government—that of a republican state—afforded a grateful opportunity to his countrymen, of which they promptly availed themselves, to acknowledge his great and patriotic service. In 1785, he was raised to the gubernatorial chair of South Carolina, being the third person to whom this honor had been accorded. During his administration, the town of Columbia was laid out for the seat of government. In 1794, he was a second time elected to this office, the duties of which he fulfilled with honor and to the satisfaction of all parties. His career, henceforward, to the close of his life, was one of uninterrupted and honorable repose. Slander never presumed to smutch his garments. Of a calm, equable temper, great good sense, a firm undaunted spirit, a kind heart, and easy indulgent moods, he was beloved by his personal associates, and revered by all. His character is one of those of which his career will sufficiently speak. He lived beyond the appointed limits of human life—dying on the 27th September, 1805, in the seventy-fifth year of his age. His name, deeds, and virtues, constitute a noble portion of American character, to which we may point the attention of our sons, with a sure confidence in the excellence of his example."

MAJOR GENERAL ANDREW PICKENS.

LIFE OF

MAJOR GENERAL ANDREW PICKENS.

CHAPTER I.

Birth and ancestry of General Pickens—His father emigrates to Virginia, and afterwards to South Carolina—Pickens serves in the French war, and in the Cherokee war—Engages in farming at the Long Cane settlement—Serves in the Revolutionary war in the South—Defeats the loyalists at Kettle Creek—Services after the fall of Charleston—At the battle of Cowpens—Attached to the main army—Detached with Marion to North Carolina—Pursuit of Tarleton, and defeat of Pyle.

This able commander was born in Bucks county, Pennsylvania, on the 13th of September, 1739. His ancestors were driven from France by the revocation of the edict of Nantz. They first settled in Scotland, and afterwards in the north of Ireland. His father emigrated to Pennsylvania, from whence he removed to Augusta county, Virginia, and soon after to the Waxhaws, in South Carolina, before Andrew had attained the age of manhood.

Like many of our most distinguished officers of the Revolution, he commenced his military services in the French war, which terminated in 1763, when he began to develope those qualities for which he was afterwards so eminently distinguished. In the year 1761, he served as a volunteer with Moultrie and Marion, in a bloody but successful expedition, under Lieutenant Colonel Grant, a British officer, sent by General Amherst to command against the Cherokees. After the termination of the war, he removed to the Long Cane settlement, and was wholly engaged for several years in the usual pursuits of a frontier country: hunting and agriculture.

At an early period he took a decided stand against the right claimed by Great Britain, to tax her colonies without their consent: and at the commencement of the Revolution was appointed captain of militia.

He served in the southern department of the United States, and rapidly rose to the rank of colonel in the South Carolina militia. At the time of the conquest of Georgia (1778–9) Pickens distinguished himself by defeating the loyalists at Kettle creek. Savannah, Sunbury, and Augusta, had successively fallen into the hands of the British; the first of these places being taken by Lieutenant Colonel Campbell, and the two others by General Prevost.

From Augusta, Lieutenant Colonel Hamilton, of the North Carolina regiment, advanced, with a suitable detachment, further west to crush all remaining resistance, and to encourage the loyalists to step forward and give their active aid in confirming the establishment of royal authority. Every attempt to interrupt the progress of this officer was ineffectual; and seven hundred loyalists embodied with the determination to force their way to the British camp.

Colonel Pickens, true to his country, and correctly interpreting the movement under Hamilton, assembled his regiment, and drew near to him for the purpose of counteracting his operations.

Finding this officer invulnerable, he suddenly turned from him, to strike at the loyalists advancing towards Augusta. He fell in with them at Kettle creek, and instantly attacked them. The action was contested with zeal and firmness; when Colonel Boyd, the commander of the loyalists, fell, and his death was soon followed by the route of his associates. Nevertheless, three hundred of the body contrived to effect their union with the British army.

After the fall of Charleston, and previous to the battle of Camden, Marion, Sumpter, and Pickens, were engaged in harassing the enemy in the Carolinas and restoring the spirits of the patriots which had been sorely depressed by the conquest of South Carolina, and the harsh measures which followed. General Lee, in his " Memoirs of the War in the Southern Department of the United States," after sketching the characters and appearance of Marion and Sumpter, thus notices Pickens and his operations at the time.

A third gentleman quickly followed their great example. Andrew Pickens, younger than either of them, inexperienced in war, with a sound head, a virtuous heart, and a daring spirit, joined in the noble resolve to burst the chains of bondage riveted upon the two southern states, and soon proved himself worthy of being ranked with his illustrious precursors. This gentleman was also promoted by the governor to the station of brigadier general; and having assembled his associates of the same bold and hardy cast, distinguished himself and corps in the progress of the war, by the patience and cheerfulness with which every privation was borne, and the gallantry with which every danger was confronted. The country between Ninety-Six and Augusta received his chief attention. These leaders were always engaged in breaking up the smaller posts and the intermediate communications, or in repairing losses sustained by action. The troops which followed their fortunes, on their own or their friends' horses, were armed with rifles; in the use of which they had become expert; a small portion only, who acted as cavalry, being provided with sabres. When they approached the enemy they dismounted, leaving their horses in some hidden spot to the care of a few of their comrades. Victorious or vanquished, they flew to their horses, and thus improved victory or secured retreat.

Their marches were long and toilsome, seldom feeding more than once a day. Their combats were like those of the Parthians, sudden and fierce; their decisions speedy, and all subsequent measures equally prompt. With alternate fortunes, they persevered to the last, and greatly contributed to that success which was the first object of their efforts.

We next find General Pickens taking an active and important part in the celebrated battle of the Cowpens, where the Americans, under Morgan, inflicted a signal defeat on the British detachment commanded by Colonel Tarleton. He there commanded the militia forces; and, animated by the spirit and courage of their commander in that important battle, they fairly won an equal share of glory with the continentals, under Colonel Howard. For his gallantry and conduct on that occasion, Congress voted him a sword.

Of his intrepid conduct at the battle of the Cowpens, it is scarcely necessary to speak. It is a well-known fact, that he not only prevailed upon his riflemen to retain their fire till it could be given with deadly effect, but, when broken, and compelled to retreat, that he rallied them; and what had never before been effected *with militia*, brought them a second time to meet their enemy, and, by continued exertion, to accomplish their final surrender.

After this battle Pickens's brigade was attached to the main army under General Greene, and remained with him during the celebrated retreat which terminated in the passage of the Dan. After this passage was effected, Lord Cornwallis, then commander of the British forces in the south, considering North Carolina to be conquered, raised his standard at Hillsborough, and invited the loyalists of the province to join him in fully re-establishing the British authority.

General Greene, aware of his movements, and believing that the people were rapidly organizing troops and joining the British army, decided to re-enter North Carolina and endeavor to defeat the measures of Cornwallis.

"Greene," says General Lee,* "persevering in his

* Lee's Memoirs.

determination to risk his army again in North Carolina, — to rouse the drooping spirits of his friends, and to check the audacity of his foes, — the legion of Lee, strengthened by two companies of the veterans of Maryland under Captain Oldham, with the corps of South Carolina militia under Brigadier Pickens, was ordered, in the morning of the 18th, to repass the Dan. This was readily performed; all the boats heretofore collected being still held together by Carrington for the use of the army.

Pickens and Lee were commanded to gain the front of Cornwallis, to place themselves as close to him as safety would permit, to interrupt his communication with the country, to repress the meditated rising of the loyalists, and, at all events, to intercept any party of them which might attempt to join the enemy.

These officers lost no time in advancing to the theatre of operations; and having in the course of the march provided capable guides, sat down that evening in a covert position, short of the great road leading from the Haw river to Hillsborough, and detached exploring parties of cavalry on the roads towards Hillsborough and towards the Haw. In the course of the evening, Greene, never avoiding toil or danger, with a small escort of Washington's cavalry left his army, and overtook the advanced corps in its secret position. He continued with it during the night, and renewed to the two commandants explanations of his plan and object. He communicated his intention of repassing the Dan with the army in a few days, directing his route towards the upper country; too remote, as he remarked, from the advanced corps to afford the smallest protection; urged cordial concert, pressed in fervid terms the necessity of unceasing vigilance, and the most cautious circumspection.

In obedience to General Greene's orders, Pickens and Lee, learning that Colonel Tarleton had just passed from Hillsborough with horse, foot, and artillery, destined to pass the Haw river to embody and bring in the loyalists, marched in pursuit of him, with a view to bring him to action. In this attempt they were not successful; but while engaged in the pursuit of Tarleton, they fell in with Colonel Pyle at the head of a body of loyalists. The surprise of this officer's corps is thus narrated by Lee.*

Lee's van officer, preceding him a few hundred yards only, was met by two well mounted young countrymen, who being accosted in the assumed character, promptly answered, that they were rejoiced in meeting us, having been sent forward by Colonel Pyle for the purpose of ascertaining Tarleton's camp, to whom the colonel was repairing with four hundred loyalists. These youths were immediately sent to Lieutenant Colonel Lee, but were preceded by a dragoon, with the information imparted. Immediately upon the arrival of the dragoon Lee despatched his adjutant with the intelligence to Brigadier Pickens, requesting him to place his riflemen (easily to be distinguished by the green twigs in their hats, the customary emblem of our militia in the South) on the left flank, out of sight; which was readily to be done, as we were then in a thick wood; at the same time to assure him that Lee was determined, in conformity with the concerted plan, to make an attempt with the legion, of

* Lee's Memoirs.

turning the occurrence to advantage. The prisoners were also reminded, as was the serjeant having them in care, of the past order. This commnication was scarcely finished, before the two dragoons rode up with the two countrymen, who were received with much apparent cordiality; Lee attentively listening with seeming satisfaction to their annunciation of the laudable spirit which had actuated Colonel Pyle and his associates, and which they asserted was rapidly spreading through the country. Finding them completely deceived, (for they not only believed the troops they saw to be British, but overlooking what had been told them, took them to be Tarleton's, addressing the commandant as that officer,) Lee sent one of them back with the two dragoons to his van, thence to proceed to Colonel Pyle with Lieutenant Colonel Tarleton's gratulations, and his request that he would be so good as to draw out on the margin of the road, so as to give convenient room for his much fatigued troops to pass without delay to their night position, while the other was detained to accompany the supposed Tarleton. Orders were at the same time despatched to the van officer to halt as soon as he got in sight of the loyalists.

As Lee approached his officer, who had halted, highly gratified with the propitious prospect, and listening to the overflowings of respect and devotion, falling incessantly from the lips of his young attendant, his comrade, who had been sent to Colonel Pyle, returned with his expected compliance, announced in most respectful terms.

The column of horse now became complete by union with the van, and Colonel Pyle was in sight on the right of the road, drawn up as suggested, with his left to the advancing column.* This last circumstance was fortunate, as Lieutenant Colonel Lee had concluded to make known to the colonel his real character as soon as he should confront him, with a solemn assurance of his and his associates' perfect exemption from injury, with the choice of returning to their homes, or of taking a more generous part, by uniting with the defenders of their common country against the common foe. By Pyle's lucky occupation of the right side of the road, it became necessary for Lee to pass along the whole line of the loyalists before he could reach their colonel; and thus to place his column of horse in the most eligible situation for any vicissitude.

They were mounted like our militia, fitted like them to move on horseback, and to fight dismounted. Their guns (rifles and fowling pieces) were on their shoulders, the muzzles consequently in an opposite direction to the cavalry. In the event of discovery, they must have changed the direction before they could fire,—a motion not to be performed, with a body of dragoons close in with their horses' heads and their swords drawn.

The danger of this rare expedient was by no means so great as it appears to be on first view.

---

* Had Pyle accidentally arrayed upon the left of the road, he would have been found on the right of his regiment, the flank first reached by the column of the horse. Some pretext must have been adopted to have moved on to the other flank, so as to place the horse in the requisite posture, before Lieutenant Colonel Lee could make the desired communication; therefore it was fortunate that he should have chosen the side of the road on which he was found posted.

Lee passed along the line at the head of the column with a smiling countenance, dropping, occasionally, expressions complimentary to the good looks and commendable conduct of his loyal friends. At length he reached Colonel Pyle, when the customary civilities were promptly interchanged. Grasping Pyle by the hand Lee was in the act of consummating his plan, when the enemy's left, discovering Pickens' militia, not sufficiently concealed, began to fire upon the rear of the cavalry commanded by Captain Eggleston. This officer instantly turned upon the foe, as did immediately after the whole column. The conflict was quickly decided, and bloody on one side only. Ninety of the royalists were killed, and most of the survivors wounded. Dispersing in every direction, not being pursued, they escaped. During this sudden rencontre, in some parts of the line the cry of mercy was heard, coupled with assurance of being our best friends; but no expostulation could be admitted in a conjuncture so critical. Humanity even forbad it, as its first injunction is to take care of your own: and our safety was not compatible with that of the supplicants, until disabled to offend. Pyle, falling under many wounds, was left on the field as dying, and yet he survived. We lost not a man, and only one horse.

The pursuit of Tarleton was now resumed, but he escaped the corps of Pickens and Lee, and by forced marches returned to Hillsborough.

"Fortune," says Lee, "which sways so imperiously the affairs of war, demonstrated throughout the operation its supreme control. Nothing was omitted on the part of the Americans to give to the expedition the desired termination; but the very bright prospects which for a time presented themselves, were suddenly overcast,— the capricious goddess gave us Pyle and saved Tarleton."

CHAPTER II.

Pickens and Lee besiege and take Augusta—They rejoin the main army—Battle of Eutaw—Pickens's expedition against the Cherokee Indians—Services as commissioner under the treaty of Hopewell—Member of the Convention of South Carolina—Of the legislature—Member of Congress—Consulted by Washington on Indian affairs—Appointed Major General—Retires from public life—Recalled to the legislature in 1812—His death and character.

AFTER the incidents related in the last chapter, General Pickens, with Lieutenant Colonel Lee, and Colonel Williams, formed a strong light corps to operate in the country between the armies of Greene and Cornwallis. General Pickens was soon relieved from this duty and ordered to assist with his militia in the capture of Augusta. Consequently his brigade was not present at the battle of Guilford.

His first object was Augusta, and in the siege of that place, he was assisted by Lieutenant Colonel Lee with his legion, who had been ordered to join him, and had arrived just before the siege commenced. The place was very ably defended by the commandant, Lieutenant Colonel Brown, and after the siege had lasted fifteen days, it was surrendered to Pickens and Lee (June 5th, 1781). After the surrender of Augusta, Pickens and

Lee joined the main army under General Greene, then engaged in the siege of Ninety-Six.

General Pickens remaining with the main army, took an active part with his militia in the battle of Eutaw, Sept. 8th. The remainder of the militia were commanded by General Marion. In the battle, "the militia," says Marshall, "being commanded by generals of experience and courage, exhibited a degree of firmness not common to that species of force, and maintained their ground with unexpected obstinacy. The result was a splendid victory. General Pickens was wounded in this battle."

General Pickens's next important service was the conquest of his old enemies, the Cherokee Indians. Lee, in his Memoirs, gives the following account of this expedition:

About this time Greene's attention to the leading object of his measures was diverted by accounts from the West, announcing the irruption of the Cherokee tribe of Indians on the district of Ninety-Six; which having been as sudden as it was unexpected, had been attended with serious injury. Several families were massacred, and many houses were burnt. Brigadier Pickens had, after his long and harassing campaign, returned home with his militia. The moment he heard of the late incursion, he again summoned around him his well tried warriors. To this officer the general resorted, when he was informed of this new enemy. Among the first acts of General Greene's command in the South, was the conclusion of a treaty with this tribe of Indians, by which they had engaged to preserve a state of neutrality so long as the war between the United States and Great Britain should continue. What is extraordinary, the Cherokees rigidly complied with their engagement during the past campaign, when the success of Lord Cornwallis, with the many difficulties Greene had to encounter, would have given weight to their interference. Now, when the British army in Virginia had been forced to surrender, and that acting in South Carolina and Georgia had been compelled to take shelter in the district of country protected by forts and ships, they were so rash as to listen to exhortations often before applied in vain. Pickens followed the incursors into their own country; and having seen much and various service, judiciously determined to mount his detachment, adding the sword* to the rifle and tomahawk. He well knew the force of cavalry, having felt it at the Cowpens, though it was then feebly exemplified by the enemy. Forming his mind upon experience, the straight road to truth, he wisely resolved to add to the arms, usual in Indian wars, the unusual one above mentioned.

* John Rogers Clarke, colonel in the service of Virginia against our neighbors the Indians, in the Revolutionary war, was among our best soldiers, and better acquainted with the Indian warfare than any officer in our army. This gentleman, after one of his campaigns, met in Richmond several of our cavalry officers, and devoted all his leisure in ascertaining from them the various uses to which horse were applied, as well as the manner of such application. The information he acquired, determined him to introduce this species of force against the Indians, as that of all others the most effectual.

By himself, by Pickens, and lately by Wayne, was the accuracy of Clarke's opinion justified; and no doubt remains, but in all armies prepared to act against the Indians, a very considerable proportion of it ought to be light cavalry.

In a few days he reached the country of the Indians, who, as is the practice among the uncivilized in all ages, ran to arms to oppose the invader, anxious to join issue in battle without delay. Pickens with his accustomed diligence, took care to inform himself accurately of the designs and strength of the enemy; and as soon as he had ascertained these important facts, advanced upon him. The rifle was only used while reconnoitring the hostile position. As soon as this was finished, he remounted his soldiers and ordered a charge. With fury his brave warriors rushed forward, and the astonished Indians fled in dismay. Not only the novelty of the mode, which always has its influence, but the sense of his incapacity to resist horse, operated upon the flying forester.

Pickens followed up his success, and killed forty Cherokees, took a great number of prisoners of both sexes, and burnt thirteen towns. He lost not a soldier, and had only two wounded. The sachems of the nation assembled in council; and thoroughly satisfied of their inability to contend against an enemy who added the speed of the horse* to the skill and strength of man, they determined to implore forgiveness for the past, and never again to provoke the wrath of their triumphant foe. This resolution being adopted, commissioners were ac-

---

* The Indian, when fighting with infantry, is very daring. This temper of mind results from his consciousness of his superior fleetness; which, together with his better knowledge of the woods, assures to him extrication out of difficulties, though desperate. This temper of mind is extinguished, when he finds that he is to save himself from the pursuit of horse, and with its extinction falls that habitual boldness.

cordingly appointed, with directions to await upon General Pickens, and to adjust with him the terms of peace. These were readily listened to, and a treaty concluded, which not only terminated the existing war, but provided against its renewal, by a stipulation on the part of the Cherokees, in which they engaged not only to remain deaf to the exhortations of the British emissaries, but that they would apprehend all such evil doers, and deliver them to the governor of South Carolina, to be dealt with as he might direct.

The object of the expedition being thus happily accomplished, General Pickens evacuated the Indian territory and returned to South Carolina, before the expiration of the third week from his departure, without losing a single soldier.

This expedition against the Cherokees was the last occasion on which General Pickens served in a separate command. It formed a brilliant close to his military career.

Peace being restored, the voice of his country called him to serve her in various civil capacities; and he continued, without interruption, in public employment until about 1801. By the treaty of Hopewell, with the Cherokees, in which he was one of the commissioners, the cession of that portion of the state now called Pendleton and Greenville, was obtained. Soon after he settled at Hopewell, on Keowee river, where the treaty was held. He was a member of the legislature, and afterwards of the convention which formed the state constitution. He was elected a member under the new constitution, until 1794, when he became a member of Congress. Declin-

THE MILITIA UNDER GENERAL PICKENS DEFEATING THE INDIANS.—PAGE 231.

ing a re-election to Congress, he was again returned a member to the legislature, in which post he continued until about 1811. Such was the confidence of General Washington in him, that he requested his attendance at Philadelphia, to consult with him on the practicability and best means of civilizing the southern Indians; and he also offered him the command of a brigade of light troops, under the command of General Wayne, in his campaigns against the northern Indians; which he declined. In 1794, when the militia was first organized conformably to the act of Congress, he was appointed one of the two major generals; which commission he resigned after holding it a few years. He was employed by the United States as a commissioner in all the treaties with the southern Indians, until he withdrew from public life.

Determining to enjoy that serenity and tranquillity which he had so greatly contributed to establish, with the simplicity of the early times of the Roman republic, he retired from the busy scenes of life, and settled on his farm at Tomussee, (a place peculiarly interesting to him,) where he devoted himself with little interruption to domestic pursuits and reflection until his death. In this tranquil period, few events happened to check the tenor of his happy and virtuous life. Revered and beloved by all, his house, though remote from the more frequented parts of the state, was still the resort of numerous friends and relations; and often received the visits of the enlightened traveler. Such was the gentle current of his latter years; still, of earthly objects, his country was the first in his affections. He viewed with great interest our late struggle, and the causes which excited it, distinctly perceiving, that in its consequences the prosperity, independence, and glory of his country were deeply involved; he was alive to its various incidents. In this hour of danger the eyes of his fellow citizens were again turned to their tried servant; without his knowledge he was again called by the spontaneous voice of his fellow citizens into public service. Confidence thus expressed could not be disregarded; he accepted a seat in the legislature in 1812, and was pressed to serve as governor at this eventful crisis, which, with his characteristic moderation and good sense, he declined. He thought the struggle should be left to more youthful hands.

General Pickens died at his seat in Pendleton District, South Carolina, on the 11th of October, 1817, at the age of seventy-eight years.

In his domestic circumstances he was fortunate: by industry and attention he soon acquired a competency; and never desired more. He married in early life, has left a numerous and prosperous offspring, and his consort, the sister of John E. Calhoun, formerly a senator in Congress, died but a few years before him.

Of his private character little need be said; for among its strongest features was simplicity without contrariety or change; from his youth to age he was ever distinguished for a punctual performance of all the duties of life. He was from early life a firm believer in the christian religion, and an influential member of the Presbyterian church. The strong points of his character were decision and prudence, accompanied, especially in youth, with remarkable taciturnity. He was of middle stature, active and robust; and enjoyed, in consequence of the natural goodness of his constitution, and from early and combined temperance and activity, almost uninterrupted health to the last moments of his life. He retained much of his strength and nearly all his mental vigor in perfection; and died, not in consequence of the exhaustion of nature, or previous sickness; for the stroke of death fell suddenly, and while his personal acquaintances were anticipating the addition of many years to his life.

GOVERNOR JOHN RUTLEDGE.

LIFE OF

GOVERNOR JOHN RUTLEDGE.

CHAPTER I.

Birth and Parentage of Governor Rutledge—Education—Practice at the bar—Resistance to Governor Boone—Member of the Continental Congress—Member of the Convention—Member of Congress—President of South Carolina—His conduct in relation to the defence of Fort Moultrie.

JOHN RUTLEDGE was born in the year 1739, and was the son of Dr. John Rutledge who, with his brother Andrew, both natives of Ireland, arrived in Carolina about the year 1735, and there practised, the one law and the other physic. Dr. Rutledge married Miss Hext, who in the 15th year of her age gave birth to the subject of this memoir. At a very early period she was left a widow, and added one to the many examples of illustrious matrons, who, devoting their whole attention to their orphan offspring, have brought forward distinguished ornaments of human nature.

The early education of John Rutledge was conducted

by David Rhind, an excellent classical scholar, and one of the most successful of the early instructors of youth in Carolina. After he had made considerable progress in the Latin and Greek classics, he entered on the study of law with James Parsons, and was afterwards entered a student in the temple, and proceeding barrister, came out to Charleston and commenced the practice of law in 1761. One of the first causes in which he engaged was an action for breach of a promise of marriage. The subject was interesting, and gave an excellent opportunity for displaying his talents. It was improved, and his eloquence astonished all who heard him.

Instead of rising by degrees to the head of his profession, he burst forth at once the able lawyer and accomplished orator. Business flowed in upon him. He was employed in the most difficult causes, and retained with the largest fees that were usually given. The client in whose service he engaged, was supposed to be in a fair way of gaining his cause. He was but a short time in practice, when that cloud began to lower which, in the course of ten or twelve years, burst forth in a revolutionary storm.

In the year 1764 Governor Boone refused to administer to Christopher Gadsden the oaths which the law required every person returned as a member in the commons house of assembly to take before he entered on his legislative functions. This kindled the indignation of the house as being an interference with their constitutional privileges as the sole judges of the qualifications of their own members. In rousing the assembly and the people to resist all interferences of the royal governors, in deciding who should, or who should not, be members of the commons house of assembly, John Rutledge kindled a spark which has never since been extinguished.

This controversy was scarcely ended when the memorable stamp act was passed. The British colonies were then detached from each other, and had never acted in concert. A proposition was made by the assembly of Massachusetts to the different provincial assemblies for appointing committees from each to meet in congress as a rallying point of union. To this novel project many objections were made; some doubted its legality, others its expedience, and most its efficiency. To remove objections, to conciliate opposition, and to gain the hearty concurrence of the assembly and the people, was no easy matter. In accomplishing these objects, the abilities of John Rutledge were successfully exerted. Objections vanished—prejudices gave way before his eloquence. The public mind was illuminated, and a more correct mode of thinking took place.

A vote for appointing deputies to a continental Congress was carried in South Carolina at an early day, and before it had been agreed to by the neighboring states, Christopher Gadsden, Thomas Lynch, and John Rutledge, were appointed. The last was the youngest, and had very lately begun to tread the threshold of manhood. When this first congress met in New York in 1765, the members of the distant provinces were surprised at the eloquence of the young member from Carolina. In the means of education that province was far behind those to the northward. Of it little more was known or believed than that it produced rice and indigo, and contained a large proportion of slaves, and a handful of free men, and that most of the latter were strangers to vigorous health—all self-indulgent, and none accustomed to active exertions either of mind or body. From such a province nothing great was expected. A respectable committee of its assembly, and the distinguished abilities of one of them who was among the youngest members of the congress, produced at this first general meeting of the colonies more favorable ideas of South Carolina than had hitherto prevailed.

After the repeal of the stamp act, John Rutledge was for some years no further engaged in politics than as a lawyer and a member of the provincial legislature. In both capacities he was admired as a public speaker. His ideas were clear and strong—his utterance rapid but distinct—his voice, action, and energetic manner of speaking, forcibly impressed his sentiments on the minds and hearts of all who heard him. At reply he was quick—instantly comprehended the force of an objection—and saw at once the best mode of weakening or repelling it. He successfully used both argument and wit for invalidating the observations of his adversary: by the former he destroyed or weakened their force; by the latter he placed them in so ludicrous a point of light that it often convinced, and scarcely ever failed of conciliating and pleasing his hearers. Many were the triumphs of his eloquence at the bar and in the legislature; and in the former case probably more than strict impartial justice would sanction; for judges and juries, counsel and audience, hung on his accents.

In or after the year 1774 a new and more extensive

field was opened before him. When news of the Boston port-bill reached Charleston, a general meeting of the inhabitants was called by expresses sent over the state. After the proceedings of the British parliament were stated to this convention of the province, sundry propositions were offered for consideration. To the appointment of delegates for a general congress, no objection was made. But this was followed by propositions for instructing them how far they might go in pledging the province to support the Bostonians. Such a discordance of opinion was discovered as filled the minds of the friends of liberty with apprehensions that the meeting would prove abortive.

In this crisis John Rutledge, in a most eloquent speech, advocated a motion which he brought forward to give no instructions whatever; but to invest the men of their choice with full authority to concur in any measure they thought best; and to pledge the people of South Carolina to abide by whatever they would agree to. He demonstrated that any thing less than plenary discretion to this extent would be unequal to the crisis. To those who, after stating the dangers of such extensive powers, begged to be informed what must be done in case the delegates made a bad use of their unlimited authority to pledge the state to any extent, a laconic answer was returned: "Hang them." An impression was made on the multitude. Their minds were subdued by the decision of the proposed measure, and the energy with which it was supported.

On that day and by this vote the Revolution was virtually accomplished. By it the people of Carolina determined to be free, deliberately invested five men of their choice as their representatives with full powers to act for them and to take charge of their political interests. Royal government received a mortal wound and the representative system was planted in its stead. The former lingered for a few months and then expired. The latter instantly took root, and has ever since continued to grow and flourish. An election immediately followed. The mover of this spirited resolution, his brother Edward Rutledge, Christopher Gadsden, Thomas Lynch, and Henry Middleton were elected. Furnished with such ample powers, they took their seats in congress under great advantages, and by their conduct justified the confidence reposed in them.

John Rutledge was continued by successive elections a member of congress till the year 1776. He returned to Charleston in the beginning of that year, and was elected president and commander in chief of Carolina in conformity to a constitution established by the people on the 26th of March 1776. His duties henceforward were executive. He employed himself diligently in arranging the new government, and particularly in preparing for the defence of the state against an expected invasion by the British. Their attack on Sullivan's Island has been already related.

On this occasion John Rutledge rendered his country important service. General Lee, who commanded the continental troops, pronounced Sullivan's Island to be a "slaughter pen," and either gave orders or was disposed to give orders for its evacuation. The zeal of the state, and the energy of its chief magistrate, prevented this measure. Carolina had raised troops before congress had declared independence. These remained subject to the authority of the state, and were at this early period not immediately under the command of the officers of congress. To prevent the evacuation of the fort on Sullivan's Island, John Rutledge, shortly before the commencement of the action on the 28th of June, 1776, wrote the following laconic note to General Moultrie who commanded on the Island: "General Lee wishes you to evacuate the fort. You will not without an order from me. I would sooner cut off my hand than write one.

J. RUTLEDGE."

The successful issue of the defence has been already related. The consequences which would probably have followed from the evacuation of the fort, may in some measure be conjectured from the events of 1780; when the British, grown wiser, passed the same fort without engaging it.

CHAPTER II.

Rutledge chosen Governor of South Carolina—Member of Congress—His important services—Minister to Holland—Judge of the Court of Chancery—Member of Constitutional Convention—Associate Judge of Supreme Court—Chief Justice of the United States—His death.

JOHN RUTLEDGE continued in the office of President till March, 1778, when he resigned. The occasion and reasons of his resignation are matters of general history. This did not diminish his popularity. Of this the legislature gave the strongest proof; for the next election he was reinstated in the executive authority of the state, but under a new constitution, and with the name of Governor substituted in the place of President. He had scarcely entered on the duties of this office, when the country was invaded by the British General Prevost. The exertions made by Governor Rutledge to repel this invasion—to defend Charleston in the years 1779, 1780—to procure the aid of congress and of the adjacent states—to drive back the tide of British conquest—to recover the state—and to revive its suspended legislative and judicial powers, form the most important part of the history of South Carolina. On the termination of his executive duties in 1782, he was elected and served as a member of congress till 1783.

MISSION OF RUTLEDGE AND CLYMER. 299

In this period he was called upon to perform an extraordinary duty. The surrender of Lord Cornwallis in October, 1781, seemed to paralyze the exertions of the states. Thinking the war and all danger to be over, they no longer acted with suitable vigor. Congress fearing that this languor would encourage Great Britain to recommence the war, sent deputations of their members to rouse the states to a sense of their danger and duty.

On the 22d of May, 1782, John Rutledge and George Clymer were sent in this character, and instructed " to make such representation to the several states southward of Philadelphia, as were best adapted to their respective circumstances and the present situations of public affairs, and as might induce them to carry the requisitions of congress into effect with the greatest dispatch." They were permitted to make a personal address to the Virginia assembly.

In the execution of this duty John Rutledge drew such a picture of the United States, and of the danger to which they were exposed by the backwardness of the particular states to comply with the requisitions of congress, as produced a very happy effect. The addresser acquitted himself with so much ability that the Virginians, who, not without reason, are proud of their statesmen and orators, began to doubt whether their Patrick Henry or the Carolina Rutledge was the most accomplished public speaker.

Soon after the termination of Mr. Rutledge's congressional duties, he was appointed minister plenipotentiary from the United States to Holland, but declined to serve.

In the year 1784 he was elected a judge of the Court of Chancery in South Carolina. The events of the late war had greatly increased the necessity for such a court. John Rutledge draughted the bill for organizing it on a new plan, and in it introduced several of the provisions which have been already mentioned as improvements on the English court of the same name. Mr. Rutledge's public duties hitherto had been either legislative or executive. They were henceforward judicial. If comparisons were proper, it might be added that he was most at home in the latter. His knowledge of the law was profound; but the talent which pre-eminently fitted him for dispensing justice was a comprehensive mind, which could at once take into view all the bearings and relations of a complicated case. When the facts were all fairly before him, he promply knew what justice required. The pleadings of lawyers gratified their clients, but rarely cast any light on the subject which had not already presented itself to his own view. Their declamations and addresses to the passions were lost on him. Truth and justice were the pole-stars by which his decisions were regulated. He speedily resolved the most intricate cases —pursued general principles through their various modifications till they led to the fountain of justice. His decrees were so luminous, and the grounds of them so clearly expressed, that the defeated party was generally satisfied.

In the year 1787 he was called upon to assist in framing a national constitution in lieu of the advisory system of the confederation. In arranging the provisions of that bond of union, and in persuading his countrymen to accept it, he was eminently useful. As soon as it was in operation, he was designated by President Washington as first associate judge of the Supreme Court of the United States. In this office he served till 1791, when he was elected chief justice of South Carolina. He was afterwards appointed chief justice of the United States. Thus for more than thirty years, with few and short intervals, he served his country in one or other of the departments of government; and in all with fidelity and ability. In the friendly competitions of the states for the comparative merits of their respective statesmen and orators, while Massachusetts boasts of her John Adams—Connecticut of her Ellsworth—New York of her Jay—Pennsylvania of her Wilson—Delaware of her Bayard—Virginia of her Henry—South Carolina rests her claims on the talents and eloquence of John Rutledge. This illustrious man closed his variegated career in the year 1800.*

* Ramsay's South Carolina.

SKETCHES OF

HEROES AND PATRIOTS OF THE SOUTH.

GOVERNOR EDWARD RUTLEDGE.

Governor Edward Rutledge, the son of Dr. John Rutledge, was born about the year 1750.

He received his classical education in Charleston under David Smith, A. M., of New Jersey college, who was an able instructor in the learned languages. On finishing his classical education, he studied law with his elder brother John Rutledge. In a due course of time he was entered a student in the temple, and proceeding barrister returned to Charleston and commenced the practice of law in 1773. The high character of John Rutledge raised the expectations of the public that his brother would support the reputation of the name and family; nor were they disappointed. His eloquence was great, but not precisely in the same line with his brother's. Demosthenes seemed to be the model of the one, Cicero of the other. The eloquence of the elder like a torrent bore down all opposition, and controled the passions of the hearers—that of the younger was soothing, persuasive, and made willing proselytes. In the practice of law, Edward Rutledge was directed by the most upright and generous principles. To advance his personal interest was a secondary object; to do good, to promote peace, to heal breaches, to advance justice, was a primary one.

His powers of persuasion were not to be purchased to shield oppression or to support iniquity. Where he thought his client had justice on his side, he would go all lengths in vindicating his claims; but would not support any man, however liberal, in prosecuting unfounded claims or resisting those that were substantially just. He abhorred the principle that an advocate should take all advantages for his client, and gain whatever he could for him, whether right or wrong; or on the other hand, to assist him with all the quirks and quibbles which ingenuity can contrive, or the forms of law permit, for defeating or delaying the claims of substantial justice.

Such honorable principles, connected with such splendid talents, procured for him the love and esteem of all good men. In the second year after Edward Rutledge commenced practice, he was called to represent his country in the congress which met at Philadelphia in September 1774. He and John Jay of New York were nearly of an age, and the two youngest members of that honorable body. In this station Mr. Edward Rutledge continued for nearly three years. Throughout that period he was one of the most influential members. He had much of the esteem and confidence of Washington, and was often requested by him to bring forward particular measures, for the adoption of which the general was anxious.

Edward Rutledge has the honor of being one of the four members who signed the declaration of independence in behalf of South Carolina. His protracted absence from home, and continued attention to public business was no small sacrifice. His talents and popularity would have commanded the first practice at the bar; but he loved his country too well to be influenced by pecuniary considerations to neglect its interests. In the year 1779 he was again appointed member of congress; but on his way thither was seized with an obstinate, tedious fever which prevented his proceeding to the seat of their deliberation. In addition to his civil employments, Edward Rutledge held a commission in the militia, and regularly rose through all grades of rank in the Charleston battallion of artillery to the rank of its lieutenant colonel. In the year 1779, when the British were defeated and driven from Port Royal Island, he as captain commanded a company of artillerists which earned its full share of the glory of that victory.

In the year 1780 he became a prisoner of war, and as such was sent to St. Augustine where he was confined for eleven months; and on his exchange, delivered above eight hundred miles from his home and friends. He embraced the first opportunity of returning to Carolina; but could not approach Charleston, for it was a British garrison. He was elected and served in the Jacksonborough assembly in 1782, and afterwards in the privy council of the state; and in both rendered essential service to his country, but was obliged to lead a desultory life till the evacuation of Charleston in December 1782. When that event took place he returned to his proper home after an exile of nearly three years. He had set out with the most brilliant professional prospects; but the Revolution deprived him for eight of the best years of his life from reaping the reward justly due to the studies of his youth. For the seventeen succeeding years he followed his profession, and at the same time served in the legislature. Though a private member, he by his persuasive eloquence directed most of the important measures adopted in that period for the improvement of the country. Many were the points which his eloquence either carried through or defeated in the legislature. For the good obtained and the evil prevented, his memory will be long respected by his countrymen. His persuasive eloquence will in like manner be held up as a model for young public speakers to form themselves upon.

Though Mr. Edward Rutledge from the year 1783 had withdrawn from the public life on a national scale, he was never absent from the public service. He was too much absorbed in his country's welfare to look with indifference on the course of her public affairs. He kept up a constant correspondence with his friends, and particularly his nephew John Rutledge, in congress. His opinions were much respected, and had great influence with a new set of members who took up the same national concerns in their progress which he had directed in their origin. He wanted no offices from the government, but ardently wished to see its national interests judiciously managed for public good. In moderating those collisions which in Carolina too often produce duels, Mr. Edward Rutledge had great address. His opinions as a man of honor were appreciated by all parties, and, being impartial, seldom failed of bringing round those explanations which without degrading were satisfactory. As a lawyer and a gentleman he was justly entitled to the honorable appellation of a peace-maker. He was eminently the friend of the distressed, and thought nothing too much for their accommodation and relief. The talents of few were estimated equally high. The virtues of none attracted a greater proportion of public love and esteem. In the last year of his life he was elected governor of the state, and died in January, 1800, when in the discharge of the duties of that exalted station.

COLONEL JOHN LAURENS.

Colonel John Laurens, son of Henry Laurens, was born in Charleston in 1775. His early education was conducted by Benjamin Lord, reverend Messieurs Himeli and Panton. In youth he discovered that energy of character which distinguished him through life. When a lad, though laboring under a fever, on the cry of fire he leaped from his bed, hastened to the scene of danger, and was in a few minutes on the top of the exposed houses risking his life to arrest the progress of the flames. This is the more worthy of notice, for precisely in the same way, and under a similar, but higher impulse of ardent patriotism, he lost his life in the year 1782.

At the age of sixteen he was taken to Europe by his father, and there put under the best means of instruction in Geneva; and afterwards in London.

In the course of his youthful studies he united the plodding diligence of the mere scholar and the refinement of the gentleman. By a judicious distribution of his time, and doing with his might whatever he engaged in, he acquired as much solid useful learning as could be expected from one, who, immuring himself in the walls of a college, renounced society; and at the same time as many accomplishments as are usually attained by those who, neglecting all study, aim at nothing more than the exterior polish of an elegant education. In classical learning, the French and Italian languages, mathematics, philosophy, geography, history, and the ordinary circle of sciences, he was an adept; and also excelled in drawing, dancing, fencing, riding, and all the graces and refined manners of a man of fashion.

He was entered a student of law at the temple in 1774, and was daily improving in legal knowledge till the disputes between Great Britain and her colonies arrested his attention. He soon found that the claims of the mother country struck at the root of liberty in the colonies, and that she perseveringly resolved to enforce these claims at every hazard. Fain would he have come out to join his countrymen in arms at the commencement of the contest; but the peremptory order of his father enjoined his continuance in England, to prosecute his studies and finish his education.

As a dutiful son he obeyed these orders; but as a patriot burning with desire to defend his country, he dismissed Coke, Littleton, and all the tribe of jurists, and substituted in their place Vauban, Folard, and other writers on war. He also availed himself of the excellent opportunities which London affords of acquiring practical knowledge in the manual exercise, of tactics, and the mechanism of war. Thus instructed, as soon as he was a freeman of legal age he quitted England for France, and by a circuitous voyage in neutral vessels, and at a considerable risk, made his way good in the year 1777 to Charleston.

Independence had been declared—the American army

was raised, officered, and in the field. He who by his attainments in general science, and particularly in the military art, deserved high rank, had no ordinary door left open to serve his country but by entering in the lowest grade of an army abounding with officers.

General Washington, ever attentive to merit, instantly took him into his family as a supernumerary aid-de-camp. Shortly after this appointment he had an opportunity of indulging his military ardor. He fought and was wounded in the battle of Germantown, October 4th, 1777.

He continued in General Washington's family in the middle states till the British had retreated from Philadelphia to New York; and was engaged in the battle of Monmouth, June 28, 1778. After this, the war being transferred more northwardly, he was indulged in attaching himself to the army on Rhode Island where the most active operations were expected soon to take place. There he was intrusted with the command of some light troops.

The bravery and good conduct which he displayed on this occasion was honored by congress. On the 5th of November, 1778, they resolved "that John Laurens, esquire, aid-de-camp to General Washington, be presented with a continental commission of lieutenant colonel in testimony of the sense which congress entertains of his patriotic and spirited services as a volunteer in the American army; and of his brave conduct in several actions, particularly in that of Rhode Island on the 29th of August last; and that General Washington be directed, whenever an opportunity shall offer, to give Lieutenant Colonel Laurens command agreeable to his rank."

On the next day a letter from Lieutenant Colonel Laurens was read in congress, expressing "his gratitude for the unexpected honor which congress were pleased to confer on him by the resolution passed the day before; and the high satisfaction it would have afforded him could he have accepted it without injuring the rights of the officers in the line of the army, and doing an evident injustice to his colleagues in the family of the commander in chief—that having been a spectator of the convulsions occasioned in the army by disputes of rank, he held the tranquillity of it too dear to be instrumental in disturbing it, and therefore entreated congress to suppress the resolve of yesterday, ordering him a commission of lieutenant colonel, and to accept his sincere thanks for the intended honor." In this relinquishment there was a victory gained by patriotism over self-love. Lieutenant Colonel Laurens loved military fame and rank; but he loved his country more, and sacrificed the former to preserve the peace and promote the interest of the latter.

In the next year the British directed their military operations chiefly against the most southern states. Lieutenant Colonel John Laurens was induced by double motives to repair to Carolina. The post of danger was always the object of his preference. His native state was become the theatre of war. To its aid he repaired, and in May 1779, with a party of light troops, had a skirmish with the British at Tulifinny. In endeavoring to obstruct their progress towards Charleston, he received a wound. This was no sooner cured than he rejoined the army, and was engaged in the unsuccessful attack on Savannah on the 9th of October of the same year.

To prepare for the defence of Charleston, the reduction of which was known to be contemplated by the British, was the next object of attention among the Americans. To this Colonel Laurens devoted all the energies of his active mind. In the progress of the siege which commenced in 1780, the success of defensive operations became doubtful.

Councils of war were frequent—several of the citizens were known to wish for a surrender as a termination of their toils and dangers. In these councils, and on proper occasions, Colonel Laurens advocated the abandonment of the front lines and to retire to new ones to be erected within the old ones and to risk an assault. When these spirited measures were opposed on the suggestion that the inhabitants preferred a capitulation, he declared that he would direct his sword to the heart of the first citizen who would urge a capitulation against the opinion of the commander in chief. When his superior officers, convinced of the inefficacy of further resistance, were disposed to surrender on terms of capitulation, he yielded to the necessity of the case and became a prisoner of war.

This reverse of fortune opened a new door for serving his country in a higher line than he ever yet had done. He was soon exchanged and reinstated in a capacity for acting. In expediting his exchange, congress had the ulterior view of sending him as a special minister to Paris that he might urge the necessity of a vigorous co-operation on the part of France with the United States against Great Britain. When this was proposed to Colonel Laurens, he recommended and urged that Colonel Alexander

Hamilton should be employed in preference to himself. Congress adhered to their first choice.

Colonel Laurens sailed for France in the latter end of 1780; and there in conjunction with Dr. Franklin, and Count De Vergennes, and Marquis De Castries, arranged the plan of the campaign for 1781; which eventuated in the surrender of Lord Cornwallis, and finally in a termination of the war.

Within six months from the day Colonel Laurens left America, he returned to it and brought with him the concerted plan of combined operations. Ardent to rejoin the army, he was indulged with making a verbal report of his negotiations to congress; and in three days set out to resume his place as one of the aids of General Washington.

The American and French army about this time commenced the siege of Yorktown. In the course of it Colonel Laurens, as second in command with his fellow aid, Colonel Hamilton, assisted in storming and taking an advanced British redoubt which expedited the surrender of Lord Cornwallis.

The articles of capitulation were arranged by Colonel Laurens on behalf of the Americans. Charleston and a part of South Carolina still remained in the power of the British. Cononel Laurens thought nothing done while any thing remained undone. He therefore, on the surrender of Lord Cornwallis, repaired to South Carolina to assist in recovering the state.

Before he entered on active military duty, he obeyed the call of his country to serve as a representative to the state legislature, which was convened in January 1782, at Jacksonborough, within thirty-five miles of Charleston, which was at that time a British garrison. His eloquence was then put in requisition for the public service. He was the advocate of every energetic measure of defence and offence, but declined all civil honors; preferring to serve his country in the field.

His legislative duty being over, he joined the southern army commanded by General Greene. In the course of the summer of 1782, he caught a common fever, and was sick in bed when an expedition was undertaken against a party of the British which had gone to Combakee to carry off rice. Colonel Laurens rose from his sick bed and joined his countrymen.

While leading an advanced party, he received a shot which, on the 27th of August 1782, at the close of the war, put an end to his valuable life in the 27th year of his age. His many virtues have been ever since the subject of eulogy, and his early fall of national lamentation. The fourth of July seldom passes without a tribute to his memory.

COLONEL JOHN EAGER HOWARD.

No man possessed, in a higher degree, the confidence of General Greene—none better deserved it. He had every requisite for the perfection of the military character—patience, judgment, intrepidity, and decision. To his memorable charge with the bayonet at the Cowpens, so nobly supported by Washington and his cavalry, that important victory is chiefly to be attributed. Nor do I regard his gallantry less worthy of admiration, when, at the battle of Guilford, following up the blow inflicted by Washington, he charged the second battalion of the British Guards, and nearly annihilated them. At Hobkirk's Hill, his efforts to rally the broken regiment of Gunby, did him high honor; nor did the bitterness of grief ever pervade the human bosom more keenly, than in his, when he found all his exertions to revive the courage of men, who, on every former occasion, were distinguished for intrepidity, were unproductive of the slightest effect. At Eutaw, he was severely wounded, but not till he had seen his regiment retrieve its tarnished reputation, and triumphantly pursue the enemy.—*Garden's Anecdotes.*

COLONEL CARRINGTON.

I wish, says Garden in his "Anecdotes of the Revolution," I could more particularly speak of the services of Colonel Carrington, as I am well apprized that he enjoyed the entire confidence of General Greene; and by his judicious counsels, and unremitted exertions as Quarter Master General, greatly contributed to the advantages gained over the enemy. It is an indisputable fact, that in a country exhausted, and deficient in all resources, he still contrived to provide such supplies for the comfort and support of the army, that he appeared to have achieved impossibilities, and not a murmur nor complaint impeded the progress to victory. A dispute, relative to rank, had called him to the North, before it had been my happiness to receive a commission in the service; but, previously to the evacuation of Charleston, he had rejoined the army, and resumed his former station; which gave me ample reason to believe that wheresoever placed, his pre-eminent abilities must have been of the highest importance to his country.

CAPTAIN O'NEAL.

O'NEAL was one of the officers of the Legion, who rose to rank and consideration by the force of extraordinary merit. He entered the army a private trooper in Bland's regiment, and was one of a gallant band who, when Captain Henry Lee was surprised at the Spread-Eagle Tavern, near Philadelphia, resolutely defended the position against the whole of the British cavalry, and ultimately compelled them to retire. Lee, on this occasion, addressing his companions, and strenuously urging them rather to die than surrender, added— "Henceforth, I consider the fortune of every individual present, as inseparably connected with my own! If we fall, we will fall like brothers! If successful in repelling the enemy, (and it needs but a trifling exertion of your energies to effect it,) my fortune and my interest shall be uniformly employed to increase your comforts, and secure your promotion." Nor did he ever swerve from his promise. Appointed, shortly after, with the rank of Major, to the command of a corps of horse, O'Neal and Winston, another of his faithful adherents, received commissions, and to the last hour of the war, by uniform steadiness of conduct, and exemplary intrepidity, gained increase of reputation. It was said, on this occasion, that Tarleton, making his first essay as a military man, but for the accidental snapping of O'Neal's carbine, would have fallen a victim to a bold effort, which he made to enter by a window at which he was posted, the muzzle of the piece being, at the time, within a foot of his head. Tarleton behaved with great calmness; for, looking up, he said with a smile, "You have missed it, my lad, for this time;" and wheeling his horse, joined his companions, who, deceived by a false alarm, were retiring with precipitation.

www.ingramcontent.com/pod-product-compliance
Lightning Source LLC
Chambersburg PA
CBHW021206230426
43667CB00006B/580